Why Rural Schools Matter

Why Rural Schools Matter

MARA CASEY TIEKEN

THE UNIVERSITY OF NORTH CAROLINA PRESS *Chapel Hill*

This book was made possible by financial assistance from the Ruth Landes Memorial Research Fund, a program of The Reed Foundation; the Roger C. Schmutz Fund for Faculty Research via the Bates Faculty Development Fund; and the Thornton H. Brooks Fund of the University of North Carolina Press.

© 2014 The University of North Carolina Press

The University of North Carolina Press has been a member of the Green Press Initiative since 2003.

Cover illustration by Sally Fry Scruggs

Library of Congress Cataloging-in-Publication Data

Tieken, Mara Casey.
Why rural schools matter / Mara Casey Tieken.
  pages cm
Includes bibliographical references and index.
ISBN 978-1-4696-1848-7 (pbk : alk. paper) —
ISBN 978-1-4696-1849-4 (ebook)
1. Education, Rural—United States. 2. Education, Rural—United States—Case studies. 3. Children with social disabilities—Education—United States. 4. Children with social disabilities—Education—United States—Case studies. I. Title.
LC5146.5.T57 2014
370.9173'4—dc23
2014020275

18 17 16 15 14   5 4 3 2 1

This book has been digitally printed

Contents

Acknowledgments

I am indebted to the following people for their help with this book:

My collaborators, reviewers, and editors, especially Joe Parsons, Kai Schafft, Pat Graham, Cheryl Mason Bolick, Matt Duvall, Sara Fabrizio, Chris Schiff, and Emily Kane, who were attentive, wise, and patient.

My mentors: Donna San Antonio, who reminded me to seek nuance and show care; Sara Lawrence Lightfoot, who revealed the art in science; and Mark Warren, who taught me how to be a good researcher and a good person.

My writing group: Liliana Garces, Cynthia Gordon, Ann Ishimaru, Sola Takahashi, and Amanda Taylor, who supported me, challenged me, and inspired me.

My students: my third graders in Vanleer, who moved me to start this journey, and my undergrads at Bates—particularly Mia, Teika, Asha, and Lizzie—who made sure that I completed it.

My family and friends: the Brocks, who motivated me with their Viking spirit and the promise of Jack; A. J., who provided enthusiasm and a sense of humor when mine were in short supply; and Chelsea, Mom, and Dad, who had more faith in me than I ever will.

And, finally, the residents, friends, and families of Delight and Earle, who gave so generously of their time, their insights, and their couches. A special thanks to Dorothy Singleton, Cyndi Moorman, and Kathy Cole. I hope that I have done justice to your stories.

Why Rural Schools Matter

CHAPTER ONE

The Meaning of a School

The drive to school was quick, just fourteen miles—U.S. Route 70 to Yellow Creek, a right onto Tennessee State Route 235, and then a left at the small red barn with the single cow at its fence. A couple of miles down on the right—after the green road sign marking the Vanleer town line, a string of apartments patrolled by cats, and a few closed shops, furniture piled in their dusty windows—was Vanleer Elementary School, an old wooden schoolhouse surrounded by a handful of trailers and a cinderblock gym. The drive from home to school was quick in the early mornings, a drive past smoke-ringed tobacco barns and long-fallow fields, just fourteen minutes down fourteen miles of empty open road.

It was still warm when I left home to get back for the school's fund-raiser supper. The sun still glinted off steep barn roofs; the afternoon shadows still stretched across the fields; and the wide pavement still baked in the warmth of October. Quick up Yellow Creek and onto an empty Route 235, left at the lonely barn and then . . . standstill—a long line of cars filling the road, with pickups sidling onto gravel shoulders and minivans pulling to a stop.

The school's lot was past full—people must have started arriving shortly after the last bell that afternoon—and cars covered the playground, the field, and the school's short drive. We parked—me, the cars before and behind me, all pulling onto the grassy roadside—and joined the crowd walking toward school. I saw a few families and students that I knew—a couple of children were my own third graders—but most I didn't recognize. They knew one another, though, shouting greetings over parked cars, children running ahead and adults balancing pies and cakes in their arms. I made my way to the back doors of the cafeteria, which stood open to release the heat of food and crowds, the clatter of dishes and voices, and the sharp smell of turnip greens. Dark piles of the steaming greens, kettledrum vats of white beans, greasy wedges of cornbread, coolers of iced tea, and endless platters of desserts covered the serving line. The supply of food was immense, enough to feed armies.

The food didn't surprise me; I'd come to expect these quantities at suppers in Tennessee. It was the crowd that astonished me—all the cars that lined the darkening road and the people that now filled the cafeteria. Adults were squeezed in at tables made for children, babies were perched on laps and shoulders, Styrofoam trays were laid end to end, and a long line of hungry people was circling the tables and snaking toward the back. Even with the preparations all week—the farmer volunteering his acres of turnips, the teachers picking their leafy tops, the washed greens lying on towels throughout the kitchen, the beans simmering on the stoves, the pile of cookies growing in the back room—I still hadn't expected this crowd. This sleepy, no-stop-light, more-closed-than-open town and its surrounding, equally sleepy hollows had suddenly yielded an entire community of people, a community of students and parents and grandparents and alumni and cousins and friends stretching back generations, an entire community hungry for beans and greens, for food and fellowship. That night, this community turned out for its school. And it would again and again—for auctions and Christmas concerts and firehouse fund-raisers, to raise property taxes and christen a new school building, to fight off consolidation one more time.

It was here, over three years of beans and greens suppers, the ground-level skirmishes and compromises of education politics, and the quiet rhythms of ordinary school days, that I—a young teacher, new to Vanleer, new to life in a rural town—began to learn just what a school means to a community. The school, it became clear, was important socially; it sustained relationships between students and teachers, sustained ties among alumni and across generations, sustained me and my quickly growing roots in this place. And it mattered economically, too, bringing business to the few gas stations, the little meat-and-three, and the small bank right down the road.

But these more obvious lessons of fellowship and finance gave way to complexities. I would soon notice other patterns—cafeteria benches lined with singularly white families, classroom desks filled with nearly all white children, crowds less striking for whom they included than for whom they didn't. I would notice the silence about race and the quiet assumption that race simply didn't matter to a rural, almost entirely white school like Vanleer. And, eventually, I would hear rumors of a lynching tree, an old tree with smooth, wide limbs standing just outside town. I would wonder about the knotty racial histories hidden below this tranquil surface and wonder how the school was tangled in these histories and patterns, too.

And I would learn more about the tensions buzzing through the hallways and classrooms, tensions fueled by the growing power of the state and federal governments, tensions that led to a constant anxiety about the future. I would learn to prominently display my blue book of Tennessee state standards on my desk, and, for a few days every spring, I would send my students home with messages about the value of a good breakfast, arrange their desks at odd angles throughout the room, refuse to answer panicked requests for assistance, and pass out the state test booklets—and I would wonder about all of the things that now weren't getting taught. I would hear the threats of consolidation, whispered fears that would ripple through the staff, fears that the district's smallest, most rural school would finally be deemed just too small and too rural to remain open and the children would be bused to other, larger facilities.

This relationship shared by school and community was complex. Built through histories of racialized inequalities and complicated by current education policies, it seemed to define and shape both school and community in meaningful and consequential ways. For better and for worse, this town depended upon this school.

Yet this relationship was also, largely, an ignored relationship. While I taught in Vanleer, legislators in the state's capital and Washington, D.C., continued to issue educational policies that seemed mostly irrelevant—at best, meaningless to this school and the community that depended upon it; at worst, impossible in their demands and damaging in their effects. The irony was striking: there seemed to be so much useful and significant in the relationship tying rural school to community—an imperfect and important relationship—yet policy makers simply failed to acknowledge it, to appreciate its possibilities or address its flaws. For all the growing attention paid to education, with policies like No Child Left Behind and debates about standards and failing schools filling newspaper headlines, these policy makers seemed to miss so much.

And when I left Vanleer for graduate school, I was disappointed again, at least at first. What the policy makers missed, many academics did, too. Education research, in its focus on urban schools, mostly overlooks rural schools and communities. The books and articles assigned in my classes failed to reflect my experiences in Vanleer and, I would wager, the lives and understandings of rural community members elsewhere. These texts never mentioned the promise of a crowded rural cafeteria or the stark reality of an old lynching tree, never addressed the messy overlap of rural community and rural school, never examined the habits of inclusion and exclusion a rural school can perpetuate in a rural community. They simply didn't cover rural geographies, simply didn't notice the urban bias of school reform. They didn't ask the kinds of questions about community and race and power that seemed so consequential here.

But the questions remained. I wanted to understand this relationship, to understand whether and why and how a rural school matters to a rural community. I wanted to understand the particulars and complexities of this relationship, to grasp its imperfections. I wanted to know what roles a public school could play in a rural community, how it could shape a community's economics and politics, its relationships and its demographics, its borders and its boundaries, and I wanted to see how context—long-standing racial contexts and current school-reform contexts—could color these roles. And, too, I wanted to return to a rural town, to know and be known in particular places and particular communities. I wanted to be back in a crowded cafeteria, sitting with a plate of beans and greens and feeling rooted once more.

RURAL TEACHER

I moved to Tennessee in 2002 to teach in a rural school. I had wanted a rural teaching job since getting my elementary teaching certification in college, since experiencing the awkward irony of reading about urban schools and talking about urban education and debating urban reform while student teaching in a small, rural Vermont elementary school. Rural teaching—even the short, sleepless stint of student teaching—seemed so different from these urban tales. Overcrowding wasn't an issue in my little Vermont school; undercrowding was. Cultural relevance meant four-wheeling and country music and hunting, never hip-hop or subways or high rises. I couldn't have avoided knowing my students if I'd wanted to. But other issues seemed strikingly, terribly similar: transience, poverty, drug and alcohol abuse. Rural teaching had all of the challenge and hard questions of urban teaching, yet remained somehow distinctive, and so, after graduation, I wanted more—more rural teaching.

I would find a rural teaching position, a position teaching third grade at Vanleer Elementary School, in Vanleer, Tennessee. But finding it—finding a *rural* position—was tricky. I was soon questioning what I even meant by "rural"—was "rural" about isolation? Sparse populations? Livestock and barns? Governmental designations were of little help. The federal government, for example, currently uses over fifteen different definitions of rural,[1] each tied to the needs and purposes of a particular organization[2]—with many locales falling into the nebulous sometimes-rural category. The most common conceptions I found—those offered by the U.S. Census Bureau, the Office of Management and Budget (OMB), and the Economic Research Service (ERS)[3]—have their own problems. The census and the OMB both rely on dichotomous classifications, with the census labeling geographic areas as urban or rural and the OMB using a metropolitan/nonmetropolitan distinction,[4] while the ERS provides a more fine-grained classification system, parsing the metropolitan/nonmetropolitan categories by size of the metropolitan area and a nonmetropolitan area's degree of urbanization and proximity to a metropolitan area. But these definitions rely upon distinctions that make "rural" or "nonmetropolitan" "residual" categories culled from what's "left over"[5]—essentially, what "urban" and "metropolitan" are not.[6] Even with all of the color-coded maps, these definitions seemed only to render rural invisible. They felt slippery and reductive; I was looking for a job in a place that wasn't there.

Ultimately, I chose Vanleer not for any official designation or specific demographics, but simply because it felt rural, in some real and authentic way. And it's this feeling—something beyond the size of a population or its proximity to a city[7]—that many rural scholars and advocates feel should actually define rural: "the *rural* in rural is not most significantly the boundary around it, but the meanings inherent in rural lives, wherever lived."[8] "Rural," then, is a matter of the commonplace interactions and events that constitute the rural "lifeworld," a value mostly overlooked by the media and academia, and a significance impossible to quantify. This understanding, shared by many of the residents of rural communities, is tied to place; it provides a geography-dependent sense of belonging.[9] Rural, in this conception, is not simply a matter of boundaries.[10] It constitutes one's identity; it shapes one's perspectives and understandings; and it gives meaning to one's daily experiences. This identity, this shared and place-dependent sense of rural belonging, gives rural its significance. It's this rural that I found in Vanleer.

And I loved rural teaching. I loved the challenge of getting multiplication to make sense to third graders. I loved the silence when I reached the last pages of *Where the Red Fern Grows* and the feel of small arms wrapped around my waist. I loved the slow time outside the classroom: picking blackberries in my students' backyards, learning to can peppers with the ladies in the cafeteria, hunting for morels if the spring rains had been just right. I loved seeing students and parents after school in the parking lot and then seeing them again at the gas station and then later at the football game and then on Sunday at Walmart. I loved that I couldn't separate the "rural" from "teaching," that teaching here was completely and utterly tied to this very particular place.

But there were parts I hated. I hated the story problem about an escalator on the state's math test, a problem many of my students would miss simply because they had never ridden an escalator. I hated feeling as though the teaching and curriculum books were never written for my teaching, the state and federal policies were never written for my school. I hated knowing that when the demographics of this little community changed, as they began to just before I left, there would be few resources available to support the necessary and hard work of changing practice, and maybe changing some hearts and minds, too. I hated that this school, by virtue of its geography, would always risk closure. I hated the rural invisibility—the neglect by policy makers that left racial and geographic inequalities unacknowledged and unchecked. I hated being a part of a system that I couldn't quite buy into. And so I left. I took all of my questions and confusions and indignations and went to graduate school.

A RURAL RATIONALE

I have now spent years flying in and out of Arkansas, years working on this study, years justifying my academic interest in rural schools and communities, years explaining to curious urbanites and race-conscious practitioners why I care about rural places. This curiosity—or incredulity—still surprises me, for rural America is hardly small or insignificant or raceless. The 2010 census recorded 51 million nonmetropolitan residents[11] living in rural communities with varied geographies, demographic compositions, economies, histories, and social fabrics.[12] Rural America covers Native American reservation communities in the West, small mostly white New England fishing villages, midwestern farm towns with growing Latino populations, African American communities scattered along the Mississippi Delta, and isolated hamlets tucked into the Appalachians and Rockies. Racial and ethnic diversity is increasing in rural areas. White residents made up 77.8 percent of the rural population in 2010, followed by African Americans at 8.2 percent and Hispanics at 9.3 percent, with

Native Americans constituting the majority of the remaining share.[13] But the proportion of white rural residents is dropping, while the Hispanic population is growing.[14] And poverty is tied to geography and race in complicated ways: 15.4 percent of the nonmetropolitan population lived in poverty in 2007, compared to a national rate of 12.5 percent,[15] though some towns—picturesque beachfront and ski towns, filled with retirees and second-home owners—enjoy resources and opportunities most communities in Appalachia and the Delta never will.[16] Rural America is a vast, diverse expanse, stratified by the same race and class lines that slice urban America.

But the skepticism I encounter is likely less about population counts and demographics than about mythology, I think. Stereotypes and assumptions about rural communities and people are laced throughout popular culture and perpetuated by mainstream media,[17] and can even creep into research and reform.[18] Two somewhat contradictory myths dominate. The first is about deprivation and decline: "rural" is backwoods, backwater, and backward, its residents assumed to be ignorant, lawless, and provincial, its communities little different than those portrayed in the movie *Deliverance*. The second myth draws from a romantic nostalgia: this "rural" is equated with uncomplicated simplicity, with some sort of lost golden age, an image that, while kinder, is no more accurate than the first. And threaded through both of these myths is the assumption that "rural" means "white," whether salt-of-the-earth white farming family or poor white trash.[19] These myths serve to ensure the status of rural communities as either relics or wretches in the public imagination, and they obscure rural complexities and realities—inaccuracies that lead to marginalizing entire communities of people and forgetting entire schools of children.

These rural schools, though, make up nearly a third of America's public schools. Rural schools educate a fifth of American students:[20] 9 million students[21] rely upon these schools to prepare them for work and ready them for civic life. And 51 million rural residents[22] rely upon these rural schools to shape and structure their increasingly diverse communities; their economies, their politics, their social interactions—the handful of businesses on Main Street, the issues on November's ballot, the quiet boundaries of inclusion and exclusion—are fueled by these schools. Fifty-one million people—the individuals that harvest America's food, care for its land, make its natural resources usable and useful, and the youth that grow up to adopt these responsibilities—depend on these schools. The quality of rural schools, the quality of this relationship shared by school and community, matters, both to rural students and rural residents, and to all of the urban and suburban families that rely on these rural communities. These schools are hardly inconsequential.

And beyond the interests of rural students, the fabric of rural communities, and the material security of this country are other reasons to care about these rural schools. Many urban practitioners, researchers, and parents worry about a fractured community-school relationship, wondering how to foster meaningful community involvement in schools during an era measured in test scores and driven by mandates.[23] Urban families often describe feeling unwelcome or unwanted, while urban teachers lament the absence of parents; urban leaders often question the political will for educational improvement, while urban students feel ignored. These stakeholders all want responsive schools and active communities, a tight and mutual community-school relationship, an education that transcends government mandates and state sanctions. The beans and greens suppers that many rural schools take for granted, the conditions that many rural communities understand as a natural and routine part of schooling, these city schools and communities crave. The legacies of oppression and challenges of poverty that many rural schools struggle to understand and confront, many urban schools also face. Rural schools, then, are consequential for urban schools, too, consequential in the possibilities they suggest and commonalities they share. Yet, for all their consequences, rural schools are often forgotten and, with today's one-size-fits-all education reforms, they remain underserved.

Here, I tell the stories of two rural communities, Delight and Earle, Arkansas, and their rural public schools, the stories of the complicated and meaningful relationships these communities and schools share, stories tied to their racialized histories and current school-reform politics. I start with context, drawing upon an often-overlooked rural education literature to trace the rural community-school relationship in the United States over the past two centuries. I then turn to these two particular communities, to Delight and Earle. After describing my approach to understanding, participating in, and studying these communities, I share these studies, stories of the many complex roles their schools play in their communities. Three more narratives follow, three narratives written across these two communities—narratives of race and racial divides, community and boundaries, the state and its power. And I end with an examination of the state's narrative of education and reform, its substance—an increasingly narrow definition of what school is and what it is for—and its meaning for those in and around these schools. These two communities and the intimate and complicated relationships they share with their schools show us—both rural and urban—the significance of a school and the vast potential it holds for its surrounding community. And they remind us that educational equity shouldn't be circumscribed by a city's limits.

School is no longer a fourteen-minute drive away, and I still get homesick for Vanleer. But I found two other communities, communities interesting and open and gracious. These communities trusted me with their stories; they believed their stories were worth hearing, worth telling and retelling. Again and again, they welcomed me with the warmth of an October beans and greens supper. For all of this, I remain grateful to Delight and Earle.

CHAPTER TWO

Rural Histories

In a small town in the hills of Tennessee, a few miles past a strong-limbed tree with a dark southern legacy, on a night momentarily free from the anxieties of state tests and school closures, cars fill a usually empty road, mountains of turnip greens steam on a serving line, and families crowd long cafeteria tables—all for a small, rural elementary school. The complex relationship shared by rural school and rural community is a particular relationship, a relationship necessarily written by local context and local history. But a wider context also patterns this particular relationship; this relationship is located within—and shaped by—a broader history of regional and national dynamics, a broader rural history tangled with race and politics and reform.

And so I start here, with this history. It begins in the schoolhouses of a new nation's farming towns and frontier settlements and cotton plantations, extends across two centuries of industrialization and rural reform, and stretches to today, shaping the relationship that ties Vanleer and its elementary school, shaping the relationships of Delight and Earle. It is a history of rural economic, social, and demographic change and also a history of American urbanization.[1] It's a history of education reform—a relentless push toward "one best system"[2]—and the rural consequences of this reform. And, too, it's the history of a long-standing struggle for control, a battle between local needs and federal priorities, between community autonomy and governmental influence.

I sketch only the outlines of this American history. This outline is necessarily general: the details of any particular relationship lie in the particulars of its context, particulars that emerge through stories told over sweet tea and supper. It is also incomplete. History is layered with racialized accounts that, despite their often-separate tellings, define and write each other. Here, I focus on only two rural histories: a largely white history that reflects the politically and economically prevailing stories and events of a growing country, and a black history that, while no less influential, is much less heard. These historic accounts, despite their generalities and incompleteness, give shape and significance to the politics and economies, the cultures and racial structures, of two rural communities tucked deep in Arkansas.

A RURAL NATION AND ITS RURAL SCHOOLS

America was once a rural nation[3]—its communities were once rural communities, and its schools were once rural schools.

The earliest frontier schoolhouses were simple structures built of logs or, on the prairie, made of sod.[4] Later, as towns grew and settled, the logs and sod were replaced with wood frames, and small belfries capped the roofs. The typical New England or midwestern schoolhouse was one room, a square or rectangle, with long windows on one or two sides. Backless wooden benches and built-in desks lined the space, and a wood stove sat near the center; a teacher's desk stood on a short platform, marking the room's front. During the 1800s, these unadorned spaces—those in wealthier communities, at least—slowly filled with dictionaries, globes, blackboards, and American flags. Most schoolhouses, though, were poorly heated, cheerless, and ramshackle[5]—conditions tolerated by communities unwilling to take on the tax increases required for improved facilities.[6]

The school year reflected the farm calendar—open for a winter session and a summer session, closed for planting and harvest—and attendance was spotty.[7] Rural teachers, mostly women during the nineteenth century, taught classes of mixed ages and wide-ranging skills, and they were also usually tasked with sweeping the floor, feeding the fire, and tending the injured child. The quality of teaching was variable, as were the resources. Instruction tended to rely on memorization and focus on basic numeracy and literacy. In the late 1800s, as textbooks became more available and widespread, the popular McGuffey reader filled children's heads with stories and poems reflecting the morals and ethics of Protestantism and patriotism. For students, these textbooks, "written by men from afar who told of distant lands, who painted gaudy panoramas of virtue and vice, who talked in language never heard on the playground or in the country store,"[8] represented a world that existed beyond the confines of their rural town. Yet, even so, these rural schools were primarily a preparation for life in the community, giving students the skills, values, and knowledge needed for a life lived here.[9]

Community Schools

These schools were also institutions of and for their communities.[10] States, not the federal government, had jurisdiction over education, and they passed most responsibility for its provision to local towns.[11] Communities, through powerful school boards and vocal residents, controlled their schools—furnishing funds, hiring teachers, influencing curriculum and pedagogy.[12] The schools served as the focus of community life, too; the schoolhouse was, as one proud Kansas resident stated, "the center—educational, social, dramatic, political, and religious—of a pioneer community."[13] There was little boundary to separate school from other community matters, and "in one-room schools all over the nation ministers met their flocks, politicians caucused with the faithful, families gathered for Christmas parties and hoe-downs, the Grange held its baked-bean suppers, Lyceum lecturers spoke, itinerants introduced the wonders of the lantern-slide and the crank-up phonograph, and neighbors gathered to hear bees and declamations."[14] The school building was typically one of the few public spaces available to rural communities, and, as such, it served as a civic and religious gathering place, as well as a site for recreation.[15] Communities often organized debates—one North Dakota school wrestled with the question of whether "the Farm Woman Works Harder and has Less Recreation than the Farm Man"[16]—and students entertained with spelling bees, recitations, and plays. These kinds of events both offered amusement and fostered fellowship.

But the school could fuel conflict too.[17] School location was often the source of community battles. Long fights about the placement of a school building could extend over years, sometimes causing districts to fracture into smaller units. Wealth often played a role in these battles, as well-resourced families might offer to donate land for the building, ensuring it remained close to their residences. In the few ethnically diverse north-eastern and midwestern communities of the mid-1800s, religion and language could also become sources of conflict, with nonimmigrant teachers suppressing children's native language or religious practices and parents and students protesting. But, typically, schools united communities, and, as Horace Mann and other reformers promoted the societal and economic benefits of public education for a newly industrializing nation, rural schools spread throughout much of rural New England and the rural Midwest.[18]

Public schools were slower to come to the rural South.[19] Before the Civil War, formal education was a privilege of the elite, with private schools preparing the sons and daughters of plantation owners for the demands of white society and, perhaps, for college.[20] Slaves typically received no schooling—many southern states criminalized the teaching of slaves—and they were forbidden from organizing their own schools, slave owners punishing those found with books or slates.[21] Yet still slaves often held lessons in secret, lessons that reinforced the enormous power of literacy.[22]

After the war, though public education was spreading rapidly throughout the North and into the West, white planters opposed its southern expansion.[23] Planters saw public education as a threat to their economic and social power and, therefore, resisted the idea of government-funded schools. And, for this very same reason, freedmen and -women wanted schools: education meant liberation. So they created their own schools, various in structure and organization. Some rural black communities accepted the support of the Freedman's Bureau and northern philanthropists to establish educational institutions, and other ex-slaves forced planters to furnish plantation schools by making it a condition of their hire. Most, though, relying on long-standing practices of "self-teaching" and "native schools," resisted any sort of white influence or control and founded their own schools, raising their own funds and hiring their own teachers. These black schools taught the same classical curriculum of northern schools, and they often focused on leadership development, because only through political and social organization, many black leaders believed, would come economic liberation. Rural black communities also focused on adult literacy, establishing Sabbath schools, sponsored by churches, that ran at night or on weekends and taught freedmen and -women the fundamentals of reading and writing. The black push for education both boosted literacy rates and challenged white assumptions of black deficiency. Schooling, for many rural black communities, meant literacy—and literacy meant freedom.[24]

URBANIZATION AND RURAL "PROBLEMS"

The rise of American industry began during the nineteenth century, leaving a changed country in its wake.[25] By mid-century, much of Europe had already transitioned from an agricultural to an industrial society, and tensions between America's agrarian and commercial interests had been simmering for decades.[26] With the economy struggling after the Civil War, the country's economic and political elites saw an opportunity: large-scale manufacturing would be the answer. Favorable economic policies and changes in the modes and methods of production—new machinery, the rise of steam power and electricity, developments in the division of labor—enticed industrialists to open large factories in this country. Soon, America's machines worked faster, its coal companies drilled deeper, and its railroads pushed farther. Small cities swelled, as factories attracted thousands of workers. Immigrants from eastern and southern Europe flocked to these urban areas—18 million from 1890 to 1920.[27] Progressive reformers turned to public institutions to address the challenges and costs of the new capitalist system,[28] and city officials scrambled to build the infrastructure and systems to support the burgeoning populations. The voluntary services of the country were replaced by professional police forces and fire departments, official sewer systems and street lights.[29] The changes were rapid: during the mid-1800s, Germany, England, and France all outpaced the industrial yield of the United States, but by the century's end, the United States led the world in production, generating as much as these three countries combined.[30] Soon, manufacturing replaced agriculture as the foundation of the country's economy, and urban interests superseded rural concerns in motivating the country's politics.[31]

These sweeping changes, reformers believed, required a new type of schooling, an education for a newly modern, urban society. By the end of the nineteenth century, city classrooms were crowded with new students, creating new demands for space, order, and efficient instruction. Many of these new students were immigrants or the children of immigrants, and they needed to learn English and patriotism. And factories needed workers—diligent, obedient, American workers. And so the task fell to schools: build a properly Americanized workforce with the right values and the necessary—if limited—skills. Reformers seized the challenge.[32] Borrowing heavily from industry and business, they pushed for a new standardized system. School administration shifted to corporate-style bureaucracies filled with professionals, and these professionals, well-versed in the science of management, were charged with overseeing the legions of teachers now produced by normal schools.[33] Teacher training was formalized, and graduates were credentialed; schools were reorganized, and graded classrooms were introduced; curricula were examined, and textbook content was standardized.[34] Community involvement diminished, as the often-informal and certainly unregulated voluntary contributions of residents—hours donated to clean a school's hallways or cook the children lunch—were replaced by the work of professional custodians and lunch ladies. And what resulted was a more uniform and formalized approach to education, a "one best system"[35] driven by the demands of the country's growing cities.

A "Rural Problem"

As America's cities thrived and its urban schools scrambled to keep pace, its rural areas suffered.[36] Despite industrialists' dependence on farms for raw materials, urban and rural interests had long been at odds. Tensions had surfaced in the founding decades of the United States with battles over the establishment of a national bank—a struggle won by rural opposition— and then again after the Civil War, when statesmen raised tariffs to protect American industry and contracted the money supply to curb inflation—a fight the farmers lost. Though these postwar monetary policies furthered urban interests, they hurt agriculture, for, as the prices of foreign goods— manufactured items needed by farmers—rose, so did farmers' debts. With an economy transitioning toward industry came "an ideology that both un- dermined earlier forms of consciousness conducive to rural America and at the same time elevated capitalist notions of progress, modernity, and the division of labor."[37] A spate of novels, newspaper articles, and magazine stories documented the "backwardness" of rural life and painted an image of the future as a life lived in cities.[38] America's rural identity was fad- ing; urban interests now captured public imagination. With its promise of prosperity and cosmopolitanism, the city enticed rural residents, too, and soon rural communities began to lose population.

By the turn of the twentieth century, the advances in transportation, communication, and technology shaping city life were also remaking rural communities.[39] Agriculture was modernizing, adopting new equipment that could cultivate more acreage and produce greater yield. Farmers were no longer tied to local markets; they now had customers in other coun- tries. Soon big commercial farms began to replace small family farms, and tenant farming increased. Many of these tenants were recent immigrants, a shift that, coupled with the outmigration of many rural youth, dramati- cally altered the demographics of thousands of rural communities. Rural America, worried one early sociologist, risked deteriorating into "fished out ponds populated chiefly by bullheads and suckers."[40]

These changes concerned politicians and reformers; they feared "the corruption of rural Eden."[41] To the social Darwinists of the era, the rural population loss, the demographic shifts, and the perceived end of the American farming family all seemed diagnostic of a larger rural sickness that threatened to compromise the health of the entire American organism.[42] These concerns were fueled by urban needs for a stable agricultural foundation[43] and played to eugenicist fears over the mixing of rural youth with new urban immigrants.[44] A "rural problem," these reformers claimed, was fast emerging—"the problem of maintaining a standard people on our farms."[45] And so began a movement to reform rural community life, a movement rooted in assumptions of rural backwardness and tinged by undercurrents of rural nostalgia that aimed to restore a rural ideal of thriving farms, solid middle-class values, and an engaged and uncorrupted citizenry.

School Solutions?

This movement targeted rural schools, the source, reformers maintained, of rural America's problems. Report after report, commission after commission, documented the failures of rural education. The first was an 1896 report by the Committee of Twelve, a committee of prominent educators appointed by the National Education Association.[46] It concluded that the country's rural schools suffered from inefficiency, a lack of standards, an absence of state oversight, a "want of official and intelligent supervision," and an abundance of "untrained, immature teachers."[47] The underlying "problem" of rural schools, they argued, was the influence of the local community. Others soon echoed these claims. In *Rural Life and Education: A Study of the Rural-School Problem as a Phase of the Rural-Life Problem*, urbanite Ellwood Cubberley argued that the rural school "has been left far behind, educationally, by the progress which the schools of the neighboring towns and cities have made. Managed as it has been by rural people, themselves largely lacking in educational insight, penurious, and with no comprehensive grasp of their own problems, the rural school, except in a few places, has practically stood still."[48] Still another reported: "That the schools, managed as they have been mainly by country people, are largely responsible for the condition in which country communities find themselves today, there can be little question."[49] The federal Commission on Country Life, convened by President Theodore Roosevelt, joined the chorus, arguing for dramatic changes in rural schooling to stave the flood of rural outmigration.

These reformers were consistent in their recommendations. They argued for consolidation—collapsing small local schools into larger facilities and small local districts into larger units. Consolidation bred efficiency, they claimed, and these new facilities and units could be put under the control of county superintendents and in the hands of trained teachers. These advocates also recommended changes in curriculum, a new, more uniform education that could compensate for the isolation and tedium of rural life. Country Life advocates, in particular, pushed for a curriculum that would stimulate students' interest in the rural surrounds, "mak[ing] rural kids satisfied and content with rural life."[50] Though "rural-school reformers talked about democracy and rural needs," one theme ran through their structural and curricular reforms: "they believed that they had the answers and should run the schools"[51]—school decisions should be left up to the urban professionals, not the rural community. The "reorganization and redirection of rural education,"[52] these activists argued, would restore rural America—and keep it where it belonged.

The effects on rural schools were dramatic, and many reforms offered their own problems. Thousands of small rural schools and small rural districts were closed or dismantled through consolidation,[53] reorganizations facilitated by the spread of the automobile and the improvement of roads[54] and often pushed by private business interests tied to construction or school bus companies.[55] Larger and larger school facilities served wider and wider rural geographies, and from 1910 to 1960, the number of rural schools staffed by only one or two teachers dropped by 90 percent.[56] Professionals working in centralized state bureaucracies appropriated schooling decisions, and they focused on efficiency and standardization: hiring credentialed teachers, organizing students into graded classrooms, and improving school facilities.[57] The experience of school changed, too. Most rural students now attended safer, more modern school buildings, and some now received a nature-filled, place-based curriculum reflecting the more sincere intentions of the Country Life movement.[58] But, for many, the instructional outcome was simply a more standardized curriculum focused on occupational preparation and cosmopolitan interests and values. And all of these changes signaled another shift, "a transfer of power from laymen to professionals,"[59] from rural neighbor to urban reformer. A community's influence over its school—its ability to determine everything from where a school was located to which books it used—faded. Much to the frustration of some localities, rural schools were no longer so closely tied to their communities: rural schools would look, it seemed, more and more like their urban counterparts.

Another formulation of the "rural problem" also shaped rural America and rural schools during the late 1800s and early 1900s: the number of rural black schools was growing.[60] Many rural southern black communities, convinced of the emancipatory potential of education, now supported common schools through donations—a double tax, in essence, since their local taxes went primarily to fund white education. A few northern philanthropists also provided for the spread of black education: nearly 5,000 rural communities welcomed new school buildings, financed through the combined efforts of the philanthropist Julius Rosenwald and local communities— "one of the largest and most dramatic rural school construction programs of the era."[61] Though these common schools lacked many of the curricular resources enjoyed by white schools, black children still often received a rigorous and nurturing education, furnished by hard-working black teachers and administrators and supported by parents and community members volunteering their time and money, adults with a common belief in the value of education.[62] Here, in the rural South, few white government officials worried about the inefficiencies or unstandardized curricula of black education; instead, many white southerners worried about the simple fact of black education. This, then, was the rural problem of the South: an increasingly educated black citizenry, and the risks this posed for the economic, political, and social order.[63]

While the white planter class continued to resist the public education of black children, white industrialists advocated a different solution to the problem of black education: a repurposing of black schools, replacing their classical liberal arts curriculum with a model designed to create docile black laborers.[64] These industrialists, both southern and northern, hoped to solidify the country's agricultural base in the wake of urbanization. Manufacturing depended upon cotton and, therefore, black labor: "our great problem," one leading reformer wrote, "is to attach the Negro to the soil and prevent his exodus from the country to the city."[65] And so they turned to the Hampton model, first proposed by white northerner Samuel Chapman Armstrong and later promulgated by Booker T. Washington— an ex-slave and a student of Armstrong—to build a black working class. This model, developed at Armstrong's Hampton Normal and Agricultural Institute and Washington's Tuskegee Normal and Industrial Institute, focused on the training of black teachers. It involved both pedagogy and ideology. The curriculum centered on a routine of farm and trade labor: as students took teacher preparation courses, they dug, plowed, and sowed. They also learned, advocates claimed, the value of hard labor, Christian principles, and discipline. It was these values that reformers hoped the new teachers, through their work with students and communities, could spread throughout "the darkest corner of the darkest South."[66]

The Hampton model supported the efforts of social engineers and rural reformers to ensure the broader health of the American social and economic enterprise, and soon a number of philanthropists were using it to structure and fund training and normal schools.[67] Officials running Indian boarding schools would also come to adopt the model as a means of bringing "civilization" to Native students and their rural communities.[68] Unsurprisingly, this industrial model encountered resistance from many African American leaders and intellectuals who believed it would ensure political disempowerment, and this ideological struggle—a three-sided battle between white planters resisting black education, white industrialists (and some black graduates) espousing the training model, and black intellectuals pushing for a classical liberal education—continued for decades. Yet the Hampton model remained the dominant influence in county training and normal schools throughout the late 1800s and early 1900s, shaping generations of rural black teachers and administrators and the rural black students and communities they taught.

RURAL SCHOOL PROBLEMS AND POSSIBILITIES TODAY

The rural problem no longer makes headlines, and today's rural schools inspire little popular debate.[69] The reforms of the late 1800s and early 1900s— industrialization and modernization, standardization and consolidation— have been so effective as to become routine, simply the way things are done, too ordinary to capture the attention of an urban-centric media. But the reform of rural schools carries on: it washed through the twentieth century and floods into the twenty-first, with groundswells of complicated effects. And, in local rural communities today, this reform remains the subject of intense debate and, often, critique.

Rural Loss

Rural America, by many accounts, continues to struggle. Farming, faced with rising land prices, foreign embargoes on American goods, and governmental agriculture policies, foundered throughout the end of the twentieth century.[70] Suburban landscapes have swallowed up rural acreage,[71] and increased mechanization has evaporated jobs in agriculture. Large corporate farms have replaced hundreds of small and mid-size family farms, and many of the farms that remain now contract with food corporations, further strengthening the reach of agribusiness.

These changes have had dramatic impacts on farm workers, with black farmers feeling these closures and losses most acutely.[72] In 1964, for example, the number of black farmers exceeded the number of white farmers in at least fifty-eight southeastern counties, but, by 1996, in no county did black farmers outnumber white.[73] Though the meatpacking industry has grown rapidly in rural areas, this expansion has done little for local employment; these corporations have imported workers to fill jobs with low wages, few benefits, and dangerous working conditions.[74] These imported workers—typically Latino immigrants—often face racism and discrimination, and, in many rural areas, resentment over unemployment has fueled racial tensions.[75] Poverty rates in rural areas outpace those of urban areas:[76] in 2007, 15.4 percent of the nonmetropolitan population lived in poverty, compared to a national rate of 12.5 percent.[77] It may be unsurprising, then, that net outmigration persists in many rural areas.[78] In the mid-1900s it was the racism and social and economic inequality of the rural South—coupled with the mechanization of agriculture—that fueled the outmigration of rural black families;[79] today, poverty and limited job opportunities feed a population bleed that cuts across lines of race.

But other factors play a role, too; rural schools may push rural children from their rural communities.[80] Rural America, in the popular imagination, is still considered "left over" or "residual,"[81] and many argue that rural schools, then, "have become the vehicle for a powerful cultural message: success means getting the heck out of here."[82] Teachers, leaders, and reformers—motivated by their own urban-centric assumptions—often urge bright students to leave, to "get out," to join "the real world."[83]

Schooling, once so tied to the local place—to the particular rural village—in which it occurred, is also growing increasingly standardized, regulated, and placeless. The latter half of the twentieth century—filled with the Soviet launch of the Sputnik satellite and the release of reports like *A Nation at Risk*, all broadcasting the failure of American public schools—was marked by public dissatisfaction with the educational system.[84] In response, state and federal governments adopted a larger role in public education, issuing state and national content standards, achievement tests, and teacher requirements. These reforms have narrowed and standardized curricula and pedagogy to further goals—national economic gain and individual social mobility—little related to the particular place in which one lives.[85] Students are taught to be placeless, to adopt placeless patterns of speech—replacing local idioms, accents, and dialects with standard English—and placeless systems of values—exchanging culturally rooted beliefs and critical perspectives for principles of competition and independence.[86] The standardization of content, tied to the goals and objectives of the state and nation, has left its imprint on both rural children and rural communities. For many rural youth, it forces an education in which "embracing the values promulgated by schools too often requires a rejection of . . . family and community values."[87] This choice may translate into an adult life lived far from a rural home[88]—a "brain drain" that depletes local talent and empties communities.[89] Or it may resign children to staying, staying simply because this mass-produced, depoliticized education does "not prepare [them] to navigate the boundaries between [their] rural community of origin and the larger world."[90] With either option, the benefits of college, of graduate school, of advanced skills and knowledge and expertise remain far from rural communities, and the inequalities of geography are reinforced.

The standardization of public education has intensified other inequalities, too.[91] While expectations for schools have been standardized, resources haven't: "efforts to standardize and homogenize output occurred in places where conditions and resources were not standard."[92] Rural communities must offer the same opportunities and produce the same outcomes as other urban and suburban districts, yet many face high poverty rates and weak tax bases and the challenges of distance and isolation. Formulas for federal education funding, which favor quantities of poor students rather than rates of poverty, further disadvantage rural districts.[93] Many rural schools and students have borne these costs in struggles to find credentialed teachers,[94] the sanctions that come with low test scores,[95] and high drop-out rates[96]— conditions that only exacerbate the struggles of rural communities.

Consolidation, Desegregation, and More School Closures

Consolidation has also continued, with little interruption, since the late 1800s, bringing additional rural school closures.[97] Sputnik and the subsequent space race renewed interest in school reform and educational efficiency, and, in 1959, Harvard president James Bryant Conant published a study linking school size to American educational excellence: only schools with at least one hundred students per grade, he argued, could provide the sort of intellectual opportunity and enrichment needed to renew America's economic and scientific competitiveness.[98] This report, coupled with the economic declines and farming crises of the 1970s and 1980s, generated new floods of consolidation. Often influenced by private businesses, many states adopted policies tied to curricular requirements or school facilities that incentivized or pushed school consolidation, and they fostered district consolidation through the establishment of district enrollment minimums, mandates that also typically led to school closures.

Despite the fact that the promises of consolidation—achievement gains, financial savings, and reductions in administration—are often never realized,[99] and despite resistance to consolidation from many rural communities,[100] the consolidation movement has been starkly effective: more than 262,000 public schools existed in 1930, and now only 86,470 remain, despite a doubling in student population, with the average district now ten times as large and the average school five times as large.[101] These results carry meaning for rural students and communities. Consolidation may bring opportunities for students, like more course offerings and new friendships.[102] But there are often drawbacks, too: long bus rides, limited opportunities to participate in after-school activities, less individual attention from teachers and staff, and reduced parental involvement in schools.[103] Communities may also lose a source of employment and revenue, an opportunity for civic participation, and an important social institution: "the loss of a school erodes a community's social and economic base—its sense of community, identity and democracy—and the loss permanently diminishes the community itself, sometimes to the verge of abandonment."[104] As rural schools have closed, so have many rural communities.

And consolidation isn't the only reform to close schools and threaten rural communities. During the 1960s and 1970s, desegregation brought its own wave of school closures, as a mostly reluctant rural South, after evading the federal mandate for years, finally submitted to the required reorganizations.[105] Rural black communities had long suffered under the separate-and-unequal system of education in the South; black schools, while important cultural and social centers for their surrounding communities, usually had shoddier facilities, older textbooks, and fewer resources than white schools.[106] But the hope that the *Brown* decision brought to many rural black communities was soon deflated, as communities realized that, more often than not, desegregation spelled the loss of jobs for black teachers, the loss of positions for black administrators and black school board members, and the loss of schools for black communities.[107] Some black residents organized boycotts,[108] protesting the much higher tolls these methods of desegregation exacted on black communities. And white families and administrators often opposed desegregation, too—though likely for very different reasons. Many white communities throughout the South closed schools rather than admit black students, and soon the cry for "local control" reverberated through many rural southern communities, taking on an anti-desegregation tenor.

But, pushed by President Johnson's Civil Rights Act and Elementary and Secondary Education Act and a 1968 Supreme Court ruling forcing the elimination of school segregation "root and branch,"[109] slowly, haltingly, southern schools did desegregate, and black children and white children began to sit side by side in their classrooms. In many districts, though, the integration didn't last long:[110] in the years since desegregation, white families throughout the South have removed their children from public schools and enrolled them in private academies.[111] And other demographic challenges have emerged. As immigration changes rural populations, many rural teachers and administrators lack the skills and resources to meet the needs of their new students.[112] Rural schools, it seems, have not escaped the racial inequality that structures so many of America's public schools.

Rural Possibility

But this depiction—rural schools as places of generic curricula and empty buildings, their relationships with communities frayed and distant—is partial, only a half-truth. By many accounts, these schools and these relationships retain their promise. Many rural practitioners and researchers challenge the apparent inevitability of educational mass production, widening inequities, and rural decline and instead push for schools that meet local economic, civic, or social needs—building the rural community-school relationship to both improve educational quality and support the economic, civic, and social viability of a local community.[113] Rural schools, they maintain, should prepare students for local employment, local jobs that reflect local economies or local iterations of a national economy, employment that supports a more sustainable future for individual and community. Or rural schools can preserve a local way of life, imparting local values and teaching local knowledge and maintaining local culture. Rural education, they argue, can and should remain a local enterprise.

There are rural classrooms and schools throughout the country that reflect these practices, that provide an education rooted in local culture and the surrounding political, ecological, and economic systems, that embrace a curriculum supported by standards both context-dependent and locally determined.[114] Through the New Mexico Rural Revitalization Initiative, students in the town of Mosquero interview community members and stage Familias Days to remember and share the community's history, and students in the western part of the state work with biologists from the local university to build Zuni "waffle gardens" and plant native species of vegetables.[115] For decades, the Foxfire project, housed at Rabun County High School in Georgia, has produced books and magazines documenting the culture and folklore of Appalachia.[116] And in a wooded area of northern Pennsylvania heavily dependent on forestry and tied to a strong fishing and hunting culture, middle schoolers learn lessons in microbiology and environmental stewardship while wading through the stream that runs through campus.[117] These place-based curricula often reflect partnerships between local businesses and institutions, community leaders, and the school system, resulting in curricular alignment between the skills and knowledge taught and the needs and desires of the community[118]—partnerships that also foster rural growth and sustainability.[119]

Other rural schools have focused on addressing the racial, socioeconomic, or geographic inequalities that divide their communities. In parts of rural Texas, schools with growing Latino populations have crafted policies and practices of inclusion. These schools address teachers' biases and misunderstandings and provide more inclusive teaching techniques, and they build parent centers and welcome community volunteers—blurring the boundaries between school and home.[120] A number of states—from Arizona to South Carolina—have begun locally based rural teacher preparation programs;[121] these "grow your own" programs both offset rural teacher shortages[122] and provide teachers with the knowledge and skills necessary for contextual pedagogy.[123] And some rural practitioners are turning to technology for educational opportunities, both to train and support rural teachers and to supplement the K-12 curriculum.[124] Rural schools, as many researchers argue and these communities show, can resist the pull of standardization and urbanization and retain their local roots; rural schools can still contribute to a more viable, sustainable, and equitable rural America.

And, even with the creep of national standards and placeless curricula and teachers bent on students "getting out," these schools still matter. Despite a century and a half of "rural problems," a century and a half of rural schools "improved out of existence,"[125] rural schools—those that remain—haven't lost their local importance. Rural schools, researchers have found, still promise advantages for a rural town's economy, such as greater housing values and lower income inequality.[126] They can still preserve a community's culture, maintaining the community's values and ethos,[127] and they may still foster a sense of shared fate.[128] And, against a national backdrop of increasing racial segregation, rural schools offer a counterpoint: "once the center of the most intense resistance," they are now more integrated than urban or suburban schools, and their levels of integration are growing.[129] Despite 150 years of rural reform, some things haven't changed from the days of one-room schoolhouses: these rural schools, though threatened, are still valued.

TRACING A RELATIONSHIP: COMMUNITY SCHOOL, STATE SCHOOLING

Embedded in these generations of change and reform, binding these acres of rural expanse, is a relationship, a complicated relationship shared by rural school and rural community. It is a dynamic relationship: as the country has shifted and changed over the decades, this relationship, too, has changed. It began, in the log schoolhouses of New England farming towns and the little plantation schools of southern black communities, as a relationship fundamentally local in its scope and meaning. These rural communities determined what was taught, who was taught, and how, and schools prepared youth for the lives they would live in their rural communities. And rural schools, too, were places of fellowship, centers of culture, sites of liberation. Schools determined—and were determined by—community.

Then, with the rise of industry, rural schools became a mechanism for broader rural reform, a way for urban industrial elites to modernize a "backward" rural society and ensure the country's social, moral, and economic health. Reformers, both corporate and governmental, identified the "problem" as rural communities—the rural black communities of the South were doubly cursed—and, with that powerful rationalization, these reformers assumed responsibility for the oversight and administration of rural schools. Rural schools adopted new roles, promoting the national economy, and presented new problems—outmigration, racial subordination, school closure—for rural communities. The relationship tying rural school to rural community wasn't quite so intimate; these schools were no longer quite their own.

The influence of reformers only expanded over the next century, as corporate farming grew and America's agricultural identity faded, as the

Soviet threat loomed and national political and economic ambitions intensified. Federal and state policies pushed and pulled curricula into alignment through content standards and achievement testing, replacing rural schools, "important *places* in which people construct a social reality," with a generic schooling, "an attempt at systematic *instruction* of predetermined bodies of knowledge."[130] These reforms—and those wrangling the rural South into a hard-fought and still-incomplete desegregation—have meant closed schools. The rest increasingly answer to state and federal entities, not their local rural communities; these rural schools are meant to foster a national economy, a national identity, a national society. A third party—the state and federal government—has now joined the relationship shared by rural school and rural community.

Yet, even with these changes, rural schools today are no less important to their rural communities, no less meaningful, no less consequential. These schools still influence local economies. Some ensure local stability, simply by offering a handful of jobs and a source of local revenue, and others manage the more difficult task of training and retaining skilled youth through locally relevant curricula. Or, in some rural communities, the economic influence of rural schools is felt differently, a darker impact, an influence wielded through outmigration and dropping populations—rural schools pushing rural youth toward other places, other jobs, other communities. And these schools still write local social and cultural dynamics. They sometimes recreate the separate-and-unequal systems of the old South and reinforce long-standing divides, or they sometimes welcome new students and include new families and build new communities. The importance of these schools is apparent in reactions to school closures—in black communities' dissatisfaction with the methods of desegregation, in rural towns' often-fierce resistance to consolidation. And this importance is clear, devastatingly clear, in the repercussions of closed rural schools, in the struggles of their rural communities to simply survive.

But, though the significance of this relationship is clear, its consequences are complicated. This dependence of community on school can lead, it seems, to either sustenance or devastation. This relationship can nourish a rural community socially, or it can cause segregation and inequality. It can fortify a rural economy, or it can produce shrinking populations and shuttered farms and rural decline.

And it's often the government—the powerful state and federal government, that new third party in this intimate relationship—implicated in these disparate consequences. Because rural communities depend so heavily upon their schools, as state and federal governments reform rural schools, they also change these communities. The effects of education policies—consolidation policies and desegregation mandates, funding formulas and state tests—reverberate through rural America. Though the current process of governmental intervention in rural schools may be less intentional than the naming of "rural problems" and rural solutions in the 1900s—and is certainly less explicit—it is no less real: school reform means rural reform.

This intervention can be necessary and useful. It was state and federal reform that forced desegregation and fostered a level of community integration, that created a wider array of economic options and future prospects for rural youth and tied rural places to global markets. But it's also governmental reform—one-sided desegregation plans and federal funding formulas that disadvantage the smallest and poorest rural communities—that has fueled many rural divisions and geographic inequalities. It's governmental reform that has hastened much of the rural outmigration, that has replaced locally relevant curricula and pedagogy with a generic preparation for national jobs in a national economy. And it's governmental reform that has closed rural schools, with rural communities slowly and quietly disappearing after.

It's of little surprise, then, that at the center of this relationship shared by school and community and government is a struggle for control: whose interests should rural schools serve?[131] Should these schools meet the needs of the larger state and country, or should they respond to the particular issues and desires of the community? Advocates of standardization sometimes pin their answer to the needs of the child, arguing that through a nationalized system of high standards and rigorous testing the country will achieve educational equity.[132] And the other side—often the rural communities themselves, the "problems" themselves—are left with little else but the language of "local control" to make their arguments.

Yet the battles of national control versus local control, of national interests versus local interests, have no simple sides. State and national control, while it may erode the political identity and power of rural communities, has often been a necessary force for equity and justice, for ending racial segregation and ensuring the rights of overlooked students and communities; for decades, "local control" was the racist battle cry of segregationists. And state and national governments, through their reforms and mandates, may push a rural community toward long-term economic viability. But sometimes it's local control that promotes justice, equity, sustenance—providing the flexibility and nuance that help teachers meet the needs of their particular students and administrators meet the needs of their particular communities, the care that nurtures generations of citizens and leaders, the ethic of interdependence and connection that sustains rural communities across the country. This debate over control isn't a matter of good and evil, a simple choice between a right side and a wrong side. Instead, the answer may be more about balance, a balance of needs and roles and purposes, a complicated and contextual balance negotiated within a complicated and contextual relationship, a balance desperately sought by thousands of rural communities today.

THE RELATIONSHIP TODAY

And so it is that, even after two centuries of rural change, even with some loss of local responsiveness, rural schools do still matter to rural communities. Rooted in a national history and written by local particulars, suspended somewhere in the tension between national and local, the relationship shared by rural school and rural community continues, playing out across complex geographies of long-standing inequality and education politics. These schools shape rural communities in profound and fraught and important ways—I saw this in Vanleer, and I would come to understand this much more fully in Delight and Earle.

Yet, with today's focus on city schools, rural schools are often overlooked. Reformers and lawmakers fail to hear the stories of rural schools. They fail to see how much these schools matter and why. They fail to understand how racialized histories and current education policies color and shape the ties of school and community. They fail, it seems, to comprehend everything at stake with this relationship.

For the relationship between school and community shapes the implementation and effects of educational policy—whether and how these policies are implemented, if the policies have the results intended, what unintended consequences arise, and how these effects ripple through communities. This relationship carries lessons for rural and urban educators and leaders alike, important lessons about race and community and power, about the costs of a narrow focus on academic achievement. And this relationship has meaning for both rural sustainability and educational justice, for these rural schools determine the opportunities of millions of children and the futures of thousands of rural communities.

CHAPTER THREE

Researching Rural

After I left teaching in Vanleer, I'd think about that beans and greens supper often—about an entire community crowded shoulder to shoulder over steaming Styrofoam trays, over decades of classroom lessons and consolidation threats, over demographic and economic change and a slowly simmering anxiety. I thought about that supper when I saw reruns of *The Beverly Hillbillies* or *The Andy Griffith Show* or heard news reports about the rural meth epidemic and ballooning farm subsidies and backwoods antigovernment extremists. I thought about it when I drove past a boarded-up schoolhouse way off the highway, miles from anything and empty inside. I thought about it as I sat in my graduate school classes or listened to the school-reform debates and heard only about the children and schools of cities. I would think about this supper because it illustrated a complex relationship shared by rural community and rural school that was usually missing from the other representations or discussions of "rural" or "education" I encountered. It was this rural—a more authentic rural, a rural deeply tied to issues of race and reform, the rural of beans and greens suppers—that interested me . . . and should interest others.

A RESEARCH RELATIONSHIP

Traditional approaches to research, in which participants are "subjects" to "access," their words "data" to "report," seemed unlikely to uncover this sort of authenticity—and these sterile, one-sided methods have perhaps fed tired stereotypes. I wanted, instead, the complicated rural that emerges through sprawling conversations and long car rides and time spent in rural places. I wanted to work *with* participants, not on them. I wanted to hear their stories, stories of rural school and rural community, stories that could reveal the roles that a rural public school plays in its rural community and show how these roles are patterned by historic racial inequalities and current education politics. And stories, I knew, require relationships, because they are not simply listened *to*—they must be listened *for*.[1]

To satisfy these methodological demands, I chose portraiture.[2] Portraiture is an ethnographic research method "designed to capture the richness, complexity, and dimensionality of human experience in social and cultural context, conveying the perspectives of the people who are negotiating those experiences."[3] The method is based upon relationships shared with participants, knowledge constructed in dialogue, and understandings shaped in context. It is distinct from other methods of social science research in its orientation toward strength: it refuses the "tradition-laden effort to document failure" and "assumes that the expression of goodness will always be laced with imperfections."[4] Portraiture involves both the science of rigorous research and the art of a reflected reality, balancing "analysis and narrative, description and interpretation, structure and texture."[5] With portraiture—with the details gathered through conversation and experience, interviews and observations, reflection and revision—I could investigate the meaning community members give to their schools and explore how these understandings correspond and differ. I could piece stories into broader narratives and retain their meaning, their cadence, their poetry.

Portraiture would also allow me to look across communities—not for comparative evaluation or judgment, but rather for greater depth and complexity. I could work with two places—towns with unique demographics and histories—and then consider how their particular dimensions might influence the roles their schools play; this pairing could offer detailed narratives located in particular rural places while also illuminating some of the broader realities of rural education. By creating two portraits, each dense with thick descriptions of a community and its schools,[6] I could document these relationships and their social, demographic, and historic details.

Portraiture focuses on authenticity,[7] the resonance that hides in details. Portraiture assumes that a person or a place or a phenomenon can only be understood in context, and so the portraitist examines the particular: these unique, contextual understandings suggest more universal truths. The researcher is very much a part of the research, conducting interviews and observations but also engaging in the life and rhythm of a community, continually working to identify and question biases and assumptions—his or her own and those of a broader public—and seek alternate explanations. With this method, I could explore and question, document and examine a more authentic understanding of rural schools and rural communities— an understanding focused on the meaning rural communities give their schools and grounded in the rural landscape. And so, as I conducted hundreds of hours of interviews and observations at my two sites, authenticity was my standard: open and honest relationships, thoughtful and genuine representation, careful and precise language.

LOCATING THE RELATIONSHIP

But, before all the interviews and observations could begin, I had to find two rural communities. I needed two sites—both readily self-identifying as "rural"—that were willing to engage these questions and open themselves to me and my scrutiny. I wanted southern towns—a rural context I knew, a rural context with a long legacy of racial exclusion—and I wanted locales with demographics and histories that complemented one another, that could offer different narratives of rural schools and communities. This search was neither short nor simple—it was more complicated than my hunt for a rural job several years earlier.[8] As a graduate student living in Cambridge, Massachusetts, I was now far removed from rural places and lives spent in and around public schools. And so I spent long, frustrating years meeting people and making contacts, chasing leads and searching maps, researching specific communities and parsing demographics, and, once again, questioning definitions of rurality.

Finally, a cold call to the Rural School and Community Trust yielded a name: Dorothy Singleton, an African American organizer working in Arkansas, helping communities fight to keep their schools—and aiding those that had recently lost them. I called her and arranged to fly down, meet her, and tag along with her while she worked. For two days we drove in and out of rural communities, passing shuttered school buildings and small active campuses, large consolidated facilities and buildings with dark windows and weed-covered parking lots. We started in the northeast corner of the state, in the Delta, and made our way southwest, to the hills, attending community gatherings and school meetings and a football game—Dorothy doing the networking and the morale boosting and the planning of her job, and me looking for a research site, a rural community that would tolerate a graduate student with questions, a rural community that still had its school. Our tour ended in Delight, a town with a school threatened by closure, a school with a surprisingly diverse student body and staff, a school, I was assured, with a story that needed telling. By that afternoon, I had my first research site.

A year later, I began searching for a second research site. I hoped to find a town with demographics and a racial history different from Delight's, where I could address other questions of race and rural schooling. I remembered that first Arkansas tour with Dorothy, remembered the different receptions that we—a black woman and a white woman—received in the nearly all-white and nearly all-black communities of Arkansas. I remembered the first "black church" I ever sat in, the "white house" that Dorothy wouldn't risk approaching. I remembered my own experience growing up in the South, a white student in a mostly white private school surrounded by a mostly black public system, an experience that, for long decades, I had never thought to see as racialized or segregated. And so I looked for a second site, a site that would complement Delight, a site where I could further explore and understand these ingrained and sometimes-unquestioned patterns of racial separation, patterns that, for reasons complex and layered, weren't so present in Delight. This second site was Earle—a rural town with schools filled almost exclusively by black children—and this site also came by way of Dorothy: I met Earle's former superintendent, now the region's state senator, at a summer organizing conference Dorothy led. The senator invited me to Earle, introduced me to teachers and principals, drove me through the town, and, soon, I had another site.[9]

Arkansas—a state of rivers swollen with floodwaters, cattle scattered on hillsides, and cotton white for harvest—would prove a fertile ground for questions of community and school and, particularly, of race and reform; it is a terrain carved into complicated landscapes of exclusion and inclusion. It is a predominantly rural state,[10] and it always has been—first a frontier state[11] with a reputation as a lawless backwoods,[12] later a state largely dependent upon agriculture and landless rural laborers.[13] The Arkansas area was originally inhabited by a number of Native tribes, primarily the Quapaws in the Delta[14] and the Caddo farther west.[15] The earliest white settlement in Arkansas—the first white settlement west of the Mississippi—was founded in 1686 as a trading post for the region's growing fur trade; the area was acquired by the United States in 1803 as a part of the Louisiana Purchase, gaining statehood in 1836.[16] The state was late to secede,[17] slow to comply with the federal requirements of Reconstruction,[18] and reluctant to desegregate its schools.[19] Today, its

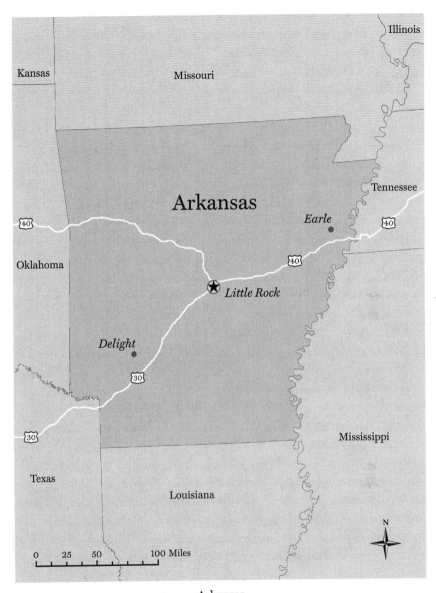

Arkansas

(map created by Mathieu Duvall at Bates College using Esri mapping software)

divisions—rifts of geography, race, and education—are entrenched, written into this state's particular history, and still today they separate the state's landscape and its communities, still mark Delight and Earle, still shape the relationships these towns share with their schools.

Divisions of Geography

Arkansas's geography is varied—mountains and flatlands, dense forest and open farmland, rolling hills and green floodplains—and these variations foster different economies, politics, social systems, and demographics. The Delta area, the area that holds Earle, stretches from the Mississippi River on the east to Little Rock on the west. The Delta is open and flat; once covered in dense forests, it is now blanketed by acres of cotton, rice, and soybeans.[20] It is distinctive, too, in its waterways, rivers that, for early settlers, held the promise of transport and travel and the danger of disease and flooding. Its warmth and humidity fuel a long growing season and, during the nineteenth century, a fledgling cotton industry, tightly tied to a plantation economy, began to thrive in the area—some early, cotton-dependent counties were the richest counties in the state. By the Civil War, many of these counties had more black residents than white, and the area was thoroughly dependent upon slavery; the Delta's leaders were enthusiastic supporters of the Confederacy and pushed for secession. After the war and the widespread clearing of the region's timber, the Arkansas Delta emerged as a one-crop economy, supported entirely by the cotton industry and the sharecropping that sustained it. African American farmers, drawn to the area by the promise of land and a flourishing industry, were soon confronted with the harsh reality of Delta life—poverty and creditors, exploitation and punitive labor, violence and uncertainty.[21] The turn of the century brought little salvation, especially for struggling black sharecroppers: the early 1900s saw floods, drought, and the Great Depression.[22] The Delta's economy foundered, and thousands of laborers left the area.[23] Remaining sharecroppers organized the Southern Tenant Farmers Union, an interracial organization that fought throughout the 1930s for better wages and working conditions and brought national attention to the plight of sharecroppers.[24] Despite their work and decades of technological change, the fortunes of most Delta residents are little different today: the rise of agribusiness and mechanization of farming have meant profits for a handful of lucky elite and hardship for the rest—a "pyramid" with "a few large agribusiness people at the top and an ever-expanding number of low-income groups at the base."[25]

The regions beyond the Delta—the other two-thirds of Arkansas—are studded with peaks and valleys. Though the jagged summits of the Ozark and Ouachita mountains crowd the northern part of this upland area, the southern half, where Delight is located, rolls with pine-covered hills.[26] After the Louisiana Purchase, white settlers and, later, European immigrants were drawn to the region, lured by the game in its forests.[27] Many established small farms, unable to sustain much more in the weak soil, and this upland area came to produce a variety of crops and goods, with timber the primary resource of the hills.[28] Without cotton, the uplands were never plantation dependent, though a few farms had a small number of slaves[29]—and today the region remains whiter than the Delta.[30] After the Civil War, the number of white tenant farmers and laborers grew, and the area shared in the economic decline of the late 1800s, when many of these white families, scattered in farms across the hills and mountains, faced poverty and financial ruin.[31]

These geographic differences, splitting Delta from uplands, also affect the state's policies and politics.[32] During the 1800s, the hill country tended to embrace a more egalitarian politics. It was reluctant to support secession,[33] a reluctance that kept the state from joining the Confederacy until after the attack on Fort Sumter,[34] and the post-Reconstruction policies and decisions that so motivated legislators from eastern Arkansas had little relevance to many Ozark families and politicians.[35] This regional divide—a "rivalry between the Delta and the hill country" defined by their separate economies and distinct politics, splitting Earle from Delight— remains today.[36]

In the decades following Reconstruction, another division emerged—a division between Arkansas's cities and its rural areas. Post-Reconstruction politicians were chiefly concerned with attracting business and industry to Arkansas and building the state's cities.[37] In adopting policies to lure northern investors, these statesmen also developed "a cavalier attitude toward protection of the South's treasured resources, an insensitivity about numerous social neglects, [an] acceptance of low-wage policies which ultimately retarded Southern economic growth, and [an] acquiescence in neo-colonialist policies of both the federal government and some Northern corporations"—all of which carried high costs for the state's rural communities.[38] The gulf between Arkansas's urban elite, an entrepreneurial class with the capital to fund urban development, and its rural residents—the

Earles and Delights of the state—only widened in the late 1800s, hastened by a return to the gold standard that sent crop prices plummeting, a railroad industry that often overlooked small rural stops, and legislation and protective tariffs that hampered the economic growth of the South. Some farmers organized into new political parties such as the Agricultural Wheel and the Union Labor Party, but these political reorganizations mostly failed to bring meaningful political power to rural farmers and instead instigated voter intimidation, election fraud, and political scrambling for votes. This agricultural decline also set the stage for a growing bitterness—a resentment felt by many poor, rural, white farmers toward the state's black residents.

Divisions of Race

This racial resentment was, of course, long brewing. After Reconstruction dismantled Arkansas's state government, the state was forced to draft a new constitution; this constitution, according to the Reconstruction Acts, would give black residents the vote, and the newly formed state government would have to ratify the Fourteenth Amendment.[39] This process, designed to empower a coalition of black legislators and extend the rule of the Republican Party, was rife with violence from the Ku Klux Klan and voting fraud, and, though black officials gained seats on a number of state boards, they struggled to leverage power over these political bodies. Reconstruction ended soon after, brought to a close with major Democratic victories in the elections of 1874 and 1875, victories hasted by fractures within the Republican Party and resentment toward its policies.

A few black officials continued to hold local offices: both Republicans and Democrats pursued the black vote, and both parties abided by a "fusion principle" that endorsed a biracial slate of candidates for local elections.[40] These conciliatory moves were motivated, it seems, by a desire for social harmony, a wish to avoid federal intervention, and the need to attract black workers to the Delta's cotton fields. Yet tensions mounted as the number of black Delta residents grew; fusion politics soon fell from favor, and black residents gradually lost their elected power.[41] Fraud and intimidation became the accepted means of tempering the black vote. Still holding the land and the means of agricultural production, the Delta's white minority wielded tight control over that region, while its black residents typically labored as tenant farmers.[42] Planters supplied the land, the mules, the plows, the seed, and the cabin; they dictated the crops grown and penalties sustained, and sharecroppers worked the fields. Not only did this sharecropping system further limit the state's economy by prolonging its reliance on a single crop and forestalling investments in new agricultural technologies, but it also perpetuated the inequities of the plantation system and left unchallenged its caste-like social mores—traditions that resonate across the Delta still today.

Divisions of Schooling

The new, postwar state constitution held one other promise: the guarantee of a free, tax-funded education for both black and white children.[43] But, because government and business leaders viewed schooling as a means of building an ample and obedient working class, this provision was little more than an avenue toward industrialization, and it did little to improve the quality of education for most children. Until nearly 1900, the state's cash-poor rural schools operated on a three-month term, while the city schools of Little Rock, funded by a strong property-tax base, ran a nine-month school year.[44] Furthermore, many white Arkansans continued to view black students as unworthy of education or unable to learn. Throughout the twentieth century, black children continued to attend plantation schools, schools that were woefully underfunded but that often managed, with the strong support of their communities and the skill and care of their teachers, to offer a sound education,[45] and a few rural black communities welcomed Rosenwald schools, built with a combination of funds from philanthropist Julius Rosenwald and local community contributions.[46] Many white Delta families, though, sent their children to private schools, which likely slowed improvements to the public system and further institutionalized the divide between white and black residents.[47]

The racial divisions of schooling reached a climax with desegregation— most notoriously with Governor Faubus's resistance to federally mandated desegregation, his decision to order the National Guard to prevent nine black students from entering Little Rock's Central High School, the ensuing violence, and a slow and public bleed of racist ideology into state education politics.[48] Arkansas, like much of the South, was unhurried in desegregating its schools after the 1954 *Brown v. Board of Education* decision; not until a 1968 Supreme Court decision forced districts to avoid delay in the creation of unitary systems did desegregation gain traction across the state. As black and white schools merged and buses crisscrossed districts to fetch their racially mixed student bodies, many white families simply moved from these districts to whiter ones, and many black teachers lost their jobs.[49] White students also fled to the private academies proliferating throughout the South.[50] These "segregation academies," often tied to local churches, provided an alternative to the newly desegregated public system, allowing white families with means to solidify their interests and resources in a private system; by 1970, the *Arkansas Gazette* counted fifteen of these academies throughout the state.[51] Occasional violence continued to break out in districts and schools, and, in the late seventies, the Klan reemerged, holding a series of meetings across the state.[52] By the late eighties, white families were leaving the Delta itself, many eager to escape the public schools.[53] Now, fifty years after the Central High crisis, many note the costs of desegregation—the violence, the growing racial resentment, the loss of a tight-knit black culture, the population bleed—and wonder, simply, whether it worked.

Today's Divisions

More recently, the state's divisions—geographic and racial—have been evident in its educational funding. After years of argument about insufficiencies in school funding and disparities between districts, the Arkansas Supreme Court ruled that the state's funding scheme was unconstitutional, both inherently inadequate and inequitable, and that the state government had failed in its obligation to educate the state's children.[54] The 2002 case *Lake View School District vs. Huckabee*, or *Lake View III*, was the last in a long series of court cases following desegregation, cases in which poor districts protested the state's funding structure. The court found that this system, which relies upon local property taxes set at a locally determined millage rate, disadvantages the state's property-poor districts—in particular, the rural, African American districts of the Delta. But in its ruling, the court failed to articulate a specific remedy, and the state remained out of compliance with the decision until 2007.

Despite the state's inability to quickly and satisfactorily meet the terms of the decision, the case did motivate some new legislation, including Act 60.[55] The act mandated the consolidation of districts with fewer than 350 students, a move that, according to lawmakers, would save the state money. It also had an academic justification, with the governor highlighting consolidation as a means to expand schools' curricula. Despite much public controversy, despite the long-standing reputation of forced consolidation as "the third rail of Arkansas politics,"[56] Act 60 passed in 2004.

Just one year later, fifty-seven districts had closed,[57] all but two of them rural, with more to follow.

Other state and federal policies also shape rural schools' finances, governance, and academics: like many other school districts across the country, Arkansas's districts have lost some of their local control with the recent rise in state and national influence. As Act 60 tightened state control over districts' structural and educational decisions, the No Child Left Behind Act mandated greater federal oversight of students' academic performance and sanctions for underperformance. No Child Left Behind (NCLB), passed with bipartisan support in 2002, requires states to administer yearly standardized tests, with the goal of 100 percent of a school's students reaching "proficiency" in reading and math by 2014.[58] As stipulated by the act, if a school fails to make adequate yearly progress (AYP) toward this goal, it faces increasingly severe punishments, ending in an abdication of all local public control and, often, school closure.[59] This threat of closure—whether by consolidation or academic sanction—blankets the state of Arkansas, hanging heavy in the poorest, smallest, most rural communities.

These divisions—divisions of geography, of race, of schooling—continue to split Arkansas. The state still feels like two, the Delta and the uplands, and its rural communities still seem quite distant from the snarl of interstates marking Little Rock, where the sun glints off a mirrored business district and gold capitol dome. It remains a state in which nearly 40 percent of its students are rural, a fifth of them minorities: over 30,000 rural students attend schools tucked in communities scattered across mountains and river valleys,[60] communities facing economic decline and population loss,[61] communities confronting school closure and instructional expenditures well short of the national average.[62] It's a state where race continues to matter: racial tensions simmer, occasionally boiling over in a violent act or tingeing political battles.[63] And perhaps race matters even more in Arkansas's schools, as large numbers of the Delta's white students still attend private schools,[64] as the state's black students still trail far behind their white counterparts on standardized tests,[65] as consolidation disproportionately impacts African American students and reduces African American leadership in schools.[66] These are the challenges that Arkansas's rural communities face: dwindling populations and consolidation fears, long-standing racial disparities and a flourishing private school system, highly publicized school improvement lists and federal sanctions that threaten takeover and closure.

And these are the challenges that Delight and Earle face, the challenges of race and reform that give texture to the complex relationship shared by these communities and their schools. Delight, tucked in the piney hills of the southwestern corner of the state, and Earle, lying in the rich Delta floodplains of the Mississippi, each share a close relationship with their schools. These are small, struggling, rural towns, with a lack of ready employment and with household incomes well below national averages, the kind of rural towns, perhaps, most dependent upon their schools, even as these communities struggle mightily to fund them. Race matters in these towns and their schools, but differently, as apparent even in Delight's racially mixed student body and Earle's entirely African American one, each representing different legacies of southern history. Both grapple with the consequences of recent education legislation—consolidation looms a constant threat in Delight, as the district's enrollment has dropped below 350 students, while the most immediate risk in Earle is about academics, as its schools have all logged time on the state's "school improvement" list—and with the slow realization that these schools, though still fundamentally and profoundly local institutions, are now state and federal entities, too. The narratives of race and reform that I would hear, then, are the narratives of a state, a region, a nation, and also narratives of much more particular places, rich narratives about space and time and community and school—a complexity that I tried to honor in my relationships with each town, in my conversations and interactions, in my analysis and writing.

A RELATIONSHIP'S DESIGN

Though I started this research in Delight in 2007 and finished it in Earle in 2010, I approached my relationship with each site similarly. I first made a few trips to each place to meet school leaders, visit the schools, drive through the towns—to begin the relationship. Then I returned for longer visits, five or six days at a time, to interview and observe, to talk with folks and spend time in the communities. Over three years spent in and out of Delight and Earle, over fifteen trips and hundreds of miles across the state, I've gone to church and shopped in the towns' stores, played with pets and cheered at basketball games, been asked over for supper and invited out to dinner. I know that Friday night is the fish buffet at Mom's in Delight, and that the women who work at Earle's Citgo gas station can tell you where anyone lives. I've witnessed the beginnings of school years, and their ends. I've spent hundreds of hours at events—ball games and parades and benefit suppers—or just in the school and town, eating lunch in the cafeteria, driving the unnamed roads, hanging out over coffee, interactions and experiences detailed in pages and pages of field notes. I've shared countless conversations with community members and outsiders, sixty-nine of them formal, tape-recorded interviews. Some participants I purposefully selected[67] for their distinct perspectives, while other participants were recommended to me. This "snowball sampling" approach[68] ensured I found "those voices that have been historically smothered"[69] by virtue of race or class, heard from the community's "native leaders,"[70] and located other sources of possibly unique or discrepant data.[71] These decisions left me with a sample that included black and white participants, adults and students, current and former school staff, retirees and business owners, newcomers to the area and long-time residents, parents and grandparents, those with children at the towns' public schools and those who had chosen to move their children from these schools.

I then examined this data, first looking at each community separately. I read and reread interview transcripts and field notes, wrote and rewrote memos about various topics and ideas, organized and reorganized all of this material—distilling themes and patterns that described the roles the schools play in each community. Some of these themes reflected topics and theories I brought to the data—my interest in school segregation, for example, or theories on social capital—but most were themes that emerged, categories and codes—like the boundaries of community or fears of closure—grounded in the words, ideas, and actions of participants.[72] I worked and reworked these themes until I felt that they accurately captured what I heard across participants, reflecting both the common understandings and the snarls of inconsistency and disagreement. I then returned to each community and gathered a group of residents. I talked through these themes, and we discussed them,[73] with community members raising questions and adding details. I also regularly sought the perspectives of a group of colleagues in Cambridge, a group that came to know Delight and Earle and their schools well. These meetings, in both Arkansas and Cambridge, helped me identify my own assumptions and biases, reexamine the language and tenor of some of these arguments, and consider other explanations.

With these perspectives and this feedback, I began to write each portrait—first of Delight and then Earle—knitting together the individual narratives I heard and events I witnessed, putting words to the communities and schools I encountered. Then I wrote across these portraits, distilling broader themes that describe the variety of roles schools play in rural communities, exploring why and how these roles arise, looking for patterns across these themes. The towns' differences complemented one another, and I tried to avoid simplistic comparisons and reductive judgments. Instead, I looked at these communities in combination, using one to better understand the other, using their differences to fully consider the range of contextual factors—historical, geographic, economic, social, demographic—that seem to affect the roles a school plays in a community.

A Relationship's Landscape

Throughout all of these interactions, both formal and informal, I have worked to maintain authentic and reciprocal relationships with participants, a personal standard and a methodological one.[74] I knew that the quality of these relationships would influence the depth of my understanding, and I wanted participants to feel heard and valued during this experience—I hoped that the sharing of stories could be an enriching, rather than depleting, experience.

Establishing these kinds of relationships has involved a fair amount of negotiating identity and labels—for me and also, I am sure, for participants. As we sat together at a classroom desk or diner booth, I wondered what a participant would see—a Harvard researcher? A former teacher? A young student? A white woman? A southerner? A northerner? And what was I seeing of them—their age, race, occupation, gender? I knew these labels would shape our interactions; they would surface in my questions, in their responses, in our ways of being and being together. I also hoped we could begin to see past these labels, to expose more complicated understandings. I learned to listen for these scripted identities, in my assumptions and theirs, to recognize them, acknowledge them, and then try to see beyond to the nuance in the story and the storyteller. The communities, I soon discovered, had overlapping identities and multiple narratives, and I tried to make room for such expansiveness, to identify and understand the contradictions, to allow for complication.

And, as my ties to each community grew stronger, I had to work to temper my affection for these places, to prevent this affection from obscuring authenticity. I genuinely liked these communities and their residents, and, sometimes, upon hearing a story of exclusion or racism or a shortcoming of the schools, I found myself feeling disappointed. I used this disappointment as an indicator that I was verging on romanticism and seeking out perfection; it was a reminder to see what was really there, rather than just what I hoped was there.

Despite their similar beginnings, my relationships with these two communities were different, necessarily so. In Delight, my connections with individuals were more personal and closer, facilitated, perhaps, by Dorothy's own personal ties to the principal and several teachers. I quickly had a "home away from home" in Delight: I'd sleep on the principal's couch when I visited, and we'd stay up late, catching up on all that had happened since my last visit. I continue to check in with a number of Delight residents—seeking updates about the community and school but also sharing news about family and friends, inquiries about health, warm wishes for the holidays. My relationship with Earle was more distant. No couch awaited me there; I stayed at a hotel in a neighboring town. This physical distance contributed to an emotional one: as much time as I spent in town meeting people and attending school assemblies and driving around, I simply wasn't as embedded in the community as I was in Delight. These differences I tried to recognize—not to eliminate, but to see—and to understand what they said about each community, about the research process, and about me. These differences, I think, reflect authenticity.

There were other particulars of relationship to consider, too. Perhaps the most salient particular was race—for me and for many of my participants, I would suspect. I am white; many of these communities' residents are black; and this is the South, where race is never far from anyone's mind. And, too, this was the *rural* South, a place that stands in stark contradiction to the assumptions of rural whiteness, a living witness to a complicated, confounding, racialized rural. Was I getting the *real* story? Whose story was it? And how would I know? I wouldn't, at least not with any certainty. But I became more accustomed to talking about race explicitly and clearly through the course of these interviews and conversations—by asking directly how race affected interactions in school, for example, or town politics outside of school—an evolution that, while not always comfortable or graceful, did feel more genuine and open. I also became more accustomed to hearing multiple narratives, both narratives and counternarratives, hearing them thoroughly and honestly.[75] I checked my own specific assumptions and understandings with participants who seemed comfortable talking about race with me, and my close relationships with Kathy, Delight's black principal, and Dorothy challenged me to identify and question my own observations and reactions.

And there were contextual particulars that, no doubt, shaped the stories I heard. Both towns were in jeopardy of school closure: in the past, the threat was "fiscal distress," but now Delight faced consolidation tied to low enrollment, while Earle's primary concern was academic sanction. I wondered how this threat colors these stories, colors the roles the schools play in these communities. In Delight, especially, with the immediacy of enrollment numbers falling around 330, conversations were often laced with anxious discussion of student counts and nervous predictions of the effects of a lost school. It's impossible, I think, to separate these threats from the focus of my inquiry—the broader meaning of these schools. It's plausible—indeed, quite likely—that the threat of closure lends a heightened importance to the roles played by the schools. But, while threat certainly gives these roles significance, it may not change the *types* of roles these schools play. Furthermore, trying to isolate the relationship shared by school and community from this threat seems a futile and meaningless exercise, for, at this point in time, these schools are schools under threat—an omnipresent, looming threat. These battles over consolidation and fears about the state's academic sanctions, I found, provided a window into this relationship: people were ready and willing to talk about their schools, and they have clearly thought about what they would lose without them—this anticipated loss, this absence, reveals the contours of what is, for now, still there. These threats, too, are the products of state and federal policies, products of today's school-reform context, and, as state and federal control over education grows, these reforms also shape and form the relationship shared by school and community. These reforms, I would come to realize, are just as meaningful, just as worthy of question and attention, as any other contextual factor—and, given their threatening power, perhaps even more so.

Language disclosed other contextual particulars, too, and, in telling and retelling these communities' stories, I tried to use the language of participants, to quote them directly, to preserve voice and tenor. Research has long ignored rural communities, lumped them into coarse categories that say little about who or what they are, misunderstood or misidentified or maligned them—with profound political, economic, and social consequences for these communities. I wanted Delight and Earle to be recognized as real places with real stories, to be seen and heard as particular places with particular stories—places and stories that couldn't then be overlooked, unheard, forgotten. And so, I realized, I couldn't hide them behind fuzzy details; I couldn't mask them with pseudonyms. Before each interview, then, I explained my intention to name these towns—and my hope to also name their residents—and I found that participants wanted their stories told; they wanted the visibility and accountability of names and details. This authenticity, I soon discovered, also kept me accountable—ensuring that I separated my opinions from those of participants, that I represented people and places fairly and accurately, ensuring, essentially, that *I* didn't hide behind fuzzy details and pseudonyms. And so, with one exception, noted and explained in the text, the names here are real names, and the details are real details.

Other naming and identifying words carry significance, meanings I also reflected in my writing. Honorifics are revealing: typically, I used "Mr." or "Ms." when interacting with Earle community members, while, in Delight, I usually called people by their first names, as they did with me—a difference that reflects both the formality of these relationships and local customs. And, frequently, the language chosen by participants was instructive: the careful use of pronouns, of "us" and "them," often indicated patterns of racialized interaction and tradition.

Two words were especially central to the stories I heard—"community" and "school"—concepts that initially appeared both indistinct and generous in their everyday, conversational usage. Community, as a construct, has long been contested and debated,[76] used variously to describe a political unit, a geographic area, or a social entity, and here, in both Delight and Earle, the ubiquity of the word made me question its meaning. "The community," it seems, generally refers to people, to community *members*—people occupying a shared space and political identity but, first and foremost, a specific group of people. I often asked about the boundaries of this group in interviews—"Who do you include when you talk about 'the community'?"—and looked for these boundaries in interactions, in patterns of speech, in the towns' places and spaces. Within each town, these boundaries were remarkably consistent. In Delight, it's the school district that makes up "the community," Delight proper, all 311 residents, plus the residents of Antoine, Okolona, the Meeks Settlement, Billstown, Pisgah, and all of the other little clusters of homes that the school buses snake through each morning and afternoon. In Earle, the boundaries are different, marked by racial rather than geographic lines. Here, "the community" is the black community, the town's black residents, those residents whose children still board those yellow buses and sit in the schools' classrooms. In both places, then, "the community" consists of the districts' students and their families; in Earle, though, "the community" excludes a number of white families zoned to the district but attending other schools.

The "school" is a bit harder to define. "School," in Delight and Earle, is a variety of things—people, structures, and space. "School" can refer to school buildings and the spaces between and around them; it is the students and teachers and administrators and aides and families and janitors, and the relationships and stories linking them; it is generations of shared history; it is the rules and norms and patterns of behaviors and ways of being. While "community" has a clearly bounded definition, "school," in both conversation and understanding, is notable for its expansiveness. Typically, though, "school" remains a local entity, separate from—and endangered by—the policies of "the state."

These contextual details—the shape and nature of relationships, the salience of race and the risks of closure, the words that reflect and construct local understandings—filled the stories I heard. And, so, as I wrote the narratives that I would tell about these places, I tried to honor these details, the meanings and language of relationship and context. Because, for all my effort to parse these semantic distinctions, to decipher the meaning of race, to filter the politics of consolidation and academic sanctions, to separate myself from the narratives, it is within these details, within these contextual particulars, that the meanings of school and community, of these rural schools and these rural communities, lay.

THE RESONANCE OF RELATIONSHIP

It's been a long time since I climbed into a car with Dorothy, drove across Arkansas, and arrived in Delight—a long time of building relationships, questioning and listening, revising and writing, talking and rewriting. Earle and Delight are familiar to me now, filled with people and places I know and care for, flush with details remembered and bits of conversations, made vividly real by dialogue and story. I'm grateful for these relationships. I think that my continued presence in each community and my genuine interest in participants' thoughts and experiences assured them that I would see beyond the rural stereotypes: that I would be careful and respectful with the insights I was gaining, that I would develop an understanding of Arkansas to contextualize these insights, that I would try to preserve the landscape of these relationships in my analysis and writing. I was not unchallenged by these relationships, for they continually pushed me to rethink and rewrite, they gently located and unseated my own assumptions, and they gradually taught me to be in relationship in new ways. I was not unchallenged, but I was grateful. And I was humbled—absolutely humbled by the sincerity and generosity with which people offered me their stories.

These towns are only two towns—only two rural communities among a vast and varied array of rural communities, communities with histories and economies and demographics all their own. Their stories are shaped by their rural geography, but also by the landscape of their state and the details of their specific contexts. Their stories, then, are not the stories of all rural communities, for their particulars are not the particulars of all rural communities. But many rural communities will share some of their particulars—a geometry of racial boundaries, ongoing struggles with state and federal school reform—and all will share one—a marginal location in an urban-centric society.[77] In these particulars, then, might reside some broader lessons of race, reform, and rurality.

And, too, hidden among the particulars of these two communities, somewhere between a teacher's luncheon in an Earle classroom and a community dinner held in the cafeteria at Delight, is a memory of a long-ago beans and greens supper. Here, in the particulars of these two places, I found the different rural I sought—a rural more complicated, more resonant, more authentic than any rural I'd see on a newscast or sitcom or find in a government's definition. In this rural, in these two rural towns, we can begin to understand the significance of these schools, the complexities of the relationships they share with their communities, and the consequence of education policies for each. These are the rural stories worth telling, the voices worth hearing, the lessons worth learning: these are the realities beyond the myths.

CHAPTER FOUR

Where the Heart Is

School, Relationships, and the Delight Community

In the darkness I can't make out any of the Delight school's thirteen build-ings. The three or four streetlights lining the narrow road separating the superintendent's office and the principal's house from the campus create only small globes of white light that hover below the pines. The town's few shops, just a block away, are all closed, and, even if open, wouldn't cast enough light to differentiate the Agri Building or the Home Ec Building from the blackness surrounding them. The night is still and quiet—though I know that its darkness hides a gym and Delight's Friday night basketball game.

Delight, Arkansas, sits in the piney, hilly corner of the state, the corner flanked by Texas and Louisiana. It's an area of poultry farming and log-ging, though both industries are shrinking under the pressures of corpo-rate farming and rising gas prices. Now only small family farms remain, and people find work where they can. This part of Arkansas is mostly white, pocketed with small mostly black areas, a segregation perpetuated by lingering distrust, strong kinship networks, and separate churches. People are friendly in their interactions, though, stopping to talk at the grocery or diner, to worry over the closed factories and few jobs.

When I got off the interstate back in Arkadelphia, under the neon glow of the Walmart sign, dusk was just settling in. Within half a mile, the sil-houettes of the tall trees are black against the gray-purple glow of the hori-zon, and, when it gets warmer, the smell of the pines will hang heavy in the humidity. From Arkadelphia I follow State Route 26 west, passing through dense thickets of trees and open pastures dotted with the dark forms of cows. And barns—barns barely visible in the dim light, the tidy shapes of small working barns and the bare ribs of abandoned barns. The towns are small, about five or ten minutes apart, with little more to announce their presence than a low speed limit and a small road sign. First Hollywood, Halfway, and Clear Spring, and then, in quick succession, Okolona, the little Meeks Settlement, the railroad tracks, and then Antoine.

Most of these towns were once bigger, as were many Arkansas communities. Back then, I hear, each had a "downtown" with two or three stores, and people would socialize there. Back then, people tell me, these towns had identities, they were communities, they had their schools. Now, though, only a small green road sign marks each handful of houses and trailers, a name on an empty place.

After five more dark miles, my headlights reveal another small green sign: Delight, Population 311. The road curves, and I see that McKnight's Grocery is dark. The road, for about three hundred yards, is lined with storefronts, some closed for the night and others empty, all blanketed in dark stillness.

Now, with the car parked in front of the principal's house, I cross the narrow street to the school. An inky blackness covers the campus. I can see neither the walkway beneath my feet nor where the sidewalk turns to grass on each side—only the purple-black of night and the even blacker shadow of the gym. The darkness seems to have swallowed up all sound and movement, all detail, all life outside. It's only at the gym's door that I finally hear something—the low noise of a crowd, muffled into one voice through the door. I fumble for the handle, and suddenly it's all bright yellow light, the squeak of sneakers on a polished floor and the clapping and shouting of crowded bleachers, the smell of popcorn and sweat, and the warmth of a packed gymnasium.

This gym isn't large, but the stands on both sides are filled. Underneath the blue and gold pennants hanging from the rafters and the large bulldog painted on the wall is a crowd wearing Delight sweatshirts and tees, ball caps and letter jackets. Some have their eyes trained to the lanky boys on the polished floor, but others, especially the teens, lean toward each other in intense conversation, and young children chase each other through the bleacher rows. Beneath all the blue and gold, it's young and old filling the gym, alumni and students, parents and grandparents and grandchildren—both black and white. And many of these same people will be back at this kindergarten-through-twelfth-grade, multi-town school tomorrow, a Saturday, to attend a benefit dinner or to play at the playground or to walk laps around the campus. They may stop by the principal's house over the weekend, just to drop in and say hello. And on Monday they will crowd the walkways, fill the street with a slow line of cars, and keep the classrooms and offices and cafeteria busy with activity. The town will awaken then, too—the neon "open" sign bright in the window of Mom's Diner, a few pickups idling in front of the hardware store, the spaces outside of McKnight's Grocery filled.

Pompoms at the game and decades of trophies dusty in their glass cases, generations gathered in the stands and students laughing in the halls, festivals on the campus and fund-raiser dinners in the cafeteria—these things anchor the community. Without them, without the school, Delight would be just another name on an empty place.

HOMELAND

Delight began as a farming town, a small community on the Arkansas frontier, an area of lush forests and little slavery, of small farms and busy sawmills. The town was incorporated in 1905, after the site was donated to the Southwestern and Indian Territory Railroad.[1] Though no one remembers much change in the community—it's never been much larger than its current 311—it once had more ready jobs: a couple mills, some poultry houses. It also used to draw a crowd on Saturdays, older white residents tell me, when everyone would flock to town for the raffle drawings at the stores; now Saturday shopping trips involve the Walmart over in Arkadelphia. The other little towns scattered around Delight—the mostly white Pisgah and Billstown, the mostly black Antoine and Meeks Settlement, and Okolona, with its white parts and its black parts—have similar stories of shuttered mills, agricultural decline, and empty storefronts. Most living in the area, both black and white, are now self-employed as small farmers or truckers or business owners, commuting to jobs in Arkadelphia or Murfreesboro, hired on at the school, or simply without work.

The Delight school, though, remains busy. Founded in 1903, it now serves all of these area towns and enrolls 332 kindergarteners through twelfth graders, about two-thirds of them white, about 65 percent receiving free or reduced-price lunch, over 90 percent continuing to graduation. Delight is also a freestanding school district employing about eighty people. Its 2008–9 enrollment of 332 is 18 short of the 350-student cut-off mandated by Act 60, a gap that puts Delight in danger of consolidation, of possibly losing its district status or the school itself.

From my very first trip to Delight, I was fascinated by the school and community and, in retrospect, a little smitten, too, especially as I began to experience the openness and generosity of community members. A resident later told me how his grandfather, originally from Brownwood, Texas—"Brown . . . wood," he said slowly, drawling out the syllables, "it's a visual thing"—helped a neighbor move up to Delight. When they arrived, his grandfather climbed out of the wagon, saw the green grass and the shade of the peach trees, and just never left. My experience has been similar; I came once and never really thought about leaving. Even in my first conversations with residents, I could tell how important this school was to those living in the community. The people I met—Kathy, the school's new black principal; Cyndi, a white teacher and vocal Delight advocate; Scott, the white coach, married to another teacher, with three children that are fourth-generation Delight residents—were genuinely kind and eager to talk, and, by the end of that visit, I had places to stay the next time I came, promises for more conversations, and feet dirty from the grass of Delight. The second visit, the trip that began in Delight's crowded gymnasium, only confirmed my desire to spend more time there. As I walked into that basketball game, I was taken aback by the number of people packed inside; as I looked across the stands and listened to the conversations yelled across rows of bleachers, the racial integration of the crowd and the warmth and familiarity of the interactions surprised me.

This community seemed to embody so many of the qualities I had enjoyed in Vanleer—a community close-knit and kind, loyal to its institutions. Yet it also seemed to counter some of the common assumptions about rural southern towns, that they were prejudiced and suspicious, segregated by their institutions. I wondered how the school shaped these qualities, these particulars, how it shaped this community. And another question floated there in Delight, unarticulated, holding a morbid and weighty finality—would the community lose its school? And what would happen then?

COMING HOME

Like many rural towns, Delight sits at an intersection, the corner where Route 19 abruptly turns west to meet Route 26. The little town received its name when an early town official declared, "I hope this will be a delightful place in which to live. We will name the town Delight."[2] It's the kind of place where people come through and then just stay, lured from the brown dust of Texas by the boughs of peach trees and the promise of a town called Delight. Railroad tracks used to cross this intersection, freighting the lumber manufactured at the local sawmills and the cotton grown on the surrounding farms. When the last mill shut down after a fire, the railroad company closed the spur, and now only a thin raised ridge traces the old tracks, separating the businesses that cluster near the intersection from the homes and school that occupy a small grid of residential streets.

The Delight school sits just over this old railroad ridge. It is an assortment of small buildings scattered across a square of grass—the noisy gymnasium I found in the dark of a Friday night; two main buildings, one elementary and one high school, each a long corridor with a handful of classrooms; a few corrugated trailers housing individual classrooms; a more permanent-looking Home Ec Building, anchored by concrete steps and brick walls; the original school, a WPA-era building that smells of must and pine and now holds the library and computer lab; and a few others, representing a range of architectural trends. A few parking lots sit in small spaces between building and street, and a fenced playground occupies the area between the gym and the elementary building. Long walkways, flanked by square poles supporting a thin sheet of metal overhead, connect the buildings, and a picnic table rests in the shade of an oak near the Agri Building. Across the back street where Coach has the PE classes run sprints during the day, behind the principal's house and the superintendent's office, are the baseball fields. Despite all of the buildings and the web of walkways, there is a sense of openness and space; the buildings are small against the stretches of grass and the people filling them.

The Delight school only takes up one block, but, to me, it seems larger. When the school year is in session, when cars line the street and buses idle in the parking lot, when parents crowd the walkways and alumni fill the gym, when teachers occupy the classrooms and students spill from the campus, I get the feeling that everybody is either here at the school, or on their way. Where else would we go, people laugh. As Coach explains, "The school's kind of a focal point; anything that happens in the community is going to happen in the cafeteria, or it's going to occur here in the gym." Kathy, the principal, agrees: community activities are held "at the school. The school is the community base of the community." She continues, describing this base as "a big stadium; the school is the stadium to the people here."

This "stadium" pulls community members together for a variety of reasons, though, as the metaphor suggests, athletics may be the most common. It's ball games that draw the crowds; that the school is too small for a football team does nothing to temper this spirit. The game schedule orders life in Delight. Fall and winter nights are basketball nights—during home games, the gym is a warm nest of activity—and spring nights last long under the bright lights of the baseball field; away-game days, whatever the season, find the town eerily empty. Basketball is the town's real passion: as a parent tells me, "During regular school time, the gym's full, because this is a basketball town." A retired school counselor explains, "When there is a basketball game going on, you are going to get those parents coming. They are there to see their children perform." The games draw people together, and even "lots of retirees go to ball games." "Ball games are social," and the game nights are an event—a time to cheer proudly when the Bulldogs score a basket or steal the ball. But I hear quieter conversations in this gym, too, worries about the price of gasoline or news about struggling neighbors or sick relatives.

Other school-related extracurricular activities also bring people to the school, as parents and relatives and friends gather to support children in school plays or attend the Halloween festival. School traditions involve members of the community, too. People turn out to watch the "senior drive around," when the graduating seniors circle the school's campus in slow laps on the last day of school. The school secretary tells me, "The school activities that the kids are involved in have a tendency to be more open to where the community can come and at least watch and participate."

It's not just school activities that use the school facilities. The "cemetery dinner," for example—a benefit dinner of chicken, mashed potatoes, green beans, cornbread, and row upon row of desserts, with proceeds going toward upkeep of the town cemetery—fills every table in the cafeteria on a Saturday afternoon. A teacher explains the hosting role that the school plays, partially due to necessity: "That cemetery dinner is not a school event; it's a community event, but the school is the place to have it. If they want to have fund-raisers of any sort, like for the Delight Fire Department or this or that or the other, they'll go to that school cafeteria or the school gym for big meetings." The campus seems to be open to anyone who wants or needs to use it: while I heard how frequently the school is used to host a wide range of events, I never learned of any process to reserve the site, and when I used the school library to meet with a group of residents, I only needed to get the building keys from Kathy's large stash and figure out which one fit the library door. And even the less formal activities of community life happen at the school. The block around the school is about half a mile, and, at all times of day, walkers circle it for exercise: "There are a lot of people, black and white, that come over there to walk. And that's just one of those small town things, 'Hey, how are you?' You visit for a minute and then go on about your walking." This kind of open, shared use seems to mark the school as a communal space. As a parent explained to me, "The school is very good about letting . . . the facilities to be used for other things. So if you have a family reunion or something like that, you are in the cafeteria. You may have a church function or something; that'd be in the gym. . . . It's just the community hub." And the possibility of losing this "community hub" to consolidation worries community members: "For such a small town, there is so much that goes on from a recreational standpoint. . . . To not have a school here to help feed that would be a tremendous blow." Without the school, the community would lose its "hub," its recreational and communal center. This school is the space where people gather, an animated and dynamic space filled with people coming together for common purposes, and in this space, as they gather, they build relationships.

FAMILY

The brick cafeteria sits aside the elementary school building, near the trailer with the music classroom. One end of the large room holds a wooden stage scattered with a few desks, reserved for students with "D-Hall"—detention. At the other side is the kitchen, and in between are four long rows of cafeteria tables. During a lunchtime in late April the row near the windows is covered with a blue paper table cloth, clusters of salt and pepper shakers, and porcelain vases of yellow and blue silk flowers—all waiting for the seniors and their senior lunch. Kathy and I wait, too, sitting and talking with a group of teachers, waiting for this graduating class and a good meal.

First, though, come the younger students. They stand, orderly and mostly patient, in a short line that snakes past coolers of milk to the counter. They leave the kitchen with a tray weighted by food, filing past Mrs. Jones, the school secretary, who checks them off her enrollment list. Most of the students, in a hurry to eat and talk, don't bother to slow as they pass her, and they don't seem to need to—she recognizes them all and crosses off their names, usually before they have even cleared the food counter.

Classes begin to fill the long tables, white children and black children leaning over trays to tell a friend about a TV show or the puppies their dog just had or plans to go hunting this weekend. One teacher—Connie, Coach's wife—stands between two of the tables, busy squirting ketchup on the trays of children with raised hands. The cafeteria isn't ready to forego bottled ketchup, and Kathy tells me that they still fry their chicken and bologna, too, giving their kids a good "Sunday" lunch. As we wait, she also tells me stories of the students, the senior girl who just won a large basketball scholarship or the pair that snuck to Mom's for a soda before lunch. The hum in the lunchroom is busy but comfortable, filled with the calm sounds of chatter, laughter, and forks on plastic trays. It only grows loud after a queasy-looking student throws up. Kathy quickly stands and announces that noisy students should sit themselves out for ten minutes of recess—and, she later learns, twenty students own up and sit their ten.

The seniors enter as the other classes are leaving, and they're louder at their blue-papered tables, chatter fueled by long friendships and the entitlement that comes with a much-anticipated tradition. They've chosen today's meal—Salisbury steak—and Mrs. Van Camp, the head cook, also brings out a blue and yellow cake, a gift from the preschool teachers across campus, the same teachers who had these seniors as three- and four-year-olds over a decade ago. Mrs. Van Camp stays with the students as they eat, wandering down the table and talking with them, joking with one about a "Got Milk?" poster with a pretty model. The Vo-Ag teacher sits down to join them; the superintendent comes over from his office for lunch; and Kathy says a few words to the group, congratulating the students on their upcoming graduation.

The entire lunch hour seems comfortable, intimate, like eating at home. Certainly the tablecloth and the real bottles of ketchup contribute to the intimacy, but it's the interactions I notice—interactions that are unremarkable for their familiarity, yet warm and thoughtful and respectful. Most of these students have been classmates since preschool, and many of these teachers have watched them grow, teaching them in more than one class or grade, and maybe teaching their siblings or parents, too. For nearly fifteen years, Mrs. Van Camp has served them breakfast and lunch, and Mrs. Jones has checked them off the lunch list. Their parents and relatives know each other, talk at basketball games or benefits, are often friends themselves. They play at each other's houses, can name each other's pets and remember each other's favorite movies, and spend days and weekends together, year after year. And they care about one another; they care enough to sit down and talk, to gently tease, to mind the staff. In fact, when I ask people to describe the school, they often talk about the relationships experienced within it; Delight is "close-knit," they say. It's the relationships I hear about, again and again, and especially from students—relationships "just like one big family," imperfect relationships but relationships built on recognition and care.

Within the school's small space, people are known. Children are greeted in the hallways, and I am, too. It's not long before I feel recognized at Delight, as I see and talk with people, again and again, in the hallways, in the carpool line, in the gym. As Coach says, "With a small school, you know everybody. There's not anybody [who, when] you hear a name, [you think,] 'Well, who's that?'" Sometimes this knowledge comes from family ties: many teachers and administrators once taught the parents, brothers, sisters, and cousins of current students. Students bring their own ties, too. One tells me, "My aunt works here, my mom's best friend, . . . so a bunch of the teachers I know personally. I like it like that because you know you can relate to them and you feel more comfortable with them. . . . I'm used to these teachers. I've known them my whole life."

And this knowledge shapes interactions between students and teachers. Teachers are attentive, I hear, anticipating students' academic struggles and challenges, playing to their strengths. They also respond to matters beyond academics, acting upon the insights and understandings gathered through interactions across years and generations, as a former school board member describes: "Let's suppose little Johnny goes into the classroom some morning. And he's not able to stay awake because, well, mom and dad fought all night last night. That teacher probably knows the reason, and it may not be little Johnny's fault. She might be able to be a little bit more concerned and know a little bit more about how to help that child than if he's just a child that comes in that she knows absolutely nothing about." And sometimes the personal knowledge accumulated within the school allows relationships to carry beyond the walls of the classroom. Coach points out that "kids can have contact with you anytime; they can call you, they know where you live." This kind of intimate understanding of a child and his or her "history"—coupled with easy accessibility—seems to build a more forgiving, more comprehensive connection between teacher and student.

These connections are not limited to staff and students. Familiarity helps students initiate relationships among themselves, too: "I have a lot of friends here. I used to have a really hard time making friends, but it seems to get easier over the years when you get to know people better." Another student says, "Everybody's known everybody since kindergarten, and everybody's all friendly. If you're here at lunch, you'll see everybody talking to everybody." Because they know one another, students tell me, their interactions are open and friendly. And familiarity among teachers and parents also shapes those interactions: it's easier "to call somebody that you personally know about a child," the school secretary explains, or, as a parent describes, "You are going to see your teacher at McKnight's, or you are going to see your teacher when your teacher is walking in front of your yard, and you can see how did your kid do." Familiarity makes interactions between parents and teachers, and students and teachers, frequent, commonplace, and unbounded: this is the kind of recognition that likely builds deeper relationships.

But familiarity can have its drawbacks. One's personal business also tends to be widely known, and "we may not want folks knowing about our situation." As a student notes, "Since [the school] is so small, they know your whole family; they know how you're going to be before you even come to class, before you start school." I wondered if this kind of familiarity could be stifling, if this sort of knowledge, especially information learned secondhand or long ago, could be straitjacketing or self-fulfilling. But I was surprised that few teachers or parents—and no students—characterize this kind of public scrutiny as problematic. Most seem to view familiarity as an asset, for a more complete understanding of one's family or background allows for a more complete recognition: when the school "know[s] what's going on in [students'] everyday life a lot more, it just does a lot better job of looking out for them away from school. . . . We're concerned about kids and kids' lives and not just their education in a book."

Though recognition may lay the foundation for the relationships developed within the school, care determines the quality of these relationships. I hear care frequently—when a teacher compliments a student for scoring in the game, when an administrator notes the voluntary recess duty of a teacher, when a staff member asks after a grandparent's health, when a pastor inquires about the progress of a child. Care originates in the classroom. As a student explains, "The teachers . . . help us; they don't just teach it to us and just let us go. They help if we need help. They show us how to do it. If I need tutoring, then we can talk to them. I just like the way they keep us safe and help us. I feel welcome here." Graduates remember the names and habits of particular teachers, like "Mrs. Deacon, a wonderful instructor. She taught English for years and years and years. Very tough, very demanding, very challenging, but very caring. She truly, truly cared you learned. And you did." Care does not imply informal or casual relationships—teachers are, without question, in charge and in control. But a genuine interest and affection seem to motivate these dynamics.

Small classes make this level of attention possible, but care, like recognition, extends beyond the classroom. A number of parents note, "The majority of [teachers] care extremely about the kids. I've heard time and time again the teachers saying, 'If you're having trouble with this, come see me after school. I'll stay here and help you and explain it to you.'" This time stretches past the typical school day, as teachers are available to both students and parents by phone or even at home. A student explains to me, "Teachers, they're very helpful when you need it. And you can always get that help. Say school isn't in, you can always still talk to a teacher." And another student agrees that the teachers are "all pretty much really nice, and they try to get to know you personally." The care and recognition of teachers, then, allow personal relationships to develop, relationships that may then stretch beyond classrooms and across years.

Care isn't only perpetuated by teachers, in their relationships with students and families. This care seems more generalized, a prevailing norm of help and support that appears to encompass the community as a whole. I hear it again and again—this is a community where folks help one another. When someone needs food, a neighbor carries it over; when someone needs clothing, a neighbor provides a coat; when someone is sick, a neighbor brings comfort. These efforts are often organized through the school, but, perhaps more important, the school generates the trust, the sense of mutual dependence, the care that makes these efforts routine and commonplace.

Students, too, share this same sort of support. Kathy sees a level of "encouragement even when they're doing PE and they have to run around the block or so. The last one that comes in, you'll see the other ones that have already ran sitting on the cars, and they're going, 'Oh, God, I'm about to die,' but they're encouraging that last one that's coming in, knowing it's going to take them a little while, . . . and they're patting him on the back and they're clapping. The coaches didn't tell them to do this. This is just the way these kids are." The care is also evident in students' actions toward those with obvious differences, as a teacher tells me about her son: "We have Brady, who is severely handicapped, and kids are very accepting of him. . . . The kids are very accepting of each other. It's like family. You have to just take everybody with their flaws and all."

This family-like quality comes up frequently, and I ask about it, trying to figure out what family means in this context. "Family," it seems, does refer to actual kinship ties, the cousins in the same class, the mother-daughter teaching team. But "family" includes the other relationships, too, the relationships between coach and player, between teacher and student, between long-serving faculty members, the relationships so close and reliable and common that they just feel like family. It's the care and recognition of the school that build these ties, cultivating connections within and around the campus, building "family."

But this "family" is not free of disagreement. Conflicts within the community exist, though it is only later that I am able to piece together the oblique references to "tensions." And students report occasional bullying—though not nearly what you would find at other schools, they are quick to assure me. Certainly some relationships are stronger than others; while students deny the existence of any "cliques," particular "groups" do "hang together." Even some teachers "keep their old, little friendships, and they really aren't accepting of new teachers," maybe the result of "work[ing] together for years and years." Many dismiss these disputes as expected, though: "Just like in any other family, you are going to have your squabbles, and you are going to have your fights, but we are still all one, big family and . . . black, white, whatever, we take care of each other." Privately I question these easy dismissals, wondering if everyone feels equally a part of this family—would "little Johnny's" parents, the ones fighting all night, feel like they belong? And what about students who feel awkward and caught in the bright glare of so much recognition and care? I wonder about these individuals, but I also note the word that students usually chose when describing the school—"welcoming." Maybe difference doesn't have to preclude membership in this family.

A network this dense and thick surely has many sources, but most participants seem to think of the school as the foundation of these relationships. As people interact within this space, as they work in class or chat on the walkway or organize a benefit supper, they are together, tied by interaction and linked by common purpose. Care and recognition foster these ties, relationships that reach beyond the campus, as well as those that carry from home into the school. What results is a dense and overlapping network of relationships, a place where "everyone seems to be so interdependent on everyone else"; what results is a family.

And this is the family that many fear losing with consolidation. For a former school counselor, the school "is a family" because "it is so close knit that everybody knows who you are, who you belong to, and some of the things that are expected of you from a family standpoint. Because if my kid got out of line, they would know, 'Call granny.'"

I am sitting with this "granny"—Mrs. Fadie Gentry—in her house on a hot summer Sunday afternoon; she's still wearing her coral-colored suit from church, and her hair still holds some of its curl. This retired school counselor, a black woman now in her seventies, has weathered two school consolidations, the first carried out under desegregation orders, and our conversation has covered forty-five years of local economics, politics, race relations, and school happenings—and so I push her. If Delight were to lose its school, I say, this "family," this network of relationships surrounding the school, could still persist, right? No, she doesn't think so—"because the bond that they had here is going to be broken." Eventually "it may mend back," but only after time. And she clarifies, "The association and the participation and cooperation that this community has with each other is going to be broken because [people] are so far apart from each other, separated." Without the school, a means of preserving existing relationships and folding a new generation into the density of these ties, the family disappears.

SHELTER

Delight's commercial district is a quarter-mile stretch of stores and businesses that neatly line the road, a stretch that gray-haired men in pickup trucks roll through slowly, two fingers lifted from the wheel in greeting, a stretch that teens in rumbly cars roar through on Saturday nights. It begins on the east with McKnight's, nestled where Routes 19 and 26 meet, and ends with Allgoods One Stop on the west. Arranged in between are a couple of restaurants, two or three flower shops, a gas station, the Delight Bank, a hardware store, a car wash, an auto parts store, a post office, a printing company, and a hair salon called Shear Delight—some located in two-story brick storefronts, others in old wooden houses or tiny freestanding buildings. Only after several visits do I notice the occasionally open town library or the new catering business; vacancies sometimes hide the smaller, still-functioning establishments. All are a little worn but tidy and looked after, even the empty spaces.

The few surrounding blocks of homes are, for the most part, just as well tended. The blocks are flat and grassy, each with a couple trees and a handful of homes and few fences. Some houses are ranch style, long with light-colored brick walls and maybe a carport to cover the Buick and mower. Others are more compact—white-painted wood, a wide front porch, a tin roof. A few have sagging steps and peeling paint, and the roof of one old house now touches the grass, a green shingled skirt covering splintered boards, arced in a perpetual bow to the street. At the edge of town stands a horseshoe of eight apartments, built recently by the USDA

Rural Development office, and beyond the town's limits I find tarp-and-rust trailers nested among tall trees.

This short string of businesses, this cluster of homes, drives much of the concern about consolidation—without the school, how long would they remain? Without the support of a school, the town's economy—and then the community itself—would unravel, and stores and houses would soon disappear, business owners and school staff members and parents fear. Their fear feeds a deeply felt need to keep the school, to support and protect it, to avoid consolidation at most any cost; it feeds—and reflects—a reciprocal and symbiotic relationship between school and community.

The school is a ready resource, both for individuals and for groups of community members. It hosts scores of benefit suppers that fund college scholarships or cover the medical bills of ill neighbors. It's also the area's largest employer—"the school probably furnishes more payroll than any other thing in town"—and it offers much-needed space and supplies to the civic groups and churches of the community. As a preacher explains, "If the city of Delight needed something from the school, if the churches needed something from the school—we all borrow tables, chairs, and that kind of stuff." Families, employees, and organizations rely on these resources of support, of salary, equipment, and space to function and live.

But the school's reach extends beyond a mere civic commitment to needy individuals and groups. Many describe the community's economy as wholly dependent upon the school. The school is the most important customer in Delight: "The school is the big business, big industry of the town." The Bank of Delight manages the school's finances, and the printing shop in town manufactures Bulldog T-shirts, sweatshirts, and ball caps. The school buses are maintained and fueled by local shops: the owner of Allgood Auto Parts tells me, "School buses have to have upkeep, so naturally they'll come here to buy parts and upkeep and things." Thus, the school itself funnels many thousands of dollars of capital into Delight's small economy.

The school furnishes these businesses with ready shoppers, too—hungry students, parents in a rush, teachers needing last-minute supplies. As the secretary describes, "All of those little businesses, even our diners, everything kind of picks up with people when school's in session. Our lunchroom, our classrooms, they use the grocery store more, be it nothing but a pizza party or chip and dip. Most people would swing by the local store here to get their Cokes and their cookies." These pizzas and cookies add up: she finishes, "It's just a trickle-down effect. . . . And then that's truly what rules whether you stay in business or you don't." A business owner agrees,

"When there are athletic events, anything going on that brings other people in, they're going to eat, they're going to buy fuel. It just brings an influx of people through." This influx packs Mom's on Friday nights; Kathy and I go, too, and the diner's two small rooms are filled with customers hungry for dinner before the game.

The school also drives the economy by keeping people anchored to the area. A former school board member estimates that the school district employs about eighty people, most of whom "also live here, grew up here, and they received their high school diploma here." These teachers and staff members buy groceries and gasoline in Delight, get their cars serviced in Delight, eat out in Delight. If "you take those [jobs], and those teachers move to another town to teach," the owner of the hardware store explains, "you're taking the whole finances of this community away."

Thus, the school provides the community's economic base. If consolidation happens, if the Delight district is subsumed by neighboring Murfreesboro, the school would likely close. And if the school goes, "you are taking the tax base away. You are taking the business away. . . . You don't have anything to hold the kids here. And there's no jobs that are going to bring more into it. It's a dead-end road after the schools go." A storeowner imagines the sequence of events:

> If a family lives one mile from school, and their kids ride the bus
> every day, and school closed . . . and there was no work here in
> Delight and they were keeping here just for the school and just
> because they own that little lot of land, and it got to the point that,
> God forbid, gasoline ever hit four dollars a gallon and we didn't
> want the kids to get on the bus at 4:30 in the morning and so we
> drive them to school, well, this little lot of land isn't worth it when
> we can get another little lot of land in Murfreesboro where we're in
> the town where our kids are going to school at and they can walk to
> school. . . . In time, because gas prices, it would be easier to move
> away. And if . . . they're living in Murfreesboro, they're not going
> to drive back over here to buy groceries. They're not going to drive
> back over here to buy a starter for their old Chevy. They're not going
> to drive back over here to get a sandwich or a burger. They're just
> going to stay over there. And it's a gradual thing. . . . I really think
> that the school [closing], in time, would devastate the community.

This spiral of decline is described to me often, and, no matter the exact chain of events described, the explanations are identical in result—"ghost town." These bleak predictions, though, reveal a particular understanding of the school's function within the community: the school supplies revenue and customers to local businesses and lends material support to local associations and organizations. The school anchors and stabilizes the community's economy. Without it, the economy goes.

It would be simplistic, though, to portray the school as simply propping up a small—and foundering—economy. Survival is a reciprocal process in this town, and school and community need and depend upon one another. The community also supports the school, through small gestures and larger tax resources, fiscal and civic and relational demonstrations of loyalty.

School support is a routine part of community life. I notice that class fund-raising coffers fill quickly and, during any school assembly, the bleachers always include some parents or relatives. Mrs. Fadie Gentry, the former school counselor, explains that community members "are real good supporters of any type of activity that goes on, athletics or community based, like fund-raising and just getting in there, being with the kids and doing things with them." Or, she continues, the support can be seen on field trips: "the parents always are there to go and chaperone for the kids. The Agri teacher always has good support from the people because if [he has] some type of event going on like judging or so forth, the parents are in support of that." It's not just parents, either. A group of elderly women, for example, is responsible for campus "beautification"; the women come, Kathy explains, "and plant flowers, get our yards cleaned up, making sure it looks good."

The most public demonstrations of support may be the repeated efforts of the community to avoid consolidation and keep the school: "Everybody's concerned about doing what they can to keep the school here." Several years ago, when the school faced closure due to fiscal distress, "the community came together and voted over 400 to like 70–something to pass the millage." In the past, too, when the school was confronted with possible consolidation, the community acted. An alumna explains, "When I was a junior or senior in school, they were trying to pass a millage back then to save our school. Those kids, they were out here on the highway with signs—'Save our school'—then the night of the election, up and down the highway." This is a community that will "go above and beyond to try to do what they can to save their school," she concludes. Usually, though, this support is less about public action and more a general sense of "community support," "amazing support," "a really good support system," a collective and assumed willingness to act should the need arise.

But the frequency with which I heard this loyalty expressed made me wonder if people wished that, just by expressing this belief, they could make it completely true. Occasionally, community members question the extent of one another's support of the school—whether loyalty would lead to action. One employee acknowledges, "There's a lot of apathy until it comes down to something, where we might lose our school." Another employee, the same to tell me that "you know that they care when they come out and vote to spend more money just to keep the school open," also notes the difficulty in keeping this support active and consistent—revealing an ambivalence that questions the community's devotion. And a few community members, especially the older members, seem to doubt the cohesion of today's community more generally, remembering, with some nostalgia, a past version of this community, "a community that had come together for a purpose."

Others question a different aspect of the interdependence of community and school—the theory that balances the community's economy upon the existence of the school. Some—the auto parts storeowner, for one—believe that industrial decline precedes the loss of the school. As we sit in his comfortably cluttered store, he recounts a conversation with another business owner, "[The business owner] said, years ago Pike City was almost chosen the county seat. Said, you see that school close and the town just died. And my question to him was, 'Wasn't there a really large sawmill there at that time?' 'Yeah.' 'Well, which one closed first, the sawmill or the school?' 'The sawmill.'" Certainly, it's entirely possible—even likely—that the decline of a town's businesses and industries precedes the loss of the school; the loss of jobs causes a bleed in population, lowering a school's enrollment, endangering tax revenue, and, ultimately, forcing consolidation. For him, factors other than school loss—factors such as factory closings—drive economic collapse.

However, later in our conversation, when we revisit the subject and I ask what would be lost if the school was closed, he states, "Well, we'd lose our sense of community; we would gradually, over time, lose our community," and he then explains just how the economy would unravel without the school. This inconsistency is unsurprising; the collapse of an economy is complicated and most likely does not occur in linear fashion. Somewhere, though, in all of these theoretical spirals of decline, is the school.

Furthermore, this interdependence is financial only in part. Ghost towns are not only absent busy shops; they're also absent people and the relationships and associations and loyalties that unite them. It is an interdependence transacted over checkout counters, but also through parents chaperoning school trips and churches borrowing school chairs and students holding "Save our school" signs. Sustenance, then—economic and relational—depends upon both school and community.

KITH AND KIN

I meet Randy Hughes, a retired superintendent of Delight, in the district office, two houses down from the small white home where he grew up. He wears a Delight T-shirt and ball cap; he'd just finished mowing his yard at his home in Nashville, about a half-hour drive away. He tells me that this is the first time he's been back to the school in a while—I would have been surprised to learn this, given his legendary devotion to the school, but I had been told that Randy avoided this side of Delight after his mother died. After introductions, I ask, "Can you tell me a little bit about your involvement with the district?" And he begins, "I was born in the house on the corner, down here. That's where my mother lived until she died at age ninety-four, two years ago. She was the oldest surviving graduate of Delight school." He goes on to tell me how, eighty years ago, his mother and some of her classmates chose the school mascot—the bulldog—and colors—blue and gold—as they rode to a ball game in Horatio.

It's a curious way to describe "involvement with the district." He doesn't begin with his retirement or his tenure as superintendent or even his time as a student; instead, he starts with his birth next door. But as he does go on to describe his experiences as a superintendent, the continual threat of consolidation, the community's steadfast support of the school, I think it's my question that may be strange to him—"involvement" is hardly a word for a life beginning at the edge of a schoolyard, for a lifetime of being a Bulldog. This school is more than a job or an institution; it's an identity. It gives the community, this network of relationships and institutions and businesses, a ready identity by providing shared symbols and traditions, perpetuating a set of common values, and establishing clear boundaries—all of which distinguish and define Delight. The school puts meaning, an identity, behind the name on a small green road sign.

Much of this identity is bound up in symbols, long-standing common symbols. Eighty years after that ball game in Horatio, Delight still boasts the same mascot and colors. An enormous gray bulldog, happily baring its teeth, now covers one of the gym walls, and blue paw prints dot the school walkways. Bulldogs emblazon most school literature, from notices sent home to the cover of the student handbook, and it seems as though, on any given day, at least half the student body is wearing some representation of this mascot or some display of the school colors—a proportion that nears totality on game days. Parents and teachers and alumni wear the tees and sweatshirts and ball caps, too, and it's not uncommon to hear people refer to themselves as Bulldogs. Displaying these symbols is a conscious way of showing allegiance; Kathy, as a new principal, deliberately chooses her Delight polo shirt when dressing for weekend events.

Just as these symbols visually identify one as being a part of Delight, traditions also link people, establishing a connection across years and generations. As a teacher explains why she remains at Delight, "It's about that tradition that we want our kids to have. . . . My kids will be fourth generation graduates here. . . . You can't put a price tag on that." Students, too, are aware of the history that precedes them: "My parents went to school at Delight. A lot of my friends' parents went to school at Delight. . . . I mean, Delight has a tradition." The specifics of this tradition are numerous and varied. Certain school events occur yearly—the Halloween carnival, with its games and haunted houses, or "the promenade," when students, in their dresses and sports coats, march together into the prom. Twelfth graders also take part in an entire series of public rituals that mark their graduation. After a week of farewell lunches and suppers, on the last day of school, they drive in a long, slow line around the school's block. And at the day's end, they stand in the school's main hallway, arms around one another and community gathered watching, counting down their last minute at the Delight school. Tears cover many cheeks in that hallway—just as they have for years and years on this last minute of this last day.

It is one of these traditions—prom—that sparks "an incident" one Friday afternoon just before I arrive in Delight for my third visit. Kathy is away for the afternoon, and, as the nurse lets me into Kathy's house to drop my bags, I hear the first details—a student we run into issues a hurried report about turpentine and asks the nurse not to tell her mother. I meet up with a teacher in her classroom, and she takes me to the parking lot where Frasier, the maintenance man, is scrubbing the surface with a hose and brush. A group of juniors, painting decorations for the upcoming prom, had spray-painted their initials on the blacktop—and tomorrow is the cemetery dinner, when the cafeteria will be packed with people. So the campus is now a flurry of activity, as teachers worry about Kathy's reaction, as students worry about punishment, and as Frasier worries about the large silver letters covering the black surface.

His scrubbing works, though, and soon the parking lot is black and shiny with puddles. But "the incident" doesn't end there. It comes up again that night when two boys, tall boys with sweaty hair sprouting from baseball caps, drop by Kathy's house after their game and, standing in her doorway with their gaze fixed on her living room floor, tell her that they were part of the group responsible for the painted initials, assure her that they know it was wrong, especially with the cemetery dinner tomorrow, and apologize. It comes up again the next day, when Kathy and I walk into the cafeteria's kitchen during the dinner and run into the mother of one of these same boys; she tells Kathy that she wants him punished, maybe with some mowing work around the school. And then I hear about it again that night—when another student, just off work and smelling of french fries, comes by to apologize for her involvement. These kids, this mother—all just want to make things right.

Within Delight there seems to be a great deal of consensus about what "right" is, especially among parents and teachers. A parent asks me if I've heard the expression "it takes a village to raise a child" and then explains, "This is our village. Everybody here has something to do with keeping an eye on your kids and helping to raise them. If they are doing wrong, they will say something to them about it." This type of communal raising of children requires a set of shared values, and, indeed, in Delight a set of common values seems to identify what is right, what is good, what is worthy and important. Kathy characterizes this value system as "a way of life" for a community of "survivors," a more "old-fashioned mindset" concerned with "living off the land" through hunting and farming, canning and cooking, giving and helping. Others articulate these values by distinguishing between small towns and big cities: "Small towns, small schools have great big hearts and they value things in a different way than you do in a larger school, larger town." Another parent clarifies, "What goes on here in this town between the moral values taught in the school, in the churches, the extra attention produced by the teachers, the care and the knowledge that the community has towards each other—all of that cannot be duplicated in any large town. . . . And to me the trade-off is more than worth it to not make as much money, to not have all the glitz and glamour that goes on, to have this kind of life and this kind of education." His wife adds, "We have to struggle every day to pay the bills and to take care of everything we need to take care of. It's worth it to know your kids are safe at school, that you don't have to worry about somebody taking a gun up there and shooting everybody." In "this kind of life and this kind of education," community members take the time to know and care about one another, to keep the children safe, to teach right from wrong, to live simply and humbly. And this simple living, although difficult, just isn't possible among the dangers—and different values—of a city.

The school reinforces these shared values. The "way of life" Kathy describes is reflected in the home-style meals cooked in the cafeteria and the Future Farmers of America club and agriculture classes the school offers. The values are also apparent in the schools' rules and discipline policies. These expectations are spelled out in the sixty-one pages of the school handbook—"the will of the community," according to Kathy. Much of Kathy's job concerns the rules and regulations of this handbook, even the dress code: "I enforce the student handbook. . . . I check prom dresses. I check homecoming dresses. . . . I don't like students, especially girls, exposing more than what they need to. I think that that is the culture that they carry here. I think that handbook makes them follow that culture." The school's rules and activities, then, reflect and maintain "the culture that they carry here," a culture with properly clad girls and without "glitz and glamour."

The culture and values promoted at school are also reinforced at home. As one parent explains, "You know when you send your kid up there those teachers know how you feel about it. Like when we send our kids up there, I expect them to act the same way they would if we were there. And I give the teachers the full support. If they're not, fire them up. Punish them or whatever needs to be done. . . . It is just that type of an environment. So it is like a whole community taking care of your kid. . . . And you can feel pretty certain that they are going to be kept in line like they should be." And perhaps that's why the "incident" doesn't end—"you'll hear about it" until it's set right, until home and school respond, until parents and teachers are satisfied, until order is restored and the values of a community maintained.

This identity, knit together by common symbols and shared values, is also clearly bounded; its boundary—distinguishing those in the community from those not—is distinct and unmistakable. In general, it is school district lines, rather than town lines, that delineate the Delight community, "because all the kids go to school here. . . . So we're all the community. We all support the school." And so, children and families living in Antoine and Pisgah, in Okolona and Meeks and Billstown, are also part of the Delight community, part of the Delight identity.

This identity becomes even more defined, its boundaries sharper, in contrast. Sixteen miles west of Delight is Murfreesboro, a town a bit larger and wealthier than Delight. With close to two thousand, mostly white residents, it has the good fortune to sit atop a diamond-filled volcanic crater. The Crater of Diamonds State Park brings some tourism to the town, supporting a regional health center, a number of restaurants and banks, and a handful of hotels and campgrounds. According to many in Delight, though, the diamond crater also brings a deep-seated "attitude." One woman who grew up in the area tells me, "I know what their attitude is about Delight. . . . They felt like Delight was more barbaric and they're more higher-class type people than Delight." And this apparent condescension continues today, another explains: "They consider theirselves on a different level than we do. They . . . kind of look down on this area compared to them. . . . Their community and our community, we just don't get along real well."

A few give specific reasons for their distaste of Murfreesboro. One woman tells me, "The people up there are just not friendly. . . . I was interviewed for a position there when I first got out of college and was not hired because I was black." A student explains that, at Murfreesboro High School, they have "gangs and drugs and killing. Half of the guys that go there have to get sent off to juvie." Even with specific reasons, some more probable than others, dislike is generalized beyond individuals or employers to most everyone in Murfreesboro, to "half the guys" or "the people up there." These entire communities, Murfreesboro and Delight, are different, they seem to say—separate and distinct. This rivalry has little to do with athletics—Murfreesboro is large enough to be in a different class in basketball and has its own football team; instead, it is a more symbolic rivalry of community-level dispositions and values and identities.

The desire to distinguish Delight from Murfreesboro may be, in part, a product of the consolidation threat. If the Delight district is consolidated, it would likely be with Murfreesboro, and many of the students—especially those from the white neighborhoods on the western edge of the district—would attend its high school. Murfreesboro's high school burnt down a number of years ago, and its "humongous" replacement cost their district millions, putting them in fiscal distress. Though larger than Delight, this school also doesn't have the size to entirely prevent worries of consolidation. The money and the boost in enrollment that would come with receiving Delight would go far to allay these twin threats and "get them out of their problems." And so, as a teacher describes it, Murfreesboro is just "licking their chops," waiting hungrily for Delight. Murfreesboro, then, may represent not only a different identity but also the consolidation threat itself.

Perhaps the people of Murfreesboro, comfortable atop their diamond mine, do look down upon Delight. Perhaps they do lie in wait, a predator stalking prey, nudging the Bulldogs together in a self-protective response. Or maybe the two communities, each strong in its own sense of self, simply cannot occupy the same space: these identities necessarily crowd one another, creating conflict and resentment. As Kathy explains, "Because [Delight] is such a close-knit family, if they . . . have to consolidate, they're . . . not going to trust . . . the [Murfreesboro] school with their kids. . . . The kids are not going to get along with other kids. It just doesn't work. You just can't put bees and wasps together and expect them to work." Perhaps you can never expect bees and wasps to get along, and identities are sharpest in opposition.

Yet this Delight identity is not without its fractures. It's late July and hot outside; the school board meets in a small conference room in the new Hendricks building. Six of the seven members are there, and the superintendent—Mr. Flaherty—and Kathy are also seated at the shiny wood table. Several other teachers and staff sit with me on the plastic chairs that ring the small room, and a family sits stiffly near the door—a man and woman and their two daughters. Halfway through "new business" we get to "legal transfers," the reason why the Smith[3] family is here. Mr. Smith rises, standing near the door and looking down the long table toward Mr. Flaherty; his girls stand behind him against the wall, and his wife remains seated in the corner. He wears jeans and an untucked polo shirt, his fresh, clean clothes a bright contrast to his five o'clock shadow.

The father is straightforward: they are seeking a transfer to Murfreesboro for the educational opportunities there, opportunities including music, choir, sports, and typing. The board votes, and it's "dead-locked"—three support the transfer, and three oppose it. A discussion ensues, and then an argument. Every parent wants his children to have opportunities, the father claims. Here in Delight they get more personal attention, a board member responds. The father says his children need these opportunities for college, and besides, other children have been allowed to leave the district. It's nothing personal, another board member answers: the children are liked here, and now we need these kids here to keep up the enrollment and save the school. The board members who support the transfer add that, though they feel it's not right to oppose a family's wishes, the family and the girls will suffer for leaving: here, the girls will get what they need. Then the girls argue their side, telling the board that they want the typing classes and junior high teachers Murfreesboro has. The mother, now crying, asks, "Why these two? Why can't they go?" Nothing is resolved, and, without a tie-breaking vote, the issue is tabled until August. The board moves on to other business, to cafeteria bids and student-athlete insurance, and the family stands there for a bit, helplessly, and then turns and leaves.

I feel uncomfortable and unsettled throughout this episode, and, given the unmet glances and averted eyes, I think others do, too. What's best for these girls is pitted against what's best for this community—and all of these "bests" are debatable and subjective. And those voting know this family; they've sat next to them at ball games, and their children play together. As the board meeting goes into executive session, a few of us gather in the hall, and they tell me that I saw "drama." It may be drama, but I also saw pain—and a community at risk of division.

This school board meeting isn't the only time I hear of "drama" within the community. As one resident shares, "Our community has been a place of lots of difficulties the past couple years. . . . The best word I can describe it with is drama. We have drama in the school, drama with the adults and stuff." The drama seems to have a number of sources, all likely related— allegations of a sexual relationship between a former coach and student a few years ago, ensuing lawsuits, a sluggishly reactive administration, leadership turnover during the preceding and following years, a school board that just wanted the entire episode to end—sources that people are to slow to name and careful to renounce. This drama has "broken the community up to some degree, . . . kind of tore things." Each issue has its sides—typically a side supporting whatever action (or inaction) the school is thought to have taken, and another questioning it—and "everybody kind of walked around uneasy because the person next to them may not agree with it." Though the school is now in the capable hands of Kathy and the stable presence of Mr. Flaherty, and these events have ended (mostly . . . the family of the involved student has filed a new set of lawsuits), some of the resentment remains: "It's had lasting effects. To this day, some people are still bitter about it. . . . It's still real."

The state's choice policy, a policy that permits students to attend a different district if they provide their own transportation and gain school board approval, has allowed some of those unhappy with Delight to withdraw from the school, most going to Murfreesboro. The explanations given for these departures vary wildly, depending upon the information's source. The parents of the leaving children often name reasons much like the Smiths'—a greater array of extracurricular activities, the chance to play on a football team, a larger student body with more opportunities for friendships. And some of those who remain acknowledge these reasons, seeing them as valid and honest. Others feel that these families simply fear what seems to be the inevitable consolidation with Murfreesboro, and they want to make the transition early, smoothly, though perhaps preemptively. And a lot simply think that these families are harboring lingering resentment toward the school and its recent "drama," or just have "some particular burr in their saddle"; these families are committing an act both deliberate and damaging by taking their kids to Murfreesboro. In this view, those that "have choiced their kid to Murfreesboro" are crossing the boundary, aligning with the rival and sealing Delight's fate. It's a clear rejection of Delight, of its tradition and history, its values and priorities, and its future. Many of those that remain feel betrayed, and even angry: "They're hurting the school. They want to send their kid there, that's fine, but you're going to have to suffer the consequences for that." Thus, while the reasons for "choicing" to Murfreesboro may be unclear, the result is often stark—a gaping division, separating the loyal from the disloyal.

To hear such absolute conclusions—those who choice to Murfreesboro are choicing out of Delight and everything Delight represents—attributed to such a muddy mess of reasons—half-true, imagined, unarticulated reasons—is jarring. I begin to wonder if perhaps Delight's identity, made resolute and tough from the threat of consolidation, has actually become rigid, inflexible to the point of fracture. Will these internal disputes, paired with a choice policy that allows people to act—or to be perceived as acting—in a public and damaging repudiation of the school, fragment this community before actual consolidation has the opportunity to? As I sit in the school board meeting, I watch the Smiths stand there naming a list of reasons they want their children at Murfreesboro, perhaps harboring a whole set of other unnamed reasons as well. I watch the board members answer back, reminding the Smiths of the attention and love their children receive at the school. It seems an onerous burden on this school board, to weigh the wishes and desires of individuals against those of a community. Perhaps it's unsurprising that this issue has been painted in such stark terms by some: it's much simpler to be angry with the other side than to be conflicted about your own.

But the suggestion that choicing to Murfreesboro is a deliberate act of betrayal and disloyalty that provokes an equally deliberate act of censure, is only that—a suggestion. I hear it only occasionally, when I catch whispered bits of the recent upheaval and scandals within the community, when people privately discuss their concerns about the district's leadership. Or it surfaces in the moments when they tell me the numbers, the enrollment that stubbornly hangs right around 330, twenty students short, and the hurt and the anger and the fear they feel about losing their school. The reality is more complicated, though. Those that have left often seem unsettled by their choice, aware that they may be a "part of the problem," Delight's imminent consolidation. And many of those who remain fully understand the wide spectrum of reasons that a family may want to prioritize certain interests of their child and move him or her to Murfreesboro.

So maybe this identity retains some flexibility, allowing for differences of opinion and even the occasional selfish act. And maybe its boundaries can be forgiving. As one parent, a woman who moved her daughter to Murfreesboro, shares, "Me and my husband both graduated from here, so my heart still remains with Delight school. My heart will not ever be a Rattler, I'll put it to you that way. It will be a Bulldog." Maybe the strength of this identity can withstand the occasional internal assault. It's the external assault—losing the school, losing this Bulldog identity—that's the real danger.

NEW GENERATIONS

The campus is dormant under the weight of the afternoon sun, still and quiet in the thick humidity. At 3:12 a sharp bells punctures the silence; the doors of the elementary school and high school swing open, and the campus is awash in a raucous flood of students. They pour from the buildings, the older students carrying textbooks, the younger ones with brightly colored backpacks. Walkways are abandoned, and the grass is covered by one wide surge of students, a laughing noisy stream that flows toward the gym and buses and cars. I watch them carefully, trying to keep pace with the happy flow, and I check, count, notice—I'm trying to figure out just how integrated this school is.

I see a pair of girls, two white teens, heads close in gossip. I see a group of boys easing toward the gym, quick jokes over shoulders and long, loping strides, seven or eight black and white boys heading to basketball practice. I see a couple groups of four or five—four black girls, five white boys. Next it's a black teenage boy with a white girl, followed by a group of international students, and then more pairs of students, pairs of white students, pairs of black students, pairs that are mixed. And then some last classroom within the elementary school must have released because another tangle of children is finally outside, running and grabbing and shouting in the heat.

Suddenly, it's over. The doors softly click shut, and the grass is clear. Over near the buses, I can see that the flood of students has separated into a few short lines, one for each bus. The jumble has sorted itself, by bus and by town and, it seems, by race.

The Delight school has grown over its years, through integration, consolidation, even the recent expansion of an international student program, expansions that have dramatically altered its racial and ethnic composition. These expansions underscore a theme that I frequently hear in interviews, especially those with students: the school is a welcoming place, a place where people "take time out of their lives to get to know new people and make them feel welcome." These expansions speak to some kind of basic openness, and they have rewritten the community's identity in some fundamental way. But have they really changed the community, this community tucked deep in the rural South? Is Delight really integrated? And so, every lunch, every assembly, every game, I keep checking; I keep counting; I keep noticing—I keep track and parse the details, wanting some clear resolution. And then, back by the school doors I notice the last two students, probably in fourth or fifth grade, no doubt supposed to be somewhere else, bent over their Gameboys—a black boy and a white boy just playing videogames.

Schools disappear routinely in states as southern and rural as Arkansas, where, for reasons of desegregation or consolidation, student bodies are often split, rearranged, bussed off to larger or whiter schools. Twice, Delight has received students from such reorganizations—once in the 1960s when, in accordance with desegregation policies, the black school in Antoine closed and the students were sent to all-white Delight, and, again in the 1980s, when the primarily black community of Okolona lost its school and a number of its students found themselves on a bus to the still mostly white Delight.

The more recent Okolona consolidation is still a part of collective memory, perhaps because the empty buildings in Okolona's center stand as a grim foreshadowing of Delight's possible future, and the topic occasionally comes up in conversation. I ask questions, trying to understand how this consolidation unfolded, what it must have felt like to those who experienced it. The entire process seems to have happened quickly—teachers and students were told of the closing the day before summer—and confusion filled the school buses that first day in September, as families tried to remain together and children tried to figure out where they belonged. But, once the buses were sorted, most people, both black and white, describe the transition as smooth and peaceful. One woman, a black woman living in the Meeks Settlement out by Okolona, explains, "We live on the other side, and they live here [in Delight]. When we consolidated, we thought it would be a problem, but it was not. . . . Everybody just does whatever they can to do what's best for the school." Randy, the white superintendent during the Okolona consolidation, adds, "When kids came here, black or white, they were Bulldogs and we all pulled together. We didn't have any real racial problems at all." And Fadie, the black "granny" who had been a counselor at Okolona and moved to Delight with the children, says, "It was a pretty smooth transition. There was a lot of cooperation among the community people. . . . We just kind of banded together and made the school what it needed to be." I push her on this, as I did when I wanted her to describe the "family" dynamic at Delight. Finding it hard to believe that such a dramatic change for the school and these children and their parents could be described as "smooth," I ask her, "Why do you think that the community went along so smoothly?" She answers, "It was the people in the area that helped to bring this. Because they just saw it as, 'This is what we got to do, and this is what we are going to do. You know, we don't have a choice. Our kids have got to go to school somewhere. So we might as well make it as easy as possible by cooperating with each other and making each other still a part of it.'" The school may have forced the change, but, according to these sources, the community cooperated and "banded together," both black and white.

The demographics of the student body continue to shift; the most recent changes have come with the growth of the international student program. Delight has always housed a handful of international students, typically current high school students or recent graduates who live with a local family, take classes at the school, and spend the year gaining English skills. At the beginning of this school year, though, the community held a meeting and decided to enlarge the program, hoping to boost the school's enrollment. Forty students arrived in Delight from countries across the world, bringing varied English proficiencies, suitcases of food from home, and stacks of phone cards. Families opened their homes, taking in a student or two; Kathy acquired five new "daughters"—one from Thailand, one from South Korea, one from Brazil, and two from Japan.

With these transitions, today's student body has a unique demographic profile, especially given its location in a town of 309 white residents and

2 black. The school is majority white, and black children typically account for 20 to 30 percent of the students. The international high schoolers are another tenth of the population. When I ask a teacher to describe the school's students, she responds, "I can't think of a kind of student that's not here by the time you figure in our exchange students. This year they're from Thailand, Japan, Italy, Sweden, Finland, Denmark, South Korea. . . . We have Latino kids, . . . black, white . . ." The halls and walkways, the gym and cafeteria and classrooms, the sports teams and student government and after-school clubs, are a mix of white students and black students, domestic students and international students. This is a student body that looks quite different from most others surrounding it in this part of Arkansas—indeed, quite unlike many other school populations in the South—where school demographics tend to match their monochromatic town demographics.

From the very first time I stepped into the gymnasium and saw bleachers full of black and white children, black and white parents, sitting and talking and playing together—and a Korean player on the court—I'd been intrigued by the apparent openness of the community and the school. Within the school, white and black occupy a shared space—they share the same classrooms, join the same sports teams, and sit in the same bleachers. I wander the walkways and notice the groups that gather: a group of black and white middle school boys horsing around, jumping to slap the metal cover over the walkway, or an older white teenage boy whispering to a black teenage girl. The cross-racial contact the students enjoy is clear, but do these interactions develop into meaningful relationships? And do these relationships extend beyond the school's small block? Do the mixed bleachers of a school in the rural South mean anything?

Conditions within the school seem ripe for developing respectful, equitable relationships. Students cooperate while working in the classroom or putting on a skit for the school. Both black and white student officers head the classes, and both black and white valedictorians have given the graduation speeches. And under the leadership of Kathy, all students are supported: as one parent notes, "She doesn't see color. It's all treated the same." A black student says, "Since we got our new principal, the rules have changed and stuff. . . . Now that we have Miss [Kathy] Cole, the rules are stricter, and I think she's been making Delight a better school by protecting everyone and making sure everybody's okay." Students are equal here; all are recognized and cared for; and they feel safe—giving them a stable and level space in which to interact.

These conditions do seem to cultivate relationships that cross lines of race. Children approach one another with kindness and respect. Kathy explains, "They treat each other well. This is the first time that I ever seen that black and white actually get along. And the kids, they don't make a difference in black and white. It does not matter, it just doesn't. They just get along. I have not seen a race card come into play yet. You watch that type stuff; by my being black, you watch that." The students at the school are, according to a student, "a bunch of different kinds of people. They're very nice; they're very friendly." Then she adds, "And there's no cliques: everybody gets along with everybody." These relationships then extend to each other's houses after school and on the weekends. A black parent explains, "All the kids seem to get along just fine. Our kids come here to Delight on weekends. Kids from over here come over there on weekends, so they're even together not during school." A white parent corroborates this, sharing, "There is not a black kid in [our son's] class, I don't believe, who hasn't spent the night in this house. . . . They all stay here. He's stayed at their house."

The international students may be less fully integrated into the fabric of the school, especially since they remain at the school for only a year, and language barriers make communication difficult. But relationships do develop between the local students and their international counterparts: a few romances have surfaced, and one local senior I interviewed had just returned from Rome, after visiting the Italian student who'd lived with his family the previous year. One night I join Kathy as she drops off her girls at a Halloween party for the international students (families hosting students are provided a stipend to pay for these kinds of events): between dark pastures hiding silent cattle was a bonfire, a huge pot of chili, a line of pumpkins for carving, a couple clusters of parents and families, and a huge crowd of costumed high schoolers, both international and local.

These student relationships that cross the embedded lines of race—and, now, nationality—are different from those experienced by older generations. A number of adults, especially those who attended the school immediately following integration, note changes in the relationships shared by current students. While interracial dating often occurred when they were students, "it wasn't accepted, . . . there was a lot of people that did not accept it." This alumnus continues, "When we were growing up, there was a distinct difference [between the races] and we maybe knew it, and you had to honor it." While this difference couldn't prevent teenage love, it did force it underground, especially when an older brother or father would take aside the young boyfriend and offer a few words of warning. Now, though, "the kids are just kids," and these relationships are more open: "I see now that . . . they're at the mall or wherever together. When I was growing up, we wouldn't dare do that."

But these adults may also enjoy the more open cross-racial relationships shared by today's students. Adults—all adults—turn out for school events: "When we have anything at school, there's as many black folks as there is white folks." And "most of the adults in the black community know adults in the white community who went to school with them. They tend to talk and get along," a current student reports. The older generation also notes the change that has come since integration. An elderly white woman, using words that speak to the social and cultural shifts she has witnessed, describes how, "when we had the big meal here in town, there was a little colored section, down along the creek, and they stayed to theirself, they didn't get out and mingle, like they do now." Such "mingling" builds relationships and leads to a general level of trust. Kathy says, "Dealing with this school, dealing with anything that goes on, whether it's black or white, they support each other. Even if they might not even like each other, or like someone, they're still going to support that person because . . . they take care of their own."

This kind of cross-racial support may have led to other changes in the community. One alumnus, a black man in his early forties, described the gossip he heard soon after his biracial son was born: "This one gentleman who I know . . . [I] hear through the rumor mill that the guy says, 'Should have strung him up.' Not those words, but the inference was there." A number of years later, the alumnus gave the school's commencement speech, voted by the senior class as "someone who has been successful in his career." This same gentleman approached him after the speech, told him, "'I really enjoyed your speech,' and shook my hand. And that was neat. I was a little bit apprehensive when he started walking to me, but . . . [he laughs and trails off]. So I think there is progress for the best." Progress is also evident in the district's leadership. Two of the seven members of the school board are black—a change from a generation ago when, according to this same alumnus, "no one would even consider a black running for school board." Kathy provides another example of such change: "Case in point, there have not been any black businesses in town, and right now there is a black female that has a business here in town." She adds, "And, myself, as the principal. I'm the first black principal they've ever had here. So that's a change. They're ready for a change. It's kind of hard to accept change, but they're doing it."

This willingness to hire a black principal, to support a black business, to elect a black school board member, to nominate a black commencement speaker, seems to speak to a change more fundamental than just more frequent or deeper cross-race friendships. The values of this community seem to be shifting, as this once-white community appears increasingly diverse, tolerant, and integrated. Indeed, every student I talk with describes the school as either "welcoming" or "friendly." Adults, too, note these qualities within the community. A storeowner shares, "Black, white, whatever, people get along. They respect each other. We don't look at color. We just don't. People get along. I'm speaking for myself and my husband and my family, and I think I've seen that in other people, too, though. We really don't have that kind of racist attitude around here. . . . There's just no difference really as far as the way people treat each other." Another business owner and parent describes Delight as "just a good place to live. It's down home Arkansas. You don't really expect it to be as open, as free and friendly as it is." Though the community may have little tolerance for a family that choices to Murfreesboro, racial difference is increasingly acceptable.

While school demographics may be driving these changes in relationships, I wonder who is responsible for effecting these changes, which generation is steadily influencing the minds and hearts of the others. Are parents raising their children differently? Are church elders changing their sermons? Perhaps, but this isn't the source that most recognize. In fact, these older generations sometimes struggle to accept development such as interracial dating, or, as a few students tell me, still "say the N-word a lot." Instead, Kathy explains, "It's the younger generation. They're enforcing that change. An outsider can't do it, but the younger generation, they're making the parents and the grandparents accept change because they're changing it. And, regardless of what goes on, those young kids are going to do what they want to do, regardless. So, you either do what—disown them? Or continue to raise them because you love them? You just get on board with them and say, 'Okay, I accept this.'" While adults may follow, it's the children in the school leading this change.

Yet still I wonder if this is real integration. It's a busy Saturday in Delight. After breakfast at Mom's, Kathy and I head over to the gym, where a three-on-three basketball tournament is in its second day. The tournament, honoring a forty-year-old black man who died last year, is raising money for a scholarship fund. Near the front doors are two young black college students, wearing their sorority letters and selling raffle tickets, and across from them another table is piled high with baggies of cookies and slices of pie in Styrofoam bowls, prepared by the many women watching the games. We buy snickerdoodles and pecan pie, and as we stand there talking to the woman selling the sweets and the families streaming by, the pile grows. In the gym, the crowd—families, children, parents, grandparents—is entirely black, as are most of the players. There's one white man watching the game, the best friend of the honoree and the organizer of the tournament.

We then walk across campus to the cemetery dinner, about fifty yards from the gym to the cafeteria, a cafeteria full of white folks in their late sixties and seventies. The rows of cafeteria tables are filled with people sitting elbow to elbow, eating from heaping trays. Kathy scans the crowd and recognizes only a few faces, although the two women behind the table at the entry appear to know—or know of—her. We don't stay long, with fewer people greeting Kathy, fewer folks to chat with. We enter the kitchen; here we find some familiar people, a couple of mothers and teachers and the school nurse, to talk to. There is one black face in the cafeteria besides Kathy's—the black student passing out rolls at the end of the serving line. With our to-go trays, we slip out of the cafeteria, through the back kitchen door. The fifty yards separating the gym from the cafeteria could be fifty miles, or fifty years, so complete and total is the separation. Is this change?

While I typically hear stories and see examples of positive and close relationships across racial lines, occasionally the evidence instead reveals a separation or tension. Sometimes these admissions come up when I ask students about cliques in the school. A black girl responds, "Not being racist or nothing, but mostly the white students hang together and black students hang together." Her classmate, a white girl, gives a nearly identical answer: "I'm not being racist when I say this, but black people mainly hang out with other black people." These students, so careful to note that their observation doesn't speak to a personal bigotry, see a racialized pattern to interactions. This pattern may also involve the international students: a male student notes, "There's the exchange students and there's the Americans."

Sometimes I also question whether the community really is all that open and accepting. The school's faculty, for example, is mostly white, with only two black teachers, two black secretaries, and Kathy—a consequential imbalance, since the district is the area's largest employer. And a few participants, students and adults, describe the "redneck mentality around here," or the way black students use "the race thing"—an attitude or "a crutch" that appears in the face of unfair treatment. Maybe values here aren't all that different than in many other communities: as one student reminds me, "We're pretty much just scared of change, I think. This is Delight; we're small. We don't have dramatic changes."

I also notice how and when racial differences are talked about: race is certainly noted, if uncomfortably and with worries that noticing race indicates racism, but the implications of racial difference—especially being black in the rural South—often seem absent from the conversation, especially with those participants I know less well. Several later explain that it is hard to talk about race and its meaning; people, both black and white, are afraid to speak up "because they just don't know how to." Only infrequently does a white participant acknowledge that the segregated neighborhoods are likely the result of racially biased land deals and lending habits, that state-mandated segregation ended only a few short decades ago, that the experience of a black child growing up in the South differs in some fundamental ways from the experience of a white child. No one really talks about why interracial dating seems limited to black boys and white girls, and, while the frequency of cross-racial friendships is cited, the quality of these relationships is less often discussed. It is as if the elimination of race, and all of its messy, painful baggage, is the objective. As one white parent puts it, somewhat wistfully, "If we could all get colorblind . . ."

Part of me—the southern skeptic—is unsurprised by these examples and characterizations of racial separation or tension or discomfort within the school. The residential segregation throughout the South is profound, and Delight is no different—Antoine and Meeks are black; Delight and Billstown and Pisgah are white; and Okolona has its white areas and its black areas. Friendships in school are a result of these town lines, participants tell me: "They're not being racist, it's just like they're from Okolona and Antoine. They grew up together, and so they like each other." And even the residential segregation is not simply a product of racism; it's also a matter of custom and family. I often hear, "It's probably because most of the people, where they live, their parents live nearby, and they just never left. . . . There's not a racist type attitude here. There's really not. I think it's just because people, they've always lived in this area or that area." It's like this everywhere, they explain. "You could go basically to any place, large or small, and you're going to find that there are certain areas where it's predominantly one race versus another. It's just the way it is." This larger context of racial segregation is hard to counteract, and it may be unreasonable to expect a small school to change "just the way it is" and the patterns of interaction that may follow. It would also be easy to view tiny

Delight's motivations for inclusion as primarily instrumental—to boost enrollment—rather than for any real desire for diversity or new perspectives. In this view, then, is it any wonder that a more authentic integration has not followed mere contact? With such utilitarian motives, in an area where blacks and whites have never lived together or attended church together, perhaps the school simply cannot be expected to be truly integrated, let alone to facilitate residential integration or truly change a community's values.

The reality, though, seems to be more complicated than a simple assessment of "segregated" or "integrated"—I see and hear examples and characterizations of each, both within the school and in the community. Sometimes groups are segregated by race, sometimes integrated: "It's like wherever they think they fit in, that's who they hang with. Sometimes it's mixed; sometimes it's just whites, sometimes just blacks." This complication is also revealed in the comments of both black and white students that simultaneously deny and affirm some racial distancing, comments such as: "There's nothing like seriously racist where it actually comes down to fighting or something like that, saying words that offend somebody else. It's never been nothing like that. . . . I mean sometimes we'll play basketball and it'll be blacks against whites. But we're just playing around." Or, "Sometimes stuff will be said between friends. There'll be kind of a racial slur, but would it be a racial problem? Not really in the school, it isn't. I mean, because most of the people here are friends and know everybody. . . . It's just like out of jokes. So like when a joke is said everything will just die down and it's pretty much well dropped after the joke is said. And they'll be like, 'Well, I was just playing.'" Even Kathy struggles to explain how the students group themselves, noting that in the cafeteria, "You have your little group here and you have your little group here, but, basically, the whole group is mixed up in the cafeteria. There is no 'all blacks are right here' and 'all whites are right here' and 'all Indians over there'; it's not that. They're mixed in there, but you have a little group here and they may be black, and you got your little five group here and they may be white. But, as a whole, they all are together. . . . They are a mixture." Perhaps it's my questions that provoke the convoluted responses; maybe I'm pushing this issue too much, asking the wrong questions and looking too hard, trying to see color when it doesn't always matter.

But "complicated," the gray area somewhere between "segregated" and "integrated," probably is the more accurate descriptor for both school and community. On my last visit, Kathy described an interaction she had with a biracial student, a second or third grader, earlier in the week. This little girl had worn to school a shirt with a picture of wide-eyed kittens on its back, and, on the front, a small Confederate flag. The other kids began to whisper and then tease her—though her white classmates wear the very same labels. Soon the girl was in Kathy's office, crying and very confused. Kathy told the upset child that it was a nice shirt, a very cute shirt, and then asked her if she knew what the flag on the front meant. The girl didn't, and Kathy explained that the flag didn't represent Arkansas and its past very well and that it reminded people of the slavery of black people that had happened there in the South. The girl's mother, a white woman, later apologized to Kathy, telling her that she really hadn't noticed the flag when she bought the shirt. And Kathy believes her—the daughter had just liked the kittens that much.

Kathy tells me this story as we are talking about race in Delight, debating whether race is a "problem" there. I am struck by the poignancy of the exchange—Kathy setting aside her own distaste and disgust for the symbol of the Confederate flag to first reassure the little girl that she liked the kittens too, and only then explaining the historical context of slavery and racism, the meaning of the flag, and why others thought it was funny that she was wearing it. This moment between a black principal and a biracial student, playing out against the backdrop of long-standing societal racism, speaks to complicated and complex interactions. This is what the students were telling me, I think, about their relationships: friendships are usually just friendships, shared by two people of the same race or of different races, but then, occasionally, through an ignorant remark or maybe something more intentional, the larger context stands out. Then the casual interactions, the small dramas of personal relationships, become colored by generations of racism and colonialism.

So I don't think that Delight is truly integrated or completely segregated, living in either racial harmony or racial animosity. But I do think that the school forces a certain amount of cross-race interaction and integration; Delight might be closer to integration—not close, but closer—thanks to the school. This seems unusual to me—remarkable—and worth not losing.

LEAVING HOME

Soon Delight will hear: the Arkansas Department of Education will take an official count, determining if, for the third and last year, the Delight school district has fewer than 350 students. No one's certain about what will happen next. Delight may face administrative consolidation or annexation, simply losing its status as a district—though many are convinced this would only be the first in a cascade of losses. Or it may lose the school directly. Most students would board buses to Murfreesboro, though given Murfreesboro's reputation and the location of Okolona, Antoine, and Meeks, many black students may instead attend nearby Gurdon. The following August may find these children split up and scattered throughout this corner of Arkansas.

From there it's only more uncertainty, the uncertainty of a community's future. Perhaps some of the ties in Delight are strong enough that families would remain in the houses scattered near the empty school. Maybe they would provide enough patronage for Mom's Diner and the hair salon to stay open. At least for a while, the churches could still use the old school gymnasium. And maybe the road sign—"Delight, Population 311"—would still stand at the intersection of Routes 19 and 26.

Or, the fear may be accurate: "Delight might dry up and blow away." Without a school, the meaning behind the road sign—the pride and the identity, the recognition and caring, the relationships that contradict years of southern history—would fade and then disappear. And then, where would this community call home?

CHAPTER FIVE

The Ties That Bind

Schools, Stories, and the Black Community of Earle

A couple of miles outside of Earle is a large white house. It's set back from Route 149, startling in its abrupt rise from the dry November fields. Six white columns stand at its wide front, sentries guarding tall, shuttered windows and a heavy door, and a circular drive wraps around a green lawn. A single-file line of pecan trees flanks the road, each with a metal rectangle nailed to its trunk: "No Trespassing," "No pecan picking." An elderly white man crouches under the reach of the trees' branches, gathering his pecans.

But the man, the trees, the stately white house are only a momentary glimpse on the way to Earle. Mostly it's acres of Mississippi Delta farmland spreading from the road, flat and spare, open and unbroken, save a distant tree line or silver silo. Miles of green growth and brown stalks, miles of flatness . . . then a horizon's promise, a few houses growing nearer, and a sign: Earle, Population 3,063.

Route 149 snakes through town, a road of sharp corners and street-sign arrows. It turns through blocks crowded with homes that bend and sag and splinter; it dips under raised railroad tracks and passes silent cotton gins and then winds around larger homes, solid homes with peeling paint and weedy yards. Then it crosses through a small downtown area—a little welding business and an auto repair shop, a short line of town government offices, a sidewalk estate sale outside a dark storefront, the central office of the school district.

I park alongside this central office, half gone after a late-spring tornado, a blue tarp covering what's no longer there. Inside I meet the superintendent, Jack Crumbly, a large African American man with a gravelly voice and passionate opinions, also a recently elected state senator, and we return outside and climb into his car, heading to Earle's middle school. He narrates the drive through town, showing me the downed trees and deserted homes left in the tornado's narrow wake, the empty silos and grass-covered tracks abandoned with an industry's decline.

Dunbar Middle School is on the other side of Earle, on the side of the tracks without the storefronts and big houses. Perched on the edge of field and town, it was once the "black school," the school for black students and black teachers during segregation. Its buildings are low, and bars cover the windows. A gymnasium sits at the center of the small campus; it is connected along one side to a building housing the library, the principal's office, and the seventh and eighth grade classrooms. A separate round structure holds the fifth and sixth grade rooms, and a few small buildings cluster near—a cafeteria, a woodworking shop, a life-skills center, some empty rooms and spaces. Bare, dusty ground surrounds the campus—and then out stretch acres of fields, a long green expanse.

We walk inside the fifth and sixth grade building; it's almost lunch. Classroom doors are open. Students hurry to the bathrooms to wash up. Teachers finish lessons and answer questions and rush through reminders and final directions. It's noisy, the happy clamor of a routine, of familiar conversation, of completed work and a promised noontime break. Here we find the principal, Ms. Smith, a small energetic African American woman in a neat suit. She whisks me from teacher to teacher, introducing me, explaining my research and visit faster than I can, pointing out students' work on the walls, noting various professional development initiatives, pausing to answer a question from student or staff. Teachers are friendly and curious, and the school seems comfortably busy and crowded with voices and people and projects.

And then, after we've seen all of the teachers and visited all of the classrooms, we enter the gym, still and silent in the early afternoon. A podium stands alone on the empty floor—student elections are later this afternoon; campaign speeches were delivered that morning. Ms. Smith had shown me the posters papering the hallway walls, hand-drawn posters for this candidate or that one, promises of hope and change, small echoes of Barack Obama's bid for the presidency. These posters hang under collections of small sepia ovals, pictures of long-graduated seniors in white mortarboards, the all-black classes from the forties, fifties, and sixties.

In the silence of the gym, under the watchful eyes of decades of alumni and the promises of a new generation, I forget about the big white home and the man's pecan trees. I forget about the blue tarps and empty shops and thick train tracks. Instead, in the silence of the gym, what I feel is hope.

Earle sits on the northwestern side of the Delta, barely within the confines of Arkansas. Memphis, Tennessee, is about thirty miles from Earle, thirty miles of open field and crowded interstate, across a wide and muddy Mississippi and a thin state line. The area was once densely forested swampland, and then cotton, the king of cash crops, arrived. The trees were cut and sold for lumber, and the empty floodplain was filled with row after row of cotton. Large plantations divided the land, slaves worked the fields, and the harvest grew.

Earle, incorporated in 1905, was named for Josiah Francis Earle, a Confederate major and active Ku Klux Klan member. An early survey describes "the City of Earle . . . as the Pearl of Saint Francis Delta, famous for the fertility of the soil surrounding this progressive city, for the genius of her cosmopolitan citizenship."[1] During this time, this "progressive city," with its train depot and movie theaters and cotton gins and sawmills, was considered the hub of Crittenden County. The black population, unmentioned in the survey, grew during the late nineteenth and early twentieth century, as African American laborers migrated to the area to work first in the timber industry and then, after the Great Depression, to begin sharecropping and cotton farming. Over the years, the demographics have continued to shift: currently, only about a quarter of Earle's 3,036 residents are white, and three-quarters are black. It's mainly soybeans and rice farmed here now, and still a bit of cotton and some sorghum and corn. The farms don't offer much employment anymore; the mechanization of agriculture has eliminated much of the need for manual labor and dried up most of the jobs in Earle. The train still runs through Earle, but it no longer stops, and the few factories in town—a mattress factory, a chair factory, a factory manufacturing laundry hampers and closet storage units—have closed.

What remains is a handful of stores, dozens of empty storefronts, and three schools. Today these schools—Earle Elementary School, Dunbar Middle School, and Earle High School—enroll just under 800 students, about 300 each in the elementary and high schools and 200 at Dunbar, nearly all African American and eligible for free or reduced-price lunch. The schools provide more jobs than any other employer in town and draw crowds for Friday night basketball games and May graduations; after the May 2008 tornado, their gymnasiums housed displaced families. Over the past century, these schools have produced thousands of graduates, generation upon generation of alumni. But now, in 2009, these schools often inspire shame and ridicule, each having recently failed to make adequate yearly progress under No Child Left Behind, with the high school now falling short for its fifth year.

For me, Earle wasn't an accidental choice. The issue that had so absorbed me in Delight—the community's racial dynamics—continued to occupy my thoughts and shape my questions. I wanted to explore this intersection of rural school and rural community and race more thoroughly, to study it differently, and needed, therefore, a contrast—a school and community with a legacy of racialized exclusion and inequality, rather than a norm of relative inclusion and equality. I had already spent time in the Delta, on its Mississippi side, for another research study, and I wanted to return, to find an Arkansas Delta town, to better understand a community surrounded by such starkness, a starkness of landscape—the long flat fields, the expansiveness of the sky, the straight furrows and endless roads—and a starkness of contrast—white and black, rich and poor, private and public. In the Delta, even a century and a half after the end of slavery, economic control typically remains in white hands, land is still owned by white families, and political decisions are still swayed by white influence: the succession of power seems as predictable and ordained as the flatness of the land. In these towns, white children often escape to private schools, leaving black children for the public schools. Here, it's easy to feel that little has changed over the past decades.

But I knew from time spent in the Delta that this feeling is only a half-truth. Yes, white landowners retain economic sway in many important ways, but these decades have also witnessed black protest and organizing; the Delta story isn't just one of white plantations and white control. During my time in Earle, I would be reminded of the incompleteness of the many Delta stereotypes—omnipotent white landowners, powerless and complacent black communities, failing black schools—again and again. Sometimes, the reminders were gentle, subtle, delivered as I stood in Dunbar's gymnasium or crowded into a black church on Sunday morning or when I finally noticed the green mold creeping up the old plantation homes. But occasionally the reminders were more explicit, a warning from Senator Crumbly against applying an "old cliché" to Earle, followed by a description of the town's lacking infrastructure and failure to attract new industry, complicated issues that likely involve race but are hardly circumscribed by it. Still, for all of the complexity that exists in Earle, the Delta's racialized history is a tight tether, still weighting Earle's story. It was this complexity, this weighty history—and the school's role in each—that I wanted to understand.

As a researcher in Earle, I was clearly, visibly—awkwardly, it often seemed to me—an outsider. In stores and on the streets I would get stares; mailmen would stop to ask me what I was doing in Earle, to tell me to be careful. Sometimes it wasn't clear what provoked the questions and stares—my newness, my unfailing ability to get lost in town, the strangeness of someone choosing Earle for a research site, my whiteness in a context so black. But often, it was quite clear: participants reacted to my race, and I to theirs. White participants would sometimes slip into "us" and "them" statements, lumping me in the "us"; black participants sometimes seemed hesitant to explicitly name Earle's racialized politics. With white participants, I could usually follow the "us" and "them" vocabulary—it felt like familiar territory, the sentiments I often heard growing up in the South—and I tried to convey nonjudgment. With black participants, I found myself working to express a lot more—that I "got it," that I "got" Earle's racialized politics, that these politics unsettled me. I wrestled with my own political views, where to put them, what to do with them; I wrestled with my conscience, when to express disagreement, how to separate beliefs from people; I wrestled with my background, the simple fact that I had once been a white girl sitting in a southern private school. Sometimes, especially at the beginning, it seemed that race was everywhere—it was the first thing I'd notice meeting someone, the first thing I'd see when entering a room, the first thing I'd listen for in an interview. I didn't realize the status I had given race until it lost that importance—the October afternoon when I walked into Earle's little Citgo gas station looking for a snack, like I had so many times before, and the first thing I saw was that the woman who had worked that morning was still behind the counter, the woman who had so kindly talked a customer into escorting me, lost again, over to Dunbar, the same cheerful woman smiling over fried chicken in the warmer and a new line of customers at the cash register—this is what I saw first . . . and I didn't see that I was the only white person standing in the Citgo. It was then that I realized how automatic and complete my response to race was—and, with this realization, I learned to more consciously and carefully see race, see myself seeing race, and then also try to sometimes see beyond both.

I grew more comfortable in Earle over a year and a half of visits, and I write this with a profound sense of gratitude, grateful to have felt welcome in places that rarely see a white woman, to have heard thoughts and reflections about race and power that typically go unspoken, to have been given the opportunity to tell a more complete story about Earle and its schools. It is a story shaped by race, though not bound by it, a story of loss, a story of resistance and hope—a story of three small schools tucked in the vast Delta floodplain.

TIED TO A LONG SEGREGATION

Mrs. Jessie Mae Maples sits on a lawn chair on a small stoop just outside her back door, sheltered by the cool shade of her covered garage. A friend sits with her, and together they gaze across the short driveway, where a few of her daughters stand talking and three granddaughters play. I follow Mrs. Maples inside, her purple-white hair bright against the brown of her skin and the darkness of her house, and we sit across from each other at one end of a long dining room table covered by glass candy dishes and punch bowls and neat piles of silverware.

Everyone has said I need to talk to Mrs. Maples. She was there "that night" in 1970, the night the black community marched through Earle, protesting a multitude of discriminatory practices and policies, protesting the likely possibility of unequal treatment in a newly desegregated school system. Over her shiny silver she describes the many injustices leading to that night—years of old textbooks discarded by the white schools, the rats that came when a landfill was opened in the black part of town, the fear of hostility "because they didn't want the black up there with them." Finally, she gets to that night, the night of the march, the night she was shot. She is brief: "This particular night that I got shot I was walking right down this street; it wasn't a street then but it's a street now. We had marched from down there; it was way down there onto Lincoln Street, I believe. And we had marched, went up town and coming back this way, and they was daring us to do everything. So we just decided we was going to march that night, and that's how I got shot that night." I'm surprised by her spare explanation, how quickly she passes over the moment that put her in the hospital for twenty days, that took her spleen, her kidney, part of her pancreas. I want to know more, to understand this night that seems to have shaped the long decades since, to know who was responsible for the shooting. Her answer is immediate, words tumbling: "I don't even know. I don't care. I don't know that." She pauses, "I never did know."

Others had described "that night" to me, too. Several months earlier I sat in the spacious living room of an elderly white couple, Jane and Bryan

Speed. Lamplight floods the room and its flowered furniture; Mr. Speed's paintings hang on the wall; and the soft carpet is marked by the tracks of a recent vacuum. Mr. Speed had been the principal of the white elementary school, and then the combined school, during the sixties and seventies. "It was terrible here one day," he begins, his thin hands fidgety. "They stormed up this street here with guns, and our law officers were out there with their guns. But we had a fire chief; he sounded the fire alarm. Of course there was no fire, but they left out. But [the chief], he came to the door, and he knocked on the door, and he said, 'Where's your fire?'" I heard this story many times, told in so many voices, in so many living rooms and dining rooms and classrooms. I would notice the pronouns—who was "us" and who was "them"—and the many ways that agency and power were tangled in these pronouns. I would also notice the sadness and trauma that seemed to tinge these stories. I would wonder what the "sides" were in this battle and how these battle lines might stretch across schoolhouse doors. I would wonder what was gained that night and what was lost.

Before the federal government forced the desegregation of Arkansas's schools in 1970, Earle's black students and white students attended very different school systems. Black students could attend the Dunbar School, a primary through twelfth grade facility located on the edge of town, a facility that, back then, had no cafeteria or gym. The younger black children would often spend their elementary years in "plantation schools," small schoolhouses scattered throughout the rural farmland, one for each of the plantations that used to control the land; later, for middle and high school, they would join their classmates at Dunbar. For these children, many the sons and daughters of sharecroppers, the elementary years were divided into split sessions, releasing in May, resuming in July, and then stopping for much of the late summer and early fall—a schedule maintained "so that the children would be able to help harvest the crops," Ms. Linda Maples, one of Mrs. Maples's daughters and a high school teacher, explains. The white students spent all of their years in town: they first went to the white elementary school located in the center of Earle and then attended the town's white high school, described in the historical survey as "a three-story structure embodying all the modern ideas of convenience, light, heat and utility . . . that contain[s] ten class rooms, a gymnasium fifty feet by eighty, an auditorium that [seats] eight hundred and fifty-four people without crowding or discomfort, a library, a teachers' rest room and the office of the superintendent."[2] "The track separated us," W. H. Johnson, a Dunbar alumnus tells me: "That's the way it was."

During the 1960s, the town, like many others across the South, experimented with different methods of desegregation, all to delay the inevitable—various classes offered at different schools; a schedule that allowed for black children and white children to share facilities though not class time; and a voluntary plan, in which students could choose to attend any school in the district, white or black, an option taken by only a handful of black students. Finally, Ms. Maples explains, "in 1970 all of that had to come to a stop, and so it had to become one school system within this small town." So in the fall of 1970, the school year was to begin at three school sites: a desegregated elementary school in the former white elementary school, a desegregated middle school at Dunbar, and a desegregated high school in the former white high school. These changes, and fears that the black children would suffer in a desegregated school, meant that the year also began with a number of protests organized by the black community—a boycott of the school, the fateful march, and the founding of a black community-run school called Soul Institute.

Desegregation was not the only issue precipitating the protests; black residents say the landfill, racial profiling by police, Earle's long history of racial oppression—as well as the examples set by Martin Luther King Jr. and Rosa Parks—all added their weight. But education, it seems, was the focus. Some black residents may have opposed integration itself. Ricky Nicks, the current superintendent and a student at the time, remembers that as black community members marched, "they carried caskets to symbolize burying the old black school; they didn't want to go with the whites." But others explain that the black community wanted integration; it was the manner in which integration would be carried out that they opposed. "It wasn't a situation where it was a merger" of the black and white schools, Superintendent Nicks reports; "it was a complete shutdown of the black culture." Many African American teachers were losing their jobs, and classes were heavily tracked with disproportionate numbers of black students in the lowest levels. The Dunbar campus was never opened, an act some view as punishment for the protests—and it would remain shuttered until the early 1990s when it became a career academy and then, later, the middle school. "The changes were not equitable as viewed by most African Americans," Ms. Maples tells me. Desegregation alone was useless; the black community wanted "integration and equal opportunity."

To me, listening to these stories four decades later, 1970 and the night of the march seem unresolved, the narrative unfinished. No one has much to say about the remainder of the school year: the protests tapered off during the fall, and, unable to receive state accreditation, the community school, Soul Institute, closed after the year ended. The violence that began the year subsided. Left little other recourse, the Earle school system was finally desegregated, even if it failed to offer "equal opportunity" to all its students.

But many members of the white community did have recourse; they left the schools. In the years following desegregation, current residents remember "a gradual exodus of people." This exodus, both black and white residents believe, was "racial." It was motivated first by desegregation itself. "When we had integration," Mike Leaptrot, one of Earle's white business owners, explains, "we had a large portion of the population that moved away. I think a lot of communities dealt with that, and it was called white flight. . . . Part of it would be racial. You grow up in the South, and white kids and black kids, they aren't raised together, they don't play together. . . . I think part probably was fear, not knowing another culture that well and how are my kids going to adapt." During the 1970s and 1980s, Earle's white population shrank, as white families moved to whiter towns and whiter school districts. In the 1990s, the schools' leadership changed from white to black; Jack Crumbly was hired as the district's first black superintendent, and African American principals led all three schools. This change, residents believe, fueled a second flight, for, as Eric Cox, an African American school board member and pastor, notes, "a lot of people would refuse to allow their child to go to school to be under the authority of a black man."

While some white families moved, others remained in Earle, just pulling their children from the schools. "Earle is, according to the 2000 census, around about 62 percent African American," Senator Crumbly explains. "So out of the 821 kids that attend, if you do a percentage, then you figure about 30 percent or close to 40 percent of that would be Caucasians. But they don't attend." This mysterious 30 to 40 percent, Superintendent Nicks tells me, is "either home-schooled or in some private institution or opted out by choice to go somewhere else." Until recently, Earle had its own private Christian academy, and other students enrolled in the nearby West Memphis Christian Academy, carried to the school, a black parent of Earle students explains, on "a bus that come to the supermarket and pick the kids up and take them to West Memphis." And others simply "choiced" to a district with a greater proportion of white students, such as the neighboring Marion.

During these decades, while the schools still maintained a substantial-but-shrinking minority of white students, alumni remember a quiet co-existence within the schools. Though some describe "a lot of interaction between black and white students," others remember division. A white alumnus explains, "Even after integration, it was really pretty much seg-regated. The sidewalk that ran down the middle of the school, at lunch-time, you'd have white kids on one side of the sidewalk, black kids on the other side of the sidewalk. . . . You didn't really have a whole lot of mixing and mingling among the races." Desegregation was accomplished, but, for many, little changed.

And, over the years, the demographics have continued to shift, slowly and steadily. The schools still bleed off students, people tell me. Now, in the school halls, the presence of a white student is startling, jarring. I sit with Ms. Claudie Forrest, another daughter of Ms. Jessie Mae Maples, another teacher, in the high school cafeteria and auditorium on a stage ready for the end-of-year play; we sit together on a sagging couch, one corner propped up with a stack of books, as she presides over lunchtime. The students talk quietly at large round tables, eating their lunches, or stand patiently in a long line that snakes into the kitchen, empty trays in hand. She scans the room, listening, able to discern single voices from the low mumble, talking briefly with those nearest us in the line. She is watchful, ready to jump on any signs of wrongdoing, and I am watchful, too, looking for white students. I see two as we sit there and the students file by, only two white students. The shift in demographics is nearly complete.

But the rationale for leaving the schools has changed—now it's about test scores. "Reading about test scores from the paper, it doesn't seem like they're getting a quality education there," these white parents say. Many who remain in the Earle schools readily acknowledge that the district's failing test scores—and a broader perception that Earle's schools provide little education—coupled with the lack of jobs and good housing, fuel the current exodus, the flight of the last of the white students. Pastor Cox, for one, admits, "Some are actually justified; the parents may work in Memphis, then they go to school in West Memphis. And actually with our test scores being the way that they had been in previous years, you really can't fault someone for wanting to put their kids in a better learning environment." But he continues, "And then some use it for an excuse." Others share this feeling, that this reasoning is little more than a new dressing for the same ugly "racial" impulse.

Surely, no single reason explains the current demographics of the school. And today's departures seem more complicated than those of years past: now, a number of middle-class black students and families have joined their white counterparts in leaving Earle and its schools—an exodus also typically explained by test scores, but one less readily apparent and less openly discussed. For the parents making these decisions, both white and black, the calculus is likely complex, filled with a variety of factors, some tied to the schools and some less related, some recognized and some hidden, some rational and some emotional. And others' understandings of these parents' motivations are also shaped by emotion and assumption. The precise numbers and true logic underlying the current demographics will likely remain hidden by polite silence and uneasy speculation, though the results are stark. As one African American teacher notes, "There has to be some reason that we have no white people that live in Earle in this school. So there has to be something going on. I just don't know what it is." But what is clear is what remains in Earle—two communities, a white community and a black community, that stay as separate as they were before 1970.

The boundaries are wide and thorough, the moments of interaction brief. Ms. Maples tells me, "We had our lighting of our Christmas tree. People were like, 'Where did all these white people come from?' because they live here. . . . They don't let their kids come to the school, but they live here." I see the separation, too—in church, where I am the one white person in a filled sanctuary; in cafés, where patrons gather by some unspoken but obvious racial logic; in the county museum, where the shelves are filled with china tea sets from the homes of white plantation owners. Two worlds seem to exist in Earle, each with its own churches, its own neighborhoods and restaurants, its own stories and photographs, its own schools. One is a white world made up of landowners and business owners, grandparents whose children and grandchildren have long grown up and moved on; the other is a black world—much larger, much younger, much more visible, and, in general, much poorer. It is this black community that is evident in Earle, a community finally "off the plantation," a community finally on both sides of the tracks. I catch only glimpses of the white community—lingering over coffee at the Bulldog Café, ordering prescriptions at the pharmacy, populating the old photographs at the county museum.

Within these communities, of course, one finds disagreement, some small squabbles and other larger rifts. Both African American and white residents describe generational divides within their communities, with the older generation still captive to an "instinct" of racial distrust and separation. Church and class lines might further fragment each. And these two racial communities do occasionally interact, and the interactions I saw always seemed polite or even friendly. Pleasantries are exchanged at the grocery checkout counter, a quick nod is offered at an intersection, and a number of teachers enjoy cross-racial friendships at the schools. Yet, for the vast majority of Earle residents, the schools are a place of division, of segregation. And many residents, black and white, describe a tension that simmers just beneath the town's surface, the thoroughness of the separation making impossible much open conflict.

Thus, the response to school desegregation—the "white flight"—seems to have perpetuated a division in Earle. Here exist two communities, a white community and a black community, attending separate schools, living separate lives. The schools, once carrying the promise of "an association of the peoples," now reflect—and maintain—the racial segregation that has always been so thorough in Earle. They have become one more wall dividing black from white.

I'm still not sure what was won in 1970, what was gained for the anger and the fear and the bloodshed, for all the black jobs lost and landfills built, for all the inequities survived. But what was lost is clear—that promise of integration. Earle's railroad tracks may have been crossed, but the boundary remains, perpetuated through the town's schools.

TIED TO A SLOW DECLINE

Just beyond the empty blocks of downtown Earle is the old high school, a red brick behemoth built in 1919 and now closed, still sitting near the end of Second Street. A wide path splits its mowed lawn; steps lead to heavy arches that shelter a set of double front doors. Cavernous windows stud the structure's solid three-story front, and a few small curves crown the façade. At one corner of the building, standing on a large base, is a broad-shouldered cement bulldog, guarding his territory. For ninety years the building has cast a shadow over this end of Second, and even with its closing and the opening of a new facility, the addition of a spindly chain-link fence, and the loss of a few panes of glass, it is no less imposing. It looks solid, lasting, permanent.

Yet it now towers over a vastly different Earle. It wasn't always so eerily quiet in Earle. Stores and businesses once lined Second Street, Mr. Irby Campbell tells me; in fact, they crowded the street right outside the little office where we sit. From here, we can see the concrete foundation that once held the service station his grandfather built, the same concrete slab that will soon anchor a new office for Mr. Campbell. A seventy-four-year-old white man, Earle's fire chief for nearly fifty years, Mr. Campbell sits behind his desk and points to where, just outside this office, all of these businesses used to be: "At one time there was a Chrysler Plymouth dealer, a Lincoln Mercury dealer, a Ford dealer, a Chevrolet dealer, a GMC truck dealer, a Ford tractor dealership, and a John Deere tractor dealership here—seven cotton gins, the largest hardwood sawmill in eastern Arkansas, a planter mill, two feed mills that made flour, horse meal feed and all the stuff related to that, a wholesale grocery company that served probably ten counties in this district, in this area. This was a booming place." Families would come into town on Saturdays, come to visit the "store after store after store" that stood along Earle's neat grid of streets. They would do their grocery shopping and visit the cafés or the barbecue places. All of this activity, all of this buying and selling and production—even Earle itself—began with cotton. "We had a whole line of cotton gins," Mrs. Speed remembers, "the cotton—the air would be so full of it in fall, when they were ginning that cotton. We had a screened-in walkway out here in the back, and that screen was just covered in little white fuzz, and it floated through the air." Earle, like most Delta towns, is tied to the rich Mississippi floodplain with deep cotton roots.

But Earle today, residents explain again and again, is "not like it was." Farming doesn't provide the jobs it used to—"the decline in the cotton growing and . . . all these mechanized cotton pickers, . . . they don't have to hire as many people." And, over the past few decades, the other, smaller industries began to leave—first the mill and then, more recently, the factories—closing their doors one after another. Connie Moore, an African American pastor, concludes, "When the economics left, people had to go find work, and they moved into those communities." Those who remain in Earle tend to fall into one of two groups: a handful of wealthy farmers who own the vast acres surrounding the town—those that choose to stay—and a much larger number of poor African American families—those that "are stuck here."

The economic decline has made its mark on the town. The considerable unemployment feeds crime and drug use, I hear, and I frequently see young men wandering the neighborhoods at midday, with nowhere else to be. With industry gone and little flow of capital, "there's just not much revenue money that comes in here," Mrs. Speed explains, "so, therefore, the town looks a little bad. The streets are bad, that kind of thing." Nothing remains to attract new residents—no "place to eat out at," Superintendent Nicks explains, no "nice comfortable home to live in." For many, the tornado that left a thin band of destruction through the town's center in May 2008 only punctuated the deterioration, closing the last factory and causing a few more families to leave. "If you drive around Earle now," a teacher tells me, "you see dilapidated buildings; industry has just left. You see boarded-up houses. It's dying. I hate to use that word, but it is."

These descriptions of the past several decades focus on what Earle once had, and what it lost—the businesses, the jobs, the quality of life. It is a narrative of decline, and it is the older residents, those who lived here in the fifties and sixties, that remember Earle before this decline. Like Mr. Campbell, these residents, both black and white, remember when Earle "was thriving downtown," and all acknowledge the enormous economic loss this town has sustained. For many black folks, these "glory days," an era spent sharecropping, evoke little sentimentality. Mr. W. H. Johnson, an African American owner of a funeral home, tells me about a large plantation house outside of Earle, one hidden back from the road, a house from "another era." "In the glory days, that yard would have been manicured . . . to a tee, but now," he flatly states, "nobody cares." In the stories of white folks, though, I hear something else; I hear nostalgia, a sadness for an era gone. Perhaps, for them, this decline marks not just the end of a period of prosperity, but also the end of a lifestyle, a time when your grown children and grandchildren lived around the corner and the air was thick with cotton fuzz.

Sitting squarely within Earle's decline are the schools—caught, many believe, in their own cycles of decline. "It just seems like some of the educational level has kind of fallen off," a white alumnus tells me. And a current student agrees, saying, "I ain't got no full education up in here." Mrs. Speed, too, was frank: "The perception . . . is not good. People tend to think that you couldn't possibly learn anything in Earle." These narratives of school failure are typically anchored by references to the test scores—the scores that, several years ago, had all three schools designated by the state as "in school improvement." These scores, widely published in the newspapers and circulated throughout the media, seem to influence judgments of educational failure, but residents cite other evidence, too. "When I was growing up, the teachers, they cared a lot more," an Earle parent shares. And a principal explains that "parent involvement is not good." These assessments are varied and often quite harsh: a level of education "gone to pot," a classroom full of "underachievers," parents that "can't pass on anything to their kids," teachers "just there trying to get a paycheck," an administration that "has failed."

I wonder how residents understand these twin declines—the decline of Earle and the decline of the school. The two are clearly tied, with the schools often featuring prominently in descriptions of Earle's last few decades. Sometimes in these narratives the schools' troubles seem to have been caused by those of the town: a dwindling tax base makes for low teacher salaries; long commutes to other towns for work preclude parent involvement; generational poverty obscures the meaning or value of an education. Superintendent Nicks, for one, describes the educational challenges—"the marginalization of the school"—as the result of Earle's economic struggles:

> Earle, the community, was an agricultural community—never
> had much industry, manufacturing or otherwise. . . . The farming
> industry became more mechanized; a lot of farm labor was lost,
> people moved out as jobs were created in the city—Memphis, West
> Memphis. We lost valuable human resources from the community
> as well as capital resources, which led to the marginalization of the
> school. Those kids that came from those families that were working
> and educated to well educated moved to the cities, and it took a
> large chunk of your critical mass of students out of here. It was a
> slow depletion; it wasn't anything that happened overnight. It was
> a slow depletion and the majority of our students now are either
> free or reduced lunch, which are poverty-stricken families, which
> means that that's the kind of family and student that you're going
> to have to educate. That's a whole lot different than educating
> students from middle-income families . . .

He sees the schools' difficulties in educating its students as a consequence of Earle's deterioration, a student body victim to a town's misfortune.

But, in other narratives, the schools are hardly victim; instead, they are the offenders, the ones responsible for Earle's decline. These are the narratives and explanations that tend to emphasize the test scores. One alumnus explained the reason he has kept his own children from the Earle schools: "I just know that, reading about test scores from the paper, it doesn't seem like they're getting a quality education there." I often hear that "people started moving off so their kids could go to better schools" and that the schools also keep residents and businesses from moving in: "People are not moving here saying, 'I want my kids to go to school at

Earle.'" One couple, a black couple with school-aged children, was thinking of leaving Earle, worried about the quality of teaching: they felt that the teachers who had been around for generations were now retiring, replaced by new teachers that don't live in the community and quickly "get burned out on their career." And even when the schools are successful, "a lot of our brightest and best move away and don't come back": even when the school succeeds, it is a loss for the community.

Usually, though, Earle's troubles are cited as neither the sole result of the schools' struggles, nor their sole origin. These twinned narratives involve a complex mix of cause and effect, of action and reaction, narratives of decline so knotted and twisted that it is impossible to trace a clear path to today. Town and school are deeply and inextricably linked, linked to the point where their relationship is simply assumed. One resident, a white farmer and alumnus who has watched Earle and the town's schools struggle through the past four decades, explains, "I think it's interlaced in a way that sometimes it's hard to discern cause and effect. . . . If you find a town that is in decline or has very little direction or is just in the same subsistence-minded focus, then I think you're gonna find a school system that is in decline, and whether it's caused by one or the other, I would say it just works together." The schools clearly play a role in Earle's decline, yet giving this role definition and boundaries, some sort of linearity, seems impossible. The schools are implicated, understood as involved, somehow a party to these messy decades of decline. The town and the school declined together, many residents believe—each disappointing the other, failing the other, linked in downfall.

Yet, a few residents do assign a cause, a precipitating event that unleashed these descents. "The school system took a nose dive in 1970," Mr. Campbell explains to me: "It's just when integration really got going and there was too many folks walking up and down the streets, having marches and all that kind of stuff." I'm startled, sitting in his little office, rattled by his boldness. White flight wasn't the problem, he seems to be saying; instead, the issue is who was left behind. When I ask him what would happen to Earle if the schools ever closed, he clarifies: "I think it would be a step in the right direction. They might as well be closed. . . . It ain't going to lower the taxes, but maybe some of the people would move from here, undesirables that are here. I don't know. To tell you the truth, they said when the schools went, the town would go, and when the school went, then the town did too." For him, it seems that "the school went" in 1970, with integration, with the "folks walking up and down the streets," with the students that now sit in those schools. And then, "when the school went," the "town did too."

I think about this conversation later that night, later as I sit with Mrs. Jessie Maples and her purple hair and her silverware, later whenever I sit with those folks who walked up and down the streets back in 1970. I think of this conversation later on my flight home and in my library and at my office, for months and months. I had long wondered how race factored into these perceptions of decline and the complex calculus of assigning blame. I had suspected that some of Earle's white residents—and certainly many of those now long gone—felt that desegregation was the beginning of the end for Earle, and I knew that Earle's schools were commonly understood as "black schools." I had noticed that judgments of school failure were more frequent—and more absolute—among members of the white community. Mr. Campbell certainly wasn't the only one to mark desegregation as beginning the "gradual exodus," but, in that conversation, he seemed to go beyond describing integration as one moment that precipitated an entire complicated series of events, events that somehow led to a town and a school system struggling to get by. Instead, it seems to me that he implies a responsibility; he lays the blame for these declines squarely at the feet of the black community. By this logic, it is the black community— the individuals who integrated the schools and sparked the white flight, the ones who now travel the schools' halls and sit in the schools' front offices, the ones who now live in the town's houses and walk in the town's streets— that is the cause of all the decline.

This logic is rarely articulated aloud, at least among the white community. Usually, when I asked questions about the effects of desegregation or tried out various explanations of what had happened in the decades since, I would get carefully measured responses, responses that avoided the subject of race altogether. Yet I doubt that this implied logic was Mr. Campbell's alone: it seemed that for many, beneath all of the evasions, "desegregation" really means *when the black folks took over and the town went.*

These black folks were less evasive in their explanations. As uncomfortable as I felt asking black participants about race and blame and decline, as much as I worried about offending a participant by suggesting that others might see only her blackness and, for this blackness, might even charge her with the town's decline, I came to realize that I wasn't saying anything surprising or new. This blame was often assumed: many black residents suspect that the white community—if not all of it, much of it—blames integration for the decline of the schools and the town itself. They recognize that the highly publicized "school improvement" list, a nationally recognized standard, is a "black list"—a list labeling the Earle schools as "black schools," "black schools" in a Delta town, failing schools in a failing town. Whether Earle's heyday ended when the white families left or whether the deterioration spontaneously arose from the black families that remained—either way, the black community is blamed; they caused the decline.

But as I think about Mr. Campbell and his concrete foundation, about all the suspicion and blame, about all the things that go said and unsaid in Earle, I remember sitting in his office, startled and confused. I remember him telling me, "I was born on the lot I live on." He had moved from Third Street to Second Street, from Second to Sixth, from Sixth again to Second, and then back to where he lives now. His entire life has been lived within these few blocks, yet he has witnessed so much change. Industries have died and factories have shut, people have marched and families have fled, school buildings have closed and tornados have hit—all within these few streets. I remember these details and realize that, for him, what was lost that night in 1970 was an era. An era ended, and his life changed, dramatically and completely.

I hear in Mr. Campbell's views the racism of that era. Part of me wants to hear that racism so I can name and acknowledge it, can separate myself from that anger and prejudice. But this may be too easy—just as it would be too easy to think of Earle as just another struggling Delta town and its schools as just another failing black district, victims of demographics and history. These labels, all of them, are stereotypes, the clichés that Senator Crumbly warned me about. They're incomplete labels applied based on partial truths or faulty information, based on ignorance. They fail to account for Earle's brutal history, a very long history of oppression, of violence, of inequity—and, also now, a history of loss. Mr. Campbell's feelings may be racist, but they also reflect sadness, fear, and loss.

It is a messy business sorting perception from reality, hearing beyond just what was said, saying aloud what is usually left unsaid. It's difficult, trying to understand the events that bring Earle from an era of cotton haziness to today, especially in a context so divided, distrustful, racially charged. Stereotypes—the inevitable failure of the black community, the predictable racism of the white community—become an easy way to understand and explain Earle's "decline," and the division, the vast space between white and black community, only perpetuates the stereotypes, the coarse assessments, and the newspaper-driven judgments of failure and neglect. The reality becomes nearly meaningless, for it is now stereotype and distrust that fuel perceptions. What complex role the schools may have actually played in any decline is forgotten; what's remembered is 1970.

The cement bulldog has waited outside the school building at the end of Second Street for decades. It still stands there, still proudly defending its territory, still solemnly protecting its charge. But it couldn't ward off change, and change made its mark—both within the school and farther down Second Street—a mark so significant that, to many, the school and the town were left unrecognizable, tied together in decline. And still the bulldog stands there, the lonely guard of an empty building.

TIED TO POWER

Coming into Earle from the east, taking Highway 64, the drive is open and expansive, a large stretch of blue, a few white and purple clouds, a bright February morning sun. Brown and blue fields spread below—tufts of forgotten stalks, furrows filled with icy shards of sky. The road, it seems, traces the spine of the earth; the ground just curves away, leaving only open blue.

Highway 64 forks from the interstate in Marion, a small city with several grocery stores and a couple hotels, a population over 15,000 and growing. Outside of Marion, there's a railroad freight yard, a vast city of train tracks and boxcars; little more than a sign marks Ebony, and there are just a few houses and a gas station in Crawfordsville. Just past Crawfordsville—but still miles from Earle—I get my first glimpse of it: I see Earle's water tower. I know the tower stands right next to the "new high school"—the school built in 1999 and dedicated by then-president Clinton, a building still known today as "new," with a spacious library and state-of-the-art culinary and cosmetic vocational facilities and wide hallways and science labs with Bunsen burners and aquarium tanks. The tower juts up from the horizon, a small flag marking Earle and this new school. It marks a story, too, a story I will hear after I drive past the high school, down six more miles of Highway 64 to the Parkin Archeological Park, and meet Faye Futch, a story about the fight for this new high school and the land it sits on.

Usually when Earle's residents describe the past several decades, I hear stories of a fading Earle. But, sometimes, I hear bits of a very different narrative—stories of marches and protest, of boycotts and union activity, stories of power and resistance. This is the narrative that Ms. Futch, a staff member at the Arkansas Archeological Survey, tells me as we sit at a table covered with pottery shards and small boxes in the back room of the Parkin site. She tells me the story of a hard-won high school, and then, later, I begin to hear these stories of power and resistance more frequently, more completely—stories that were always present, though now I'm reminded to listen. These stories piece together a narrative of black political power—and the schools feature prominently in this narrative, too.

This narrative has deep roots. Long after the Emancipation Proclamation and the end of the Civil War, Earle remained "a plantation-operated town." "At one time Earle was strongly racial," Pastor Moore tells me: "Where I'm living now, blacks couldn't live here. Matter of fact, there were times when African Americans could not even be on this side of town walking. They would get arrested. It was highly controlled by the Caucasian population, and government, education, economics, as well." Historically, white residents have held power—both the formal power of town leadership positions and the less obvious, more ingrained power of systemic oppression. Jessie White, a white farmer, explains that until 1978 when an African American mayor was elected, the town "was very much white-dominated. I mean everything: politically, legally, it was very white dominated. And that created a lot of the racial tension because of their abuse of power, which comes along with small town politics."

But this legacy of white power isn't Earle's only history; Earle's black community has its own legacy, a long legacy of resistance and activism. Ms. Futch, an African American woman with close-cropped hair, reading glasses, and an encyclopedic knowledge of the area, begins this history just after the Great Depression. She explains that President Roosevelt "paid the farmers to turn their land under," and that these farmers were supposed to pass the money along to the sharecroppers who worked their land. Many failed to, though, and a number of black sharecroppers, members of the Southern Tenant Farmers Union, staged a strike. Sheriff Paul Preacher tried to break the strike by jailing "any black people that weren't working in the fields," and thirteen men filed a lawsuit against him—and won in the federal courts. In Earle, Ms. Futch assures me, "protesting goes way back." Here, "leaders and people . . . believed in the cause."

Claudie Forrest, a former student of the segregated and the desegregated systems, as well as Soul Institute, tells me about the empty buildings in downtown Earle. Her story begins where many others also start: "At one time there were stores on all sides; when you go down, you'll see where some of those buildings have burned." But she continues: "I know what happened, I'll tell you what happened there." She explains the old credit system in Earle, the way black sharecroppers would come into town on Saturdays to buy supplies and food from the stores, and many would charge their bills to a store account, a practice encouraged by storeowners. Interest would swell the debt, keeping these black farmers in a perpetual state of poverty and indebtedness. But, Ms. Forrest explains, "We had a man that came here . . . back in 1970, and he awakened the black man's ears: 'If you want to get your independence, you've got to stop going up there and charging those grocery bills because when you go back the next time it's $15 more than what you had before. You've got to start paying cash.' And when people started paying cash and stopped charging, a lot of those businesses folded because you don't have the extra money. And so that's part of the reason people would come off the farms, so therefore they didn't have that servitude anymore." Others underscore this desire to "get off the plantation." African American pastor Eric Cox notes the growing disinterest in farming jobs, for "farming really doesn't pay too well to just common everyday laborers." With this autonomy came an implicit demand of the white storeowners and white farmers: "Recognize me for who I am, what I have." "Inspired by Dr. King and other things that were going on," many within Earle's black community began "to get up and start doing something"—seeking financial independence, demanding recognition, protesting and marching.

By the late seventies, they were also voting, and the black community began to gain control over the ballot box. Superintendent Nicks explains that "the power of the town changed hands due to voting and African Americans understanding what it meant to vote, and becoming educated to that fact, and they understood that their numbers meant more to them than having any wealth or land." This new political force named African American Sherman Smith mayor in 1978, and other elected positions followed, including those positions tied to the schools.

Election to the school board was particularly contentious. After integration, when "African Americans wanted to become parts of the school board, they decided they would pick a token rather than let us do like that. They thought that would satisfy us," Ms. Futch tells me, "but it wouldn't." A series of lawsuits in Earle and the surrounding area gained greater African American representation on the board, and today, all five of its members are black. Finding a political voice through the schools "was a paradigm shift," says Pastor Moore, himself a former school board member. With the election of African Americans to the school board came the appointment of an African American superintendent—Jack Crumbly in 1990, followed by Superintendent Nicks this year. All three schools are now headed by African American women—Carloss Guess at the elementary school, TaGwunda Smith at the middle school, and Phylisitia Stanley at the high school. The superintendent's position led to another political role for Crumbly—his 2006 election to the state Senate, representing Arkansas's 16th District. "He went there," explains Ms. Futch, "because he wanted to fight for the schools."

The leadership of the schools is intimately tied to "the politics of the town," according to Superintendent Nicks. The schools influence the town's economic welfare, giving the schools' leaders an important political and economic responsibility. Because "we're the biggest employer in town," Superintendent Nicks explains, "we're going to have to help direct policy and go after funding for projects." Ms. Futch also underscores the power held by the school leadership: "I think the economic interest lies in the school right now, because it employs so many people. The superintendent writes grants that help employ so many people. They have so many different programs going on, but he's able to hire a lot of people in the town." Through the schools, Earle's black community, with its long history of fighting for power, of creating power where once little existed, has now gained a substantial measure of influence and political control.

But political power had its costs: with it "came resentment." "The capital was still in the other hands," Superintendent Nicks notes, "and so, therefore, they could control the capital. We may have controlled the ballot boxes, but you had a stalemate." Though black residents no longer depend upon the credit of white storeowners, Pastor Moore explains that white folks "still dominate the economics of the city because they hold the money. . . . They own property; they are the bigger farmers. Those are the people that really control the banking interest." These property owners also resist increases in property taxes, the economic foundation of a school district. "Every time the school bumps up the millage," Mr. Mark Clark, the white pharmacy owner tells me, "it hits those property owners, and so all they see is, 'Here comes another tax from the school, and I don't even have kids going there.'" Yet these white property owners lack the voting power to defeat these measures, feeding a "resentment over tax issues" and leading, Mr. Clark believes, to a more generalized bitterness toward the schools. These sorts of power struggles, some believe, may fuel the recent controversies surrounding Senator Crumbly—accusations of voting fraud following his 2006 Senate election, tension with the school board, an allegation of sexual harassment pressed by a substitute teacher, later dropped. And it is also around the school that Earle's simmering racial tension may emerge: "There has been a breakdown between the city and the school and it goes back to the racial thing," explains Pastor Moore. "We got whites on the city council; we have no whites on the school board."

Conflicts between the town's educational and economic interests occasionally surface in Earle; a long public battle accompanied the new high school under the water tower. Ms. Futch is the first to hint at the controversy; she tells me that Superintendent Crumbly "got that land by eminent domain from the white farms." I hear other details later. The decision to fund a new facility itself was a fight. According to Mr. Mike Leaptrot, a white business owner, the administration directly appealed to the majority of Earle's propertyless voters, telling them that "they'll have a better school system to go to"—"not really a better education," Mr. Leaptrot clarifies, "but maybe just a better school to go to." The administration ended its pitch with, "And you won't have to pay for it because you don't own the real estate. It's real estate taxes that pay for this, so we can get an all-new school, and somebody else will pay for it for you." Property owners—members of Earle's white community—were outnumbered, and outvoted. And then came a battle with these landowners about the location of the facility, one that the superintendent ended, Mr. Leaptrot explains, when he "had to take some land from a farmer that didn't want to give up his land." Senator Crumbly further angered many local businesses when he hired contractors from outside of Earle.

Now landowners and the schools seem to have reached an uneasy stalemate, a mutual detachment. The boys' basketball team's win at state went largely unrecognized by Earle—no signs downtown, no banners on Route 149 or Highway 64. There's little willingness among business owners to offer monetary support, either, as Mr. Campbell tells me: "They poke big building programs down our throats that we didn't need and raised our taxes to just absolute maximum limit. Just got all we could stand on us as far as school taxes go, and then they still call, or advertisement companies want us to take ads and stuff like that. This time you're going to take it out of the tax money." As I hear the story of the high school, I wonder how these battles pit the town's businesses and farms against the town's schools, whether they play into the controversies plaguing Senator Crumbly and the recent school board decision to place him on indefinite leave from his position as superintendent. I wonder if this political divide perpetuates the distance between the white and black communities in Earle. Whatever the source of these tensions, whatever the division between white and black, what is clear is that the schools have provided the black community a source of political power—one that seems to threaten the status quo in Earle.

This power has another check, though, one beyond the town itself—the state government. "The state" is often viewed as an adversary of Earle, facing the schools in another economic standoff. Over and over, administrators, teachers, and parents tell me how the state has failed to provide the schools with the funds they need. "Earle has the potential of any other school in this county or in this state," one parent assures me, "if given the resources that is necessary for our kids to excel." Earle, with its cheap land, cannot generate the same kinds of revenue from property taxes that other districts can—even the districts right next to Earle. Earle's starting teaching salary, for example, is several thousand dollars below that of nearby, wealthier Marion and West Memphis, making those districts more desirable teaching locations. "So what do I say to the parents there in Earle," Senator Crumbly asks me, "when they say, 'Okay, Crumbly, we don't have much. Our assessment is low. We don't own any of the property, really; it's an agrarian community. But we're willing to vote the millage. . . . We want the best for our kids.'" If education really is the state's "first priority," he argues, "if they are still kids and citizens of the state, I think the state has to come in because, simply, we can't generate it locally." Pastor Moore also views the disparities in funding as an equity issue: "Even though we have the same demands as Marion and West Memphis, we don't get the same funds, so we have to make good with what we have. That's offensive and it's affecting our Delta children because the funds are not equal and they are basically racially divided." Whiter districts are richer, blacker districts are poorer—and the state is silent in complicity.

Though unwilling to equitably fund small, property-poor Delta districts, the state is, residents fear, quite willing to close them. The state has an arsenal of rationales for closure at its disposal; fiscal distress is just one of them. Two others—low enrollment and academic distress—are also concerns in Earle. "We're fighting for survival," Mr. Johnson tells me: "they've been gunning for this school." The state has recently consolidated three nearby districts, and many worry that the same fate awaits Earle. Pastor Moore is blunt: "You got Crawfordsville that was east of you. You got Parkin that was west of you. They've taken both of them . . . , and you got Turrell that's north of us. . . . . Somewhere, the agenda is 'Get rid of small, rural school districts.'" The district's shrinking population, questionable tax base, and history of low achievement scores—on tests that many feel are inaccurate measures of African American achievement—plague the district. These factors give urgency to the district's most immediate need: "to produce strong numbers in terms of our performances, so that we give the state nothing to work against us."

The high school, now in year five of school improvement, may feel this pressure most acutely. Over the summer, the state, acting under guidelines set forth by the No Child Left Behind Act, forced the school to replace its principal, and state representatives came up to Earle, taking over the conference room in the central office, there to conduct a scholastic audit of the high school. I meet the new principal, Ms. Stanley—an African American woman who was the district's director of special education services, a passionate woman who answers the school's phone with "It's a great day to be a Bulldog!"—in her office at the high school. She shows me the state's report, a thick binder filled with red and black, the colors that designate "no evidence" or "little evidence" of meeting standards, a report that "pretty much said that we, as a student body, did not know the importance of an education." At the first faculty meeting, she took that report and presented the findings to the teachers, telling them, "This is how we are viewed at the state level." But, she explains to me, "when I came into position on July 1, I have no excuses, I believe there are no excuses. I believe that our students here at Earle High, that those students, that our students, are capable of meeting the standards, just as students in other parts of the state." Others may doubt this school, may doubt these students, she tells her staff—but this is our school, our students, and we will succeed.

In Earle, in a town where "the parts that can be controlled are still being controlled," the schools have provided the black community with power and political voice. Yet this authority is not without limits. Earle's landowners and its school leaders often find themselves at odds, fighting public battles over property taxes and school funding. And another threat looms outside the town—a state that appears anxious to close one more Delta district. Both of these stand-offs may have another layer, a racialized element: Earle's black community and its "black schools" face two white adversaries, Earle's own white landowners and a state "controlled . . . by whites." Arkansas's racial conflicts may be far from over.

But whatever political turmoil roils around Earle's schools, within the schools still sit young children wearing little backpacks, teenagers ready for graduation, African American students with entire futures ahead of them. Earle's black community has suffered many losses in the decades after 1970. With desegregation, ironically, cruelly, they lost the possibility of integration, of being the worthy classmates of white students, of being included and recognized as equal, of being seen for more than skin color—the possibility, some would argue, of equitable resources and just funding. Yet the black community has gained political power, much of it through the schools themselves. And they also may have gained back their schools; as Ms. Futch tells me, Earle is "the one school [district] that we look at as what we used to have. . . . It's closer to us. It looks more like us. It's predominantly African American, and that's why we just cherish it and take pride . . . because it represents us."

In Earle, this narrative of representation and political agency is often muffled, drowned out by the frequent telling and retelling of Earle's other narrative, the one of decline. Yet it offers another, a very different, story of the past four decades in Earle. This is the story I think of when Tiffany Williams, a young African American teacher and alumna, tells me, "The majority of the people on the outside, looking at us, pointing, they're laughing, 'This small school, how long is it going to be before they go down,' because every city around us has lost their school. But we consider ourself as being the small town with the big heart and the most determination, because we have overcome quite a bit to be as small as we are, and we're going to keep climbing until we reach the top." This story casts Earle's history as a struggle for empowerment and agency, as a sometimes-heated battle for power and control, as a long quest to open a new high school under the water tower of Earle.

TIED TO HOPE

"The bell rang," a student tells me—my untrained ears hadn't heard it—and, then, they're gone. All five of the students I'd been talking with—three boys, two girls—quickly file out of the small computer room to take their fifth period end-of-the-quarter tests. They had just been heatedly complaining about the dress code and the new rule that has students walking on only the right side of the hallway, a level of order and direction that irritates them. But then the bell rings and all rise, uncomplaining, to take their tests. And when they return—and all do, except for one student who also has a sixth period test—we resume the conversation, and I hear more complaints about how boring and strict the school is. I ask if it's always been so strict. "No," one of the girls answers quickly. "It's just this new principal," a boy clarifies. Things have changed this year, it seems, changed when Ms. Stanley arrived. The students are animated and comprehensive in their critique of the school, touching on the school's food, many of its teachers, its small size, the frequent tests. Some of the criticism is debated—whether, for instance, they'll be prepared for the years following graduation—but they are unanimous on one point: Ms. Stanley is all about the academics, and all of this discipline, "she's doing it for academics." "It's good," one student says, "because we just need to learn more about our books and stuff." Yes, the rules "are kind of off," but it's for the academics, they tell me. And besides, another adds, "she take up for Earle. . . . She fight for her 'hood." This new principal has faith in them, faith in her school—there's a hope here.

I see this hope as I watch Ms. Stanley preside over dismissal, standing just inside the front door as a hallway of high schoolers streams around her, joking with some, reminding others to keep moving, solid and sure within the flood. I see it at the elementary school, the day before Christmas break, as parents and teachers and volunteers set up tables with pizza and tinsel in classrooms wallpapered with projects, as children struggle to contain their jumpy excitement. And I see it at Dunbar the afternoon of student elections, when this hope hangs thick around a podium in a quiet gymnasium. Despite the political battles and the feeling of despair that may surround Earle's schools, within these schools a hope and faith remain. Earle's future—the future of its residents and of the town itself—is still tied to these schools.

Sometimes, this hope seems an obligatory hope, a sense that "the city is all the school has, and the school is all the city has . . . the school has to become the hero of the day." It's a hope born of history—"We've survived this long; we'll keep surviving"—and necessity—"That's why education was so stressed in our schools, in African American schools, to get off the plantation." It's the hope that hangs with the graduation pictures on the walls of Dunbar, the hope that rests with the knowledge that "we have doctors who've come from here, lawyers, educators." This hope understands that the school is "the heartbeat of the city of Earle. . . . It creates jobs, it also creates a quality of life, and it creates education." It is the kind of hope that can be found in the high school gymnasium on a Friday night—"that's where the heart and soul of the community is, one thing that the people feel passionately about." But for others, this hope is deeper; it is a deep and abiding faith in the ability of the schools—in the abilities of their leaders and teachers, their students and families—to prove that decline isn't imminent, to provide an education that can uplift their graduates and the town itself.

And so the schools are focused on a turnaround: "The ship was a little bit off course," Ms. Linda Maples explains, "so we need to get the ship back on course." The test scores, though many feel that they may not capture the abilities of Earle's students and teachers, have been a motivator. "We've had several different encounters with the state department," Pastor Moore explains, "that demand that average is not good enough; we'd have to be above average and better." Parents understand, "I want my kid to be able to compete when he goes to college, so give him what he need now so he won't be so lost when he get to college." And so, a teacher tells me, "our focus is to improve the state test scores, and so we basically have our curriculum and everything geared towards that to motivate the students into getting the score they need."

This new focus is clear, from orderly hallways to motivational assemblies, from after-school tutoring to drill sheets tucked in backpacks. The schools have adopted a new district-wide curriculum that is "aligned, horizontal and vertically, for literacy and math." Cash and classroom parties are given to students with high test scores and classrooms with good attendance at parent-teacher conferences; recognition of teacher dedication and student performance feature prominently in frequent assemblies. In all three schools I hear talk of college: "We're making the progress with the students," Dunbar principal Ms. TaGwunda Smith explains, "as far as preparing them for college and talking with them in regards to college and setting up programs and college tours so that they actually go and see various colleges." And the community itself seems to be rallying behind the schools: church pastors are walking the halls, and the newly formed Earle Booster Club is providing the "monies and whatever the school cannot afford for its athletic extracurricular activities." "We're moving in the right direction," a Dunbar teacher tells me. "Our schools are coming off of the improvement list. The elementary school is off. They're now an achieving school, and if we make AYP, we're going to be an achieving school. The only one that's left is the high school. . . . I believe that we can have a really positive future, if our administration continues on the path that they're on as far as really helping us get the things that we need. I believe that we'll be fine." The work may go unheralded; this sort of effort doesn't make newspaper headlines. But, within the schools, the hope is palpable and the changes notable.

This work is crucial, too, given the size and weightiness of the aspirations tied to the schools. Many of these aspirations focus on the fates of individual students. Repeatedly, parents tell me of their desires and plans for their children: "I would like to see them go on to better than what I've achieved. I work and I try to take care of them to the best of my ability, so I'll be there for them, but I want them to excel higher." For many, this "better" means college; higher education is widely recognized as the key to a stable, lucrative job. This understanding comes from experience: "If you don't have that college degree, they kinda look you over and get somebody that have the college degree. . . . That's how they do my husband sometime. He know how to do the work, but he don't have the degree." And so they tell their children, "Go here and get that degree and you have the whole package." The school staff realizes this priority. Some foster it through their own words and actions in school, emphasizing graduations and part-nering with local community colleges, though others seem to temper it with the reality that "everybody doesn't have to go to college." The high school has a number of vocational programs—cosmetology, shop, culinary arts—that provide the certifications necessary to obtain jobs, programs housed in brand-new facilities with shiny silver ovens and long rows of salon chairs.

Parents and teacher recognize—even hope—that these aspirations, whether for college or jobs, will take these children far from Earle. Stu-dents say that their families and teachers emphasize the need to leave Earle, that there's little here for a promising graduate. "First thing is to get out of Earle," they're told; "Earle ain't going to do nothing for you." One parent lectures her children, "There's something better out there than Earle. Earle's a good little community but it's other stuff out there beside this little island." She concludes her advice: "Come on back to visit me, though. Do all you can. Just learn all you can. Learning's gonna help you in the long run."

Hopes for the community, too, are tied to the schools. Many teachers and administrators dream that "the Earle School District would be one of the model school districts in the state" and that staff from other schools would visit Earle "to see what's been working for us." Ms. Maples explains: "I'd like for us to have a wonderful, fantastic, marvelous school that everybody will look at. 'What are they doing?' Because we do have a 95 percent free and re-duced lunch, . . . we do have 95 percent African American students, . . . and if we're scoring 80 percent or so on our standards test . . . , I think people would want to come. Those people who generally service white kids and can't get a handle on what they're doing with their African American kids, I think they would be wanting to look at what we do—'How you're doing that, what are you doing, can we look at what you're doing?' And I think we could be there. I know we could be there." There's a resonance that I hear in many of these hopes, a pride, a desire to speak back to the stereotypes often applied to Earle and, perhaps, the low expectations the community may hold for itself. As Pastor Moore tells me that he would like to see Earle "become a school that stands out," he emphasizes that just "because we're small, because we are a African American school, doesn't mean that we have to be just average. We can be an upstanding school." Then, once all of Earle's schools are "achieving schools" and the district is a "model district," maybe then "people will want to move to Earle . . . and maybe that'll bring in industry."

Both school administrators and business owners recognize the important role the schools play in drawing new industry. Earle has empty facilities, and the state provides attractive tax breaks to relocating companies. Now all the town needs is to improve—and promote—the quality of the school district, for "when people relocate to an area, the first thing they want to look at is the school system and what the city has to offer." Senator Crumbly imagines a sales pitch that runs: "Come to Earle! A great place to live, a good school system, low crime rate, great real estate prices! Get twice the home for the same amount of money! Less than thirty minutes from downtown Memphis!" A school system with a good reputation could go far to reverse Earle's economic decline.

And many of Earle's parents and teachers, a handful of pastors and business owners, understand Earle's future as dependent upon the graduates themselves, upon graduates embracing "the tremendous opportunity to make a positive impression and impact upon this community." Mr. Johnson hopes that Earle's alumni will attend college and "then try to come back here and give back to this community, rather than go on away and say, 'I just don't want to go back to Earle; that place is dead.'" These adults, many who attended college and returned to Earle "to uplift the city and uplift the school," see that Earle needs leadership. The town hungers for alumni with "the vision, the skills in order to move the community to another level." Mr. Mark Clark, the white pharmacy owner, describes the necessary role these kinds of graduates can play: "I think the big challenge is to sell to these kids that there is a big world out there, . . . go out there and get an education, and you have a town here that has a need for so many things that you could be successful right here. You could come back to Earle and put in a dry cleaners or put in whatever. There's a need for just about everything, and we just need to figure a way to get our kids to come back here and do those things. That's the only hope for our community, I think." These adults pray that graduates won't just leave Earle but that they'll also return, drawn by commitment and equipped with talent, ready to "uplift" the community. And, just maybe, they'll also return with the "ability to interact with people of other races, other cultures," able to bridge the divide between white and black, ready to "join together and do what's in the best interest of the city."

Sometimes, as I hear these aspirations for Earle and its children, aspirations so dependent upon the schools, I wonder about the limits of possibility. Sometimes I feel that these hopes and aspirations are clearer and more considered than the path to realizing them. Contradiction is scattered throughout many conversations: a teacher might condemn her students' laziness yet still advocate college attendance; a parent might criticize the high school's test scores but recognize that the school is still the only way out of Earle; a business owner might describe a detailed plan for Earle's future, a plan carefully balanced on the draw of the schools, and then quickly dismiss the schools' potential. Are these hopes of widespread college-going and renewed economic growth unrealistic, given the challenges facing the schools and the heavy-hanging cloud of despair? Some of Earle's more cynical residents would argue that focusing on these hopes is distracting the school from the fundamental work it needs to do—work that is more about basic reading and writing skills than preparation for college and advanced degrees. So when does hope become a delusional, or even dangerous, fantasy? And, too, buried beneath all of these hopes is a heartbreaking tension—both wanting youth to leave and needing them to stay. If the schools succeed in sending more and more graduates to college, graduates who have long heard "get out of Earle," will these talented alumni ever return? And if not, what will happen to Earle? Could the "success" of the schools seal the "decline" of Earle?

Maybe, though, just the fact of the hope is something. For so long, this school, this black community, this town have been disregarded—by those outside and, more painfully, by those within. Doubt fills the shadows and corners of Earle: families distrusting teachers, and teachers, families; business distrusting school, and school, business; white distrusting black, and black, white. "To really understand our town," a young black teacher tells me, "you would just have to see it as a town that is filled with people that want more but . . . are all kind of stuck in that place where they may not believe that it can happen. . . . A lot of people just don't believe big things can happen for our town. And so that may be the one thing that's stopping it." Doubt, then, is the enemy of progress . . . and hope is the answer to doubt.

And hope remains. It is a hope that has long sustained Earle and her schools—a faith that the way off the plantation lies through the schoolhouse, a faith that educational justice is worth protest and pain, a faith that leading the schools empowers the community, a faith that a town's future depends on rising test scores. It is a brave hope, a hope that has weathered decades of racial turmoil and years of economic loss and unemployment and absent paychecks. It is an abiding hope, a hope that launched a march one night in 1970 and a hope that keeps a high school principal anxiously, excitedly, awaiting this year's test scores.

Much was lost in 1970, but maybe one thing wasn't: maybe hope wasn't lost. And maybe hope is a place to begin.

TIED TO THE SCHOOLS

And so it goes in Earle—school and town, past and future, hope and despair—all tied so tight. These schools have shaped this town. They have been used to separate white and black, to keep white children and black children apart, to keep their families and their communities apart, to maintain a historic, gaping division. These schools are also the leading character in a story of Earle, a story of decline—for most, a messy story of circling, spiraling declines of both town and school, declines linked in their descents; for some, a simpler story of a decline that began one night in 1970. Others, though, tell a different story of Earle, a story that explains the schools as a source of influence and control for the black community, political leverage within a system designed to withhold power. And now, the schools offer hope—both a necessary hope, the realization that the schools must lure business, bring stability to this town, and a bolder hope, the hope that these schools will ensure the future success of their graduates, the hope that these schools will save Earle itself. Much depends on these schools.

Yes, history hangs heavy in Earle. But as the decades accumulate, eras end, and others begin. Power and politics change, and a green shadow of mildew creeps up the side of a big white house on Highway 149. Different stories emerge—new stories not yet told, oft-told stories not yet heard, stories that begin to reflect and explain this change, this history. History is never over, but neither is it finished, fixed, permanent.

CHAPTER SIX

The Topography of Race

Delight and Earle—and the thousands of other rural schools serving millions of other rural children and families—sit on the fringes of today's public school debates, relegated to a lonely location past all of the worry and argument about city schools, beyond all of the anticipation and hope for urban education. Their stories—their rural stories—typically go unheard, and the worries and arguments and anticipation and hope they provoke go unrecognized. The few rural stories that bubble to the surface of public consciousness are often stories of rural backwardness or tales of an idealized rural past that never really was, stories twisted by censure or longing, stories used to justify decade after decade of rural reform.

These aren't the stories of Delight and Earle. Their stories are fuller, unmuted, authentic and complex. Flush with detail and complication, these stories of cemetery suppers and water towers and consolidation threats and marches crowd out the myths; they clear the misrepresentations and misunderstandings, complicate the decline that hangs over Earle and Delight's hazy nostalgia. These are necessarily particular stories, particular stories of the particular roles these particular schools play in these particular towns. And they are important stories, for they detail the particular meaning these schools have for these two rural places and suggest—in that yawning gap between popular myth and grounded reality—just how misunderstood many rural communities may be.

But these stories matter for more than just their particulars: these particulars also reveal common narratives, narratives that echo across these two rural places. These three narratives—narratives of race and community and reform—underscore the fundamental importance of these rural schools and delineate their threatened condition. And, though they are grounded in these two particular rural places, they likely resonate with other rural places, especially those so tied to state and regional histories of inequality and exclusion.

The first is a narrative about race. Glaringly absent from the stories usually told about rural communities, race is consequential and present in Earle and Delight: race—racialized histories and inequalities, racialized identities and interactions—gives each town a shape and topography. Yet race operates differently in these two spaces, differences that are striking and startling. In Earle, the town is split in two, one white community and one black community, one white reality and history and future and a separate black reality, history, future. And it's the school that plays this role, that separates this town, that maintains—or is used to maintain—this division. This role is often expected: from the beginnings of capitalist society to the years leading to *Brown*, from the days of cotton to today, academics and practitioners have noted the stratifying function of schools, and communities have felt their effects.

Yet Delight suggests another role that schools can play. Here, this rural school knits together white towns and black towns, creating a common, cross-racial community. This role seems unexpected, a lucky happenstance. But is it? Why do the schools of two districts, located within the confines of the same southern state, districts both rural and small and poor, serve functions so different?

SCHOOLS' PARADOX

Schools, rural and urban, have long been associated with division. Society is rife with stratification, as the economic divisions of capitalism also cut social and cultural cleavages.[1] These divides persist over generations, preserving the unequal distribution of power and resources. Schools, conflict theorists argue, perpetuate this stratification.[2] Children from different class or racial backgrounds receive different educations: poor or working-class children, segregated into poverty-ridden neighborhood schools[3] or lower tracked courses,[4] are taught information and behaviors that prepare them for work at the lowest occupational strata, while affluent children develop the skills that ensure success in elite jobs and the highest rungs of society.[5] The differences also extend beyond tangible skills and academic knowledge: schools may provide different types of cultural and social capital to their different students, with wealthier children developing the language, social contacts, aspirations, and sense of entitlement that will preserve their class status.[6] Schools, according to these theorists, offer only a myth of equality, an American Dream deferred; their true function is to preserve the economic and social inequity that stratifies society.

The South's racial segregation of schools is perhaps one of the clearest— and most deliberate—demonstrations of this stratifying function.[7] De jure segregation ensured that black and white children learned different curricula from different textbooks in different classrooms with different teachers, giving many black children an education and training designed to breed docility and inculcate limited vocational skills.[8] Segregation, though, wasn't simply about encouraging separation and imparting different proficiencies. Segregation also enacted a more immediate inequity: black school buildings were often dilapidated and sorely in need of repair; black school teachers were typically underpaid and using outdated texts; and black school buses were frequently too small or too broken to safely transport all students—and even these modest conditions required the double taxation of many black residents.[9] Segregation, and the limitations it inflicted upon black education, ensured the political power of white elites and bore enormous costs for the educational and career prospects of black students. It had social effects, too: it prevented the creation of cross-racial relationships that can foster social mobility and build a more unified society. School segregation thus preserved both economic inequity and social division.[10]

The South's educational segregation came to a legal end with the Supreme Court's 1954 *Brown v. Board of Education* decision. But resistance to integration was widespread, and desegregation often happened slowly, fitfully, contentiously, freighted by the pull of white students to Christian "segregation academies"[11]—and nowhere more so than in Arkansas, with roiling, public battles fought on the steps of Little Rock's Central High and smaller skirmishes waged in towns across the state.[12] And today the struggle to achieve school integration continues: the South, once plodding toward integration in the decades after *Brown*, has reversed course.[13] Now, in the part of the country most scarred by racism and prejudice, more and more students experience racially separate educations. In many southern towns, white students still attend well-resourced private schools, black students are still enrolled in the underfunded public system, and white control of public offices still perpetuates this inequity.[14] Schools, then, continue to stratify society, and students of color continue to bear the brunt of this injustice,[15] stuck in an education system that fails to prepare so many of them for college, for work, for the future. And all students, both white students and students of color, fail to experience the cross-racial contact promised by *Brown*, the contact that can reduce prejudice, make residents more willing to live in interracial neighborhoods, and improve intergroup relations more broadly[16]—the contact that can eradicate society's divisions. Throughout much of the South, the promise of *Brown* remains largely unrealized, and towns remain racially divided, split by their schools.[17] Many schools, then, play this role—this dividing role.

But schools don't always stratify. They have also been associated with another function, with uniting, rather than dividing. Nearly a century ago, L. J. Hanifan, West Virginia's supervisor of rural schools, described the role of the rural school in building the "goodwill, fellowship, mutual sympathy and social intercourse among a group of individuals and families who make up a social unit, the rural community."[18] She argued that the rural schoolhouse, as the site of student performances, community meetings, adult literacy classes, and athletic competitions, is the "logical center" of the rural community; that it helps to "satisfy that desire which every normal individual has of being with his fellows, of being a part of a larger group than the family";[19] that it serves to unite the rural community. And this kind of social contact has benefits beyond personal satisfaction; with it comes an "accumulation of social capital, which may . . . bear a social potentiality sufficient to the substantial improvement of living conditions in the whole community. The community as a whole will benefit by the cooperation of all its parts, while the individual will find in his associations the advantages of the help, the sympathy, and the fellowship of his neighbors."[20] In the one hundred years since Hanifan described the social capital a rural school can foster, researchers have refined the concept, and largely forgotten its rural-school roots. Today, social capital is understood as the capital of relationships— "social networks and the norms of reciprocity and trustworthiness that arise from them."[21] Social capital is the assumption that favors given are eventually returned, that collective well-being comes before individual self-interest; it is the faith and trust that accompany mutuality and interdependence.[22] And this capital is useful, for it can provide access to information, facilitate cooperation, and foster individual and collective productivity.[23] It carries distinct economic advantages, as economic transactions are embedded in social networks and trusting, reciprocal networks can facilitate these exchanges.[24] And it brings political benefits: high social capital is associated with greater civic engagement and participation.[25] Social capital, then, is both an effect—the consequence of relationships—and a cause—generating its own cascade of social, political, and economic effects.

Social capital takes two forms—bonding and bridging—each with its own rewards. Bonding social capital comes from relationships that are "inward looking and tend to reinforce exclusive identities and homogenous groups,"[26] dense ties within a particular community or group, and it fosters solidarity and support, providing a base for cooperation and collective action.[27] Bridging social capital is more "outward looking and encompass[es] people across diverse social cleavages";[28] these are the norms and trust rooted in looser connections linking various groups—racial groups, social classes, ethnic organizations—into larger networks. This type of social capital, though often scarce in the United States, promises greater access to resources and diminishes prejudice.[29] These benefits suggest, then, that social capital—and, specifically, bridging social capital—may play a role in repairing racial rifts. And so, if schools could manage to foster the relationships that build this kind of social capital, if they could generate a "goodwill" and "fellowship" expansive enough to unify a town across its "social cleavages," if they could again play the role that Hanifan identified so long ago, might schools—rural schools—carry a unique potential to unify?

So, though research indicates that schools often replicate the divisions of society, promoting social inequity and prejudice, it also indicates a gleam of possibility—the possibility that schools could unite rather than divide, expanding stores of social capital and reducing discrimination. Walls or bridges, then—schools can set up walls dividing racial groups or build bridges uniting them. And, in many respects, Earle and Delight seem to substantiate this contradiction, as Earle's schools separate the black community from the white community and the Delight school pulls together racially disparate towns. So how do these schools serve these functions, and why? And could Earle's schools one day unify the town?

THE WALLS THAT DIVIDE

The gym is packed on a fall night in Earle. Parents and students and cousins sit tight together, watching the boys' team run and shoot and pass on a basketball court, dominating the opposing team, growing one win closer to a state title. The students are enthusiastic; the parents are proud; the gym is noisy—and the crowd is black: black families crowding bleachers, black players sweating on the court. A white coach might pace the floor, or maybe a white teacher sits in the stands; otherwise, the white community is absent, busy attending other games in other gyms.

The white families began leaving shortly after desegregation, as white families did across the country,[30] throughout the South,[31] and in the Delta.[32] Some moved from Earle; others simply placed their children in private schools or neighboring districts. This "gradual exodus of people," stretching over decades, was mostly "racial," Earle's residents explain—first sparked by shared classrooms, and then by the black leadership. Now it's the media-generated perceptions of educational inadequacy that fuel the flight[33]—because "reading about the test scores from the paper, it doesn't seem like they're getting a quality education there." Over the decades, the white population in Earle and the surrounding area has dropped;[34] its presence in the schools is now close to zero.

And this school-fueled division corresponds to broader divisions. Like many Delta towns,[35] the white and black communities in Earle maintain separate existences, with separate neighborhoods and separate churches. Now, when a white resident stands next to a black resident in line at the Mad Butcher, one of the few places where residents may interact across color lines, they have little to say to one another, no relevant school gossip to share, no common basketball team to speculate about. In fact, the only thing the white resident knows well about Earle's schools are their test scores; the local paper thoroughly covers those failures. This resident never learns that, after several years of hard work, the elementary school was removed from the state's list of schools in need of improvement, that it made adequate yearly progress for two years, and that the middle school made AYP, too. He never hears that the high school basketball team won the state championship. He only knows the failures, and he keeps sending his children to the private academy—it's expensive, but worth it.

Political tension accompanies this segregation. White residents may have fled the school system—they may have even moved from the town itself—but many still own the land, run the businesses, and pay the property taxes. They have little incentive to invest in a school system their children don't attend, a school system that, as far as they know, seems to continually fail to make any educational progress. Struggles over tax rates and millages are painful and bitterly remembered. The fight for the new high school facility continues to cloud the perceptions and decision making of business- and landowners: they're frustrated, angry, fed up.

And the black families watch the simmering resentment, the "gradual exodus" of white families, the slow abandonment of the school and town.

They know the political battles that divide the town's government, the gloomy economic forecast, the harsh depictions of the schools and community. They may never have wanted desegregation, or they may have questioned the motives and the method; they may now wonder what became of the promised equity. Some black community members realize these inequities, these challenges, these unfair portrayals, and still hold on to the strength and power in their schools and their community. They maintain a hope, a hope of becoming "an upstanding school," and their work as pastors and teachers and administrators and parents is a testament to this hope. Other black families, those with the economic resources, may join their white counterparts, worried that their children won't receive the quality of education they deserve and fearful that they won't ever learn to think or see beyond Earle. These families may be eager to avoid the battles over taxes, ready to have a superintendent whose integrity and leadership skills aren't questioned, impatient to escape all the decline. And some do feel "stuck here" in Earle, stuck in a place that "ain't going to do nothing for you," stuck in a town without a future and a school without a prayer, stuck behind a wall of racial distances fortified by school politics and prejudices.

Segregation's Consequences

And Earle seems stuck, too. It once had the shops and the movie theaters, the car dealerships and the factories, the businesses and the prosperity. Now, the town is "dying." It's difficult to pinpoint when the economic decline began, but desegregation—and the immediate resegregation—has, no doubt, contributed. With desegregation, racialized fears were stoked and racial rifts grew, obstructing the development of mutual trust and collective obligation within Earle, preventing the growth of social capital. Decades of white flight have only perpetuated economic and civic degeneration, and today the wealthy are reluctant to invest their financial resources in the town, long-standing political battles paralyze the town's government, and customers feel little allegiance to local businesses. Residents, too, feel the stagnation, stuck without the educational and material resources to escape the decline.

Research underscores this sense of stagnation. Certainly school segregation is associated with a whole host of damning academic effects, including lower achievement test scores,[36] that limit students' occupational possibilities and attainment potential. And beyond simply compromising the education of individual students, these academic consequences, many researchers argue, replicate an entire system of economic stratification.[37] If the quality of the schools is as poor as many residents believe, Earle's students may be prepared to do little more than scramble for the handful of jobs at the Mad Butcher, commute to factory work in Memphis, or simply collect unemployment—truly stuck in the bottom rungs of an economic hierarchy.

And so, Earle's racial rifts are also economic divides, divides between the haves and have-nots, divides that are great and, it often appears, insurmountable. Influence, wealth, and land are concentrated in the hands of a few white families, typically held there for generations, and racial difference only reinforces economic disparity. Without the opportunity for contact between black and white residents, between the haves and have-nots, bridging social capital—and access to resources it provides—is nonexistent. Without the ties that allow for some sharing of wealth, for some social mobility, for some escape from poverty, the have-nots likely *are* stuck.[38] And Earle, too, it seems, may remain stuck in its cycle of economic decline.

Furthermore, school segregation is consequential also for what it precludes: it prevents the kind of meaningful cross-racial contact that reduces prejudice.[39] Without this kind of interaction, without the schools to foster these relationships, the racial divide remains . . . and grows. Many white residents remain convinced that Earle's decline began with desegregation; many black residents remain wary, distrusting. It's little wonder, then, that tensions between white landowners and black school leaders run so high, that political decision making often ends in stalemate, or that racial stereotypes are more pervasive, more common, than tolerance and understanding. Back before 1970, the schools held promise; they represented the possibility of an integrated society. But this promise was lost in the subsequent decades, lost somewhere in that gradual exodus. Left without any vehicle for fostering relationships across its color line, Earle, it seems, will continue to live out her plantation legacy, always partly stuck back in the cotton days.

Yet not everyone feels stuck in Earle, or in its schools. Historically, the black schools of Earle played an important role in fostering a bonding social capital within the black community. Researchers have documented the academic, social, and motivational importance of all-black schools in the rural segregated South,[40] and Earle was no different: before integration, residents describe the black schools as centers of black culture. These institutions, no matter how poorly funded, provided for the black community—offering a sense of belonging, a feeling of ownership, a standard of academic excellence, a way "off the plantation." They generated the collective resistance and protest—the march, the boycott, Soul Institute—of the early 1970s, and today's schools may continue to tie the black community together a bit more tightly, rallying parents and teachers to focus on improving test scores and motivating academic achievement, building some bonding social capital.[41] And this bonding social capital fosters a relational power[42] that has won the election of a black school board and the appointment of black superintendents and principals. Indeed, these schools appear to have built enough of this resource to lay a political base and develop leadership, to stave off state take-over and past consolidation and fiscal threats, at least for now. And, for many, it fuels a hope, a hope of "uplift," a hope for a better future for the community and the town.

But, sometimes, even this bonding social capital seems limited. Students see little of their teachers after school; they've left for their own homes in Marion or West Memphis. Residents often don't know their neighbors, black or white, and unfamiliar faces fill the annual Christmas tree-lighting ceremony. Many feel uneasy at home, worried about gangs, drugs, or petty crime, and the "brightest and best move away and don't come back."

And maybe asking these schools to build a sense of mutuality and interdependence within the black community is simply asking too much: these schools are institutions the black community was forced to attend— it was this community that had its school closed, this community that was then abandoned, left alone in an institution that had never really seemed to want it. It may be little wonder, then, that trust is sometimes in short supply—trust within the black community, trust across racial lines, or trust in the schools.

THE BRIDGES THAT UNITE

A fall Friday night in Delight would find that school's gymnasium just as packed as Earle's, the stands just as filled with parents and teachers and families and students. Yet, in Delight's gymnasium, the parents and teachers and families and students are both black and white, watching a team both black and white. The ball falls in and the noise is deafening, a single, loud voice filling the gym, a community united behind its players and its school. These families will scatter after the game, the white families walking a few streets over to their nearby houses or driving home to Bill-stown and Pisgah, the black families heading back to Okolona or Meeks. The racial integration is far from complete, yet there is still something remarkable about this school and its gymnasium, something unpredicted by conflict theorists and much of the education literature: this school has built bridges across racial divides, bridges that change and shape this small part of Arkansas.

Stores of Social Capital

The school seems to be the center of the Delight community, the "com-munity hub," generating a social capital that fortifies and sustains the community.[43] Past consolidations have dramatically altered the school's demographics; they forced an all-white school to integrate and six towns, towns both white and black, to come into much closer, more meaningful contact. And an expanded international program has contributed ethnic variation. Despite these racial lines, even lines of nationality, this collec-tion of thirteen small buildings provides a forum, a space for all commu-nity members—black and white, local and international—to gather. And gather they do: students crowding the hallways between classes, families waiting on the walkways or in the pickup line after school, alumni fill-ing the cafeteria during weekend benefit suppers. They gather and talk, maybe about prom or the rain that hasn't let up or lumber prices. And they work and play together, collecting raffle money for scholarships, swinging on the swing set, writing scripts for an assembly skit.

The school fosters relationships through these interactions, maintain-ing long-standing ties and fostering new ones, relationships with "a social potentiality."[44] Friends see one another in the lunchroom, neighbors share a table at the benefit supper, a preacher asks the nurse to keep her eye on a sullen teenager, a teacher edits the college essay of a senior, the cafeteria ladies explain the senior lunch tradition to the new principal, and team-mates spend the weekend at one another's houses. The school fosters an identity, instilling shared values and local norms, socializing generations of youth, and it nurtures a culture of recognition[45] and care,[46] a sense that one is known and looked after, that one is "welcome." Adults, too, know that they are also recognized and cared for; it is at school that individuals learn about the illness of a community member and organize a commu-nity supper to support her. There's an economic benefit to this common identity and care, as well. The school provides financial support to a small cluster of businesses: it is the largest customer in Delight, the auto parts store kept busy with the school buses and the printer generating stacks of Bulldog T-shirts, and it releases an entire campus of hungry customers every afternoon. The school cultivates a sense of mutual dependence within the community, both social and economic, a sense that one's well-being is tied to the well-being of others.

And, importantly, this trust and mutuality extend across racial lines, so that, residents explain, "black, white, whatever, we take care of each other." The school, it appears, does more than facilitate interracial contact; it also fosters the type of meaningful interaction—white kids spending the night at the houses of their black friends, Korean kids and local kids playing together on a basketball team, a black administrator facilitating a staff meeting of white teachers, parents and grandparents gossiping across race lines at the games—that is known to reduce prejudice and improve race relations.[47] These interactions, researchers have noted, must have a number of features: the groups must have equal status and must cooperate around common goals, the interactions must be supported by authorities and shared norms, and there must be opportunities for personal acquaintances that counter stereotypes and for friendships that cross racial lines.[48] And, mostly, the Delight school seems to foster these conditions, with administrators and teachers who usually treat white and black children and parents fairly and equitably and promote tolerance and acceptance within the school, with common educational and athletic goals and a shared vision for the continued existence of the school that link community members and students and staff, and with thousands of opportunities, from the cafeteria to the gymnasium, for genuine—if still tentative—relationships. And so, amid the lasting prejudices of long-standing separation, despite the occasional bigotry and the slow progress of complete tolerance, the school begins to build relationships between black families and white families, between the Meeks Settlement and Pisgah, tying residents together in a shared community. The school, then, both fosters deep and trusting bonding relationships, strengthening ties of friendship and family, and promotes looser, bridging relationships across lines of race and geography,[49] providing community members with stores of useful social capital.

The Benefits of Social Capital

The social capital fostered by the school pays dividends to the Delight community. Some of these benefits are economic: the school anchors several small towns full of customers to the handful of shops sitting at this highway intersection. The school facilitates the social ties, interactions, and allegiances that gird these businesses' transactions,[50] thus sustaining these businesses and also maintaining Delight's physical presence on this stretch of highway. It is this economic anchor—weighted by the school— that, residents believe, keeps Delight from simply disappearing. And the school also encourages a network of more individualized help. Community members describe, for example, the support that was provided for an ill child or after a house fire, support largely coordinated through the school and its relationships. A norm of reciprocity[51] seems to characterize these exchanges, an understanding that favors will be returned, should the need arise. Likewise, it is assumed that time, work, and resources offered to the school—field trips chaperoned, property taxes increased, foreign exchange students hosted—will also, eventually, in some manner, benefit the community and its members. This trust, this reciprocity, this economic sustenance—these are the spoils of social capital, the rewards of the stores of social capital the school has built.

And there's another reward, a reward precious in a state of National Guard–enforced desegregations. It's the benefits of bridging relationships that seem so significant here in Delight. These relationships, linking one to a variety of individuals from a variety of groups, widen the community. This type of social capital ties needy residents and threatened businesses to the pooled assistance of *six* small towns, towns both black and white; it expands the set of social and economic resources one has access to,[52] resources that are often scarce in such a rural area. And, these resources benefit the school, too. For decades, this bridging social capital has likely kept the school open: the tolerance and acceptance that come from these relationships have anchored a diverse group to the school and pushed the community to build its international program, providing a student body large enough and a tax base broad enough to stave off consolidation. Though recent rifts, fractures caused by the consolidation threat and decisions to choice to Murfreesboro, may threaten these political and relational resources, so far, together, these six towns and their values have kept one another on the map.

And, finally, importantly, these bridging relationships seem to have reduced racial prejudice. Black or white, they get along, students tell me, and their interactions, their choices of gym partners and lunch companions, seem to support their claims. Interracial dating and friendships— and, now, relationships between local and international students—are common, and parents' and grandparents' acceptance of these relationships is becoming more common, too. And this older generation, through waves in the carpool line and gossip in the bleachers, is gradually learning to forget some of the distrust and suspicion it may still carry. This bridging social capital, the cross-racial acceptance and trust that the school builds, counters the racial stratification and inequality that divides so many southern towns. These bridges are fragile, most anyone will tell you. Racial cliques still exist, Kathy still has to reprimand students for the occasional racial epithet, and many adults still harbor deep-seated racial stereotypes. And these relationships, no matter how strong, have done little to address the residential and religious segregation that still divides the area. But they are a tentative, hopeful beginning. The school has created a small space where, despite a southern tradition of racism and bigotry, people can learn to negotiate the individual relationships that slowly dismantle this past.

A MOMENT IN TIME, A LONG HISTORY

Overlooking, for a moment, some of the nuances of these roles—the incompleteness of integration in Delight and the moments of unity in Earle—it seems remarkable that schools in two rural towns in the same state could function so differently. Why do the Earle schools create walls that split the town, while Delight's school builds cross-racial bridges?

The details of desegregation—how desegregation was carried out, who was involved, what policies precipitated the process—certainly matter. The segregating role of the Earle schools seems inextricably tied to desegregation, a moment in 1970, a moment contested and sanctioned, a moment that may have set the schools on a path to merely continue the community's racial divides, coloring their function for decades after. In Earle, after a number of unsuccessful voluntary attempts, 1970's desegregation plans stipulated that the white schools were to contain the desegregated elementary and high school, and the black school would become the middle school. This plan was abandoned, though, a decision likely made in response to protests within the black community; white students never had to attend Dunbar, and the black school was closed. And so, within an angry and fearful town, black students were divided among the white elementary and high school, quickly and abruptly bringing a demographic balance to these institutions. But this desegregation, Mr. Nicks, today's black superintendent, notes, "wasn't a situation where it was a merger."

Even as Mr. Speed, the white elementary principal at the time, tried to make desegregation academically profitable for all children, he also, however unintentionally, participated in separation. Even as he focused on ensuring "our kids would profit from it, as well as theirs," he maintained "ours" and "theirs." And the changes were dramatic. The two racial populations were relatively equal in size, a balance that may have felt threatening to white students and families. This parity also allowed for the maintenance of segregation within the schools, with white students and black students each on their side of the school's sidewalk, each with their part of the school's campus. And, when white families did remove their children, there were a number of private schools and an array of other, whiter districts to choose from. Together, these details—community members resentful and nervous, promises unfulfilled, leaders unsupportive, a student body split—compound into a moment that shook the town and continues to reverberate, a moment that may have propelled the schools to continue, rather than dismantle, segregation.

In Delight, though, this moment is different—both in its details and its recollection. Desegregation itself is only vaguely and sketchily remembered by residents, mentioned infrequently during interviews, an event confused with the area's other consolidations and district reorganizations. But from these hazy memories a few key details emerge, details that differ markedly from Earle's. After voluntary desegregation in the late 1960s, during which the area's brightest black students were encouraged to attend the white schools, the racial restructuring was accomplished through two consolidations: the black schools in Antoine and nearby Simmons were closed, with Antoine students bused to Delight and Simmons students bused to Okolona. The number of black students involved was small; in Delight, only a few black students joined each grade. The anecdotes I heard—a terrified black second grader peeing in his pants and a white teacher buying him a new pair, black teachers hired by the formerly white schools, fights in the high school—portray an uneven and bumpy start, especially for the black students involved. This rocky beginning, though, seemed to soon level into a smoother restructuring. Some white families left Okolona, precipitating that town's shift from all white to more racially mixed, but few families moved from Delight. These stories and details of desegregation are often muddy and poorly recalled, though, and it is usually the consolidation of Okolona with Delight that is remembered as the event that changed the school's racial make-up. After the earlier desegregating consolidations, the Okolona school grew blacker, the Delight school whiter; with this 1987 consolidation, most of Okolona's students came to Delight, bringing the Delight school's demographics to about two-thirds white, one-third black. Though Okolona students and residents mourned the loss of their institution—the town is now little more than a loose collection of houses—residents describe the transition as easy, with "a lot of cooperation among the community people," since, as Fadie Gentry notes, "we were just like a family more or less because everybody knew everybody." Randy Hughes, the white former Delight superintendent presiding over this consolidation, appeared dedicated to creating a cohesive student body: "When kids came here, black or white, they were Bulldogs and we all pulled together. . . . I was really proud of how our kids handled it." And so even this consolidation, with students and teachers hastily informed on the last day of the school year, with a substantial drop in the proportion of white students, with the end it may have brought to the town of Okolona, feels unremarkable when compared with Earle's.

There are several, marked differences between the details of the Delight and Earle reorganizations. In Delight, the schools involved were smaller and the number of students fewer, and the children all attended a single campus—perhaps making it easier for students and teachers to begin the work of cross-racial bridging. The changes also accumulated slowly, through several reorganizations spread over many years, a pace that may have accommodated slowly changing minds and hearts. White students remained in the clear majority throughout Delight's reorganizations, while in Earle desegregation created a student body about half white, half black. This sort of racial parity may have unsettled white families, threatening old racial orders and pushing them to leave; indeed, research has noted a "tipping point" of around one-third, with larger black proportions sparking waves of white flight.[53] Also, though the black schools in both Delight and Earle were closed and white students in these towns never had to attend a "black school," in Earle this was an unplanned change, an unmet commitment—a change made, perhaps, to mollify the fears of white parents, a change that angered many black residents. And so, while black students carried the burden of desegregation in both towns, in Delight black families were never promised otherwise and the fears of white families were never stoked. And, too, the schools' leaders seemed to approach desegregation differently. For interracial contact to improve racial relations, this contact must have institutional support[54]—a leadership that is concerned with racial merging rather than racial separation—and Earle's white leaders did not appear to share this priority, worried instead about "ours" and "theirs." And, finally, until recently, Earle had its own local private school, with a number of others within a close drive; in Delight, the closest private school is nearly thirty miles away.

Yet still, the fact remains: avoiding a district's public schools has never been a challenge for a determined white family in Arkansas—the state's abundance of Christian academies, school districts' loose choice policies, a relative's willingness to provide an address in a nearby district all ensured the option of flight. White students in both Delight and Earle had this option . . . and, in Delight, they didn't choose it. It also may be too simplistic to reduce a school's role in a community to a particular moment and the circumstances surrounding it. Centuries of history weighed on this moment of desegregation and the decades since, and a town's history can have a profound influence over its public organizations and their functions, its institutions and their ability to build social capital.[55] For, as much as leadership and racial tipping points and the details of desegregation matter, the role of Earle's schools, in many respects, may remain shaped by its location in the floodplains of Arkansas, by the Delta's long legacy of racial exploitation.[56]

From the first cotton plantations, slavery powered the Delta economy and organized Delta society. Black residents were less than human; they were a source of cheap labor used to manage hundreds of acres of cotton.[57] After emancipation, sharecropping replaced slavery, leaving intact the underlying structure of economic and physical exploitation and the dehumanizing ideology that sanctioned it.[58] Jim Crow laws both required and justified the racial separation necessary to maintain this system. Separation, economic and social, has defined race relations in Arkansas for centuries,[59] and this separation fueled suspicion, distrust, unease. And so, when the legal boundaries that maintained this separation were finally removed, the separation was so solid, so rooted, that it needed no governmental supports to stand. Earle's schools reflected this separation, the segregation that, by virtue of history, may feel more natural than desegregation ever could. And, eventually, the schools not only reflected the segregation, they actually maintained it—the white flight from the school system a simple and effective way of keeping white child separate from black child, white family separate from black family, white community separate from black community, white prosperity separate from black poverty. Earle's schools thus became a means to preserve the economic structure and power differential of the old South.

Delight, though, never had the plantations, the slavery, the structural and institutional racial exploitation. Delight was located in a very different Arkansas, in the state's hill country, the frontier. It had timber, poultry, small farms and homesteads—not much but enough to structure a relatively horizontal economic system. There weren't many haves and have-nots, just a large number of have-a-littles. The rigid divisions of the Confederacy—the plantation homes and acres of cotton and the racial exploitation that supported these estates—were hundreds of miles away. Here, out in the hills of western Arkansas, the prevailing politics was characterized by a more egalitarian independence;[60] here, nature's submission was the battle to win, not a slave's submission. And so black families worked alongside white families. Page after page of local history lists both black and white homesteaders, and reprints of old, weathered photographs show loggers and lumberjacks, black and white, standing shoulder to shoulder before vast tree trunks.[61] Black and white community members certainly led separate social and religious lives, and their educations, too, were separate, with a number of black students attending the Rosenwald school in Antoine. But most of these residents were not tied to an economic structure that relied upon separation and stratification, a system of white ownership and black exploitation, a mindset of white superiority and black intellectual deficiency. When it finally came time to integrate the schools, there was little racialized economic stratification to maintain, no institutionalized power differential to preserve. The area lacked the historical momentum that would push families to use the school to separate. Desegregation didn't threaten to topple a centuries-old plantation system, and so, looking back, it seems relatively unremarkable. Desegregation, as an event, occupies little of the community's collective memory; it remains a hazy recollection rather than a defining moment. And yet, to some extent, it seems to have worked: it created the bridges envisioned by the *Brown* decision.

In both towns, desegregation was a risk. Children were exposed to new people and new places, black institutions were closed, long-standing customs were questioned. Yet in Earle white residents, by virtue of generations of Delta history, had something else at stake: their power. To hold this power, the white community believed it had to maintain separation, and so that became the function of Earle's schools—to preserve the racial divide. Some particulars of desegregation certainly influence whether a school builds bridges or walls between racial communities: the demographic balance, the reaction of the leadership, the expectations and sentiments of the communities, the organization of the actual restructurings. But this historical factor—the structure of power and wealth in Earle—is also consequential. And a history of inequality is a formidable force to which a rural school must answer.

A DIFFERENT FUTURE

But what if . . .? What if the schools of Earle could somehow keep the town's white children? What if rising test scores could persuade white students to return to their classrooms? What if the schools did suddenly find white families sitting next to black families inside the gymnasium? What if the schools were to somehow lay bridges between the town's white community and its black one? Would it matter? Would the frustration and stagnation of the black community, the poverty and the powerlessness, suddenly dissipate?

No—I think that history is too long, too heavy. The economic, political, and social dynamics in Earle are entrenched, and they are rooted in inequality. Delight's bridging relationships—in a town tied to the relatively egalitarian timber industry, a town with a relatively egalitarian political and social history—are relationships among equals—distant equals, wary equals, unfamiliar equals, but equals. In Earle, though, these bridging relationships would have to straddle not only distance and suspicion, but also entrenched inequalities—inequalities that would not suddenly disappear. Relationships, then, would still reflect this inequality: businesses would still remain under the ownership of white proprietors, land would still remain in the hands of white families, white interests would still remain pitted against black interests. These relationships could only foster a polite paternalism,[62] a shiny veneer for an old oppression; they won't level the jagged disparities of influence and privilege in Earle. Social capital does not erase racial inequality,[63] and bridging ties are poor substitutes for power.[64]

It's the bonding relationships—the relationships tying Earle's black residents and families together—that the community so needs. Bonding relationships are a foundation for collective action;[65] they anchor mutual goals and collaboration, link common histories and shared futures. These relationships elected a black school board and fueled a march one night in 1970, and they now shape town politics and inspire a shared focus on academic achievement. A relational power resides in these ties within the black community,[66] a power that comes from coordination and organization and resistance. This is a "'power to' act together,"[67] a "power to" exert influence and control through action, a "power to" restructure old inequalities. In these relationships, with this power, hope—for higher test scores, for a stronger economy, for a better future—lives.

And it's the schools that have fostered this power. The influence that the black community has wielded in Earle—limited though it may be—has originated in the schools: within the school walls, around school issues, through school leadership. The schools have upset the traditional dichotomies of Earle: for many white residents, "black" no longer means "passive" or "defenseless." Like rusty gears creaking into motion, the town's well-worn dynamics are beginning to shift; the work of accounting for centuries of oppression is simply long, slow, and hard. But this work—the work of tying the black community together, of fostering mutual goals and imagining a common future, of building a relational power that carries political influence and economic leverage—is necessary, important work, work that will, eventually, bring opportunity and equity. It's this work that make the schools so necessary.

So, yes, the schools of Earle divide. They distance, they split, they segregate; they are used to perpetuate the distances that have separated black from white in this town for generations. Perhaps someday the schools will repair these rifts, but, for now, I don't think it's bridges they must build. For now, they must continue to build power.

THE RURAL POSSIBILITY

The social, economic, cultural, and political welfares of Delight and Earle seem tied to—dependent upon—their schools. Without these schools, parents and residents told me, these towns would "shut down," "disappear," "dry up and blow away." These schools are important, I'd hear again and again—consequential, significant. And this significance seems true not just in Earle and Delight, but in other rural areas, too. Housing prices, for example, drop in rural towns without schools, and the gap in income between rich and poor is larger.[68] And, nearly two centuries after log schoolhouses and frontier classrooms, rural schools remain the cultural centers of many rural communities.[69] These schools provide a sustenance, and fears of losing this once caused black communities to protest desegregation throughout the rural South[70] and often fuel resistance to consolidation today.[71] The very futures of these rural towns, it seems, depend on these schools—what happens within and around these schools ripples throughout the surrounding town, a wake with little else to interrupt its swells.

But beyond simply carrying a general sort of import, these rural schools seem specifically and uniquely situated to play two particular, racialized roles: to either reinforce social cleavages or to bridge these divides. Despite the varied demographic, economic, social, and political details of rural locales,[72] some of the conditions shared across rural areas may predispose many rural schools to maintain divisions. Remoteness shapes the political and economic organization of rural towns, sometimes precluding a highly developed civic structure or an economic impartiality. Bridging social ties, the weak ties that allow for social mobility, are often scarce, neither spontaneous nor accidental in occurrence.[73] Economic stratification can maintain an iron hold in rural areas from Appalachia to the Delta,[74] from small mountain hamlets to tiny floodplain towns like Earle. In these places, economic influence is concentrated in the hands of a local elite and a remote state government, providing the rural poor with little opportunity to right these inequities. In the Earles of the rural South, it's the white community that retains the economic power: an inability to attract and sustain new industry and business can mean that a racialized plantation system still structures the economy.[75] Here, the divides that slice much of the rural South—old plantation lines now reinforced by neighborhood, town, and county borders[76]—also perpetuate isolation, especially for the poorest residents. And many rural residents, both white and black, still captive to their fear and distrust and prejudice,[77] are eager to continue the racial separation. In these rural towns, the few public institutions— churches, diners, senior centers—remain as segregated as they've always been: in Earle, the Bulldog Café, the Earle Baptist Church, the Crittenden County Museum are white; L&J Soul Food, Mt. Beulah MB Church, the Earle Senior Citizens Center are black. Here, the public schools are just another racialized rural institution, so much so that, throughout much of the rural Delta,[78] it seems that "the public school system" is merely code for "black schools." In these towns unable to escape a history steeped in racial oppression, in these Earles where the economic structure is entrenched and the power structure impermeable, where so many white families rejected the public schools after desegregation, the one institution that once held the promise of bridging long-standing racial divides instead began to reinforce them. And this stratification isn't limited to the rural South. In other rural towns, it may be the coal company or the food processing industry instead of the old plantation owner, yet still, economic and social stratification is thorough.[79] The schools, as public and visible local institutions, as somewhat captive and singular institutions, can be used—can be abandoned and underfunded, can be contested and controlled, can be maligned and compromised—in ways that maintain the stratification that divides so many rural areas.[80]

Yet many rural schools and communities—towns like Delight—seem to have escaped this fate;[81] instead, their rural nature appears to have provided a potential for bridging social divisions. This possibility, it seems, comes from the singularity of rural schools: they are one of the few open, public spaces in their communities. And so, in those communities without a deep-seated racial rift or a demographic drain, schools can be a place to gather across race and class lines. They offer the sorts of shared activities with common goals—fund-raising for a class trip, playing on the same basketball team, gathering for the same graduation—that tend to build relational ties, linking together a diverse group of individuals. Other spaces cannot play this role: in Delight, people gather at Mom's Diner, but these are small, predictable groups—the same handful of men talking loudly over eggs and coffee at breakfast, the usual group of older women meeting for an early buffet dinner—and Mom's doesn't make one feel a part of a larger collective. Church, too, is very much a part of the spiritual and social lives of many rural communities,[82] but these communities often have countless churches and even more informal living-room services, isolated gatherings that are usually defined by family or town or race lines. In rural communities, the school has a unique capacity to create a broader community, to be a space occupied by a wide network of people from different families, different towns, different races, and different congregations, to knit together a wide and diverse network into a larger community.[83] In those rural communities where, for whatever reason, white families remained in the public schools, these schools have an opportunity—an opportunity to repair generations of racial rifts.

And these communities are not anomalies: counter to assumptions of rural homogeneity, rural schools—rural southern schools, in particular—are among the most integrated schools in the country, more integrated than urban schools in cities large and small.[84] Many rural southern locales, it seems, have the demographics and enough residential diversity—even segregated towns in close proximity—to allow for the desegregation of their schools. And then, these schools, like Delight's, have the potential to foster the meaningful cross-racial contact[85] that can dislodge long-held prejudices, that can lead to more interracial marriages and more multiracial churches.[86] Desegregated schools cannot, alone, create a de-segregated society,[87] and integration is far from complete in Delight. Yet, as one of Delight's former superintendents explains, "schools have done more to foster good race relations than any other institution in our coun-try," and in a rural town, where schools are so central to a community's social and cultural context, their potential for bridge building[88] might be particularly unique.

So the paradox remains: rural schools can build bridges or walls. What may be consistent, though, is the magnitude of these schools' potential to have an effect on their community, whether in the mountains of Vir-ginia or on Native reservations out West. Schools matter to urban and suburban communities, too, but in rural communities across the country, they may matter more. The ingrained power structures and divisions of many rural areas—set deep by history and isolation, left untouched by the myriad political, economic, and social influences crowding a city—can cause rural schools to have a particularly divisive impact on their towns, maintaining and reinforcing these rifts, adding to these long walls brick by brick. Or, in other rural towns, schools' distinction as the singular pub-lic institution, the one institution that can foster relationships and create a common identity, allows them to bridge racial lines and build a more integrated community. Rural schools may be different from urban and suburban ones, different not in role necessarily, for urban and suburban schools, too, can stratify and unite—but distinct in the degree of this role, in their ability to have a consequence. And what this consequence will be, whether the school will build bridges or walls, is a complicated response to the particulars of how and why and when a policy was enacted and to a long legacy of history.

RURAL AND RACIAL

It would be easy to dismiss Delight, to think of it as an exception, an excep-tion to an entire research tradition, an exception to the usual assumptions of stratified schooling and stratified communities, an exception to the usual stereotypes of southern racism and division. But I don't think that's the story; instead, this narrative is about potential, the potential for rural schools—and perhaps urban and suburban schools—to serve as bridging institutions, to pull a diversity of people together for shared purposes. In these school spaces, there is a possibility, the possibility for relationships and support, for a collective identity that bridges social divides. Delight, then, is a lesson in how a school can shape the racial landscape of a town, how it can foster a community dense with social capital and that much closer to integration—and, now, a community with a future made uncertain by consolidation. This might soon be a story of potential lost.

Earle's story, too, might seem simple—a story of a fated community, a rural community "stuck" with a bleak and fractured future, a future written long ago by its history and now enacted by its schools. But this isn't the story, either—or, at least, not the most important story. Earle has never remained circumscribed by its fate: instead, it has worked to revive test scores, to gain political influence, to rewrite narratives. Its story, too, is one of possibility, the possibility of establishing a new identity, of righting an old inequality, and of creating a better future. Its schools, like Delight's, are its possibility and its salvation, and Earle still has time; closure—whether from academic sanctions or due to dwindling Delta populations—is not an imminent reality. But crucial to the town's future will be the schools' role in building relational power—strengthening bonding relationships within the black community and motivating collective action to improve the schools' academics, to leverage their political influence, to foster economic and social equity. Then, perhaps, the schools can focus on cross-racial bridging; then, perhaps, the schools can lay tenuous ties between a white community and a black community, each with some measure of power, ties that heal and repair and rebuild. Then, perhaps, after so many decades of delay, these schools could finally desegregate.

Together, Delight and Earle tell a story of rural towns and their schools, their histories and their possibilities. It's a story about race, an untold story about the rural that exists beyond the lily-white assumptions. And, too, it is a story about what schools do and what they can accomplish, a story of why a rural school matters to a rural community. But it's not just at the possible cleavages and fractures that a school matters, not just at the racial lines. The school doesn't just build bridges or walls, lending a particular shape to this community. It also gives substance to this shape; it *creates* this community.

CHAPTER SEVEN

The Substance of Community

The school is like a big stadium.
It's like a family.
Our center.
Home.
Bulldogs . . . they stand their ground.
A safe haven.
I just wish that there was some way that you could see how a school has just been the heart of a community, you know?

I write these metaphors in the margins of my notebook, a catalog of schools articulated through image—stadiums and families, bulldogs and hearts. The list grows over the months, and the metaphors crowd into long, vivid inventories of meaning and relevance, as children and adults grope for the right image, one with enough visual heft and emotional impact to finally make me understand.

One phrase, though, is different. It's unusual in its plainness, in its complete lack of imagery—it's not, actually, a metaphor at all. *The school just is the community.* This was the conclusion that teachers or students or alumni would often reach, after they had exhausted all of their creative capacities, all of their colorful prose, when they were just beginning to lose patience with me and my questions: *the school just is the community.*

And it is. These schools define these communities, giving them substance, boundaries, and meaning. They pull together a particular group of individuals and knit this assortment of residents into a collective, a unit, a community. They supply this community with an identity, a way to be known and recognized, and they write its boundaries. These communities look different: in Delight, the school constructs a new, cross-racial community, and Earle's schools re-create a black community. Yet, together,

Delight and Earle tell a second rural narrative, a narrative about the definition, construction, and survival of community.

DEFINING COMMUNITY AND DELINEATING BOUNDARIES

Delight and Earle are communities; in these towns, community is the organizing unit. It is the word that residents use to describe themselves and their surrounds, the concept that makes sense of place and relational ties, the lines that separate "us" from "them." And in both towns, community is clearly defined, bound by school enrollment—a community black and white in Delight, an all-black community in Earle.

The definition isn't nearly so clear in the research literature, though. This research is littered with questions about the definition and substance of community, and its longstanding ubiquity as an academic concept camouflages a contested terrain of assumptions and a messy litany of proposed characteristics. But these definitions do share some qualities. Looking across nearly one hundred definitions of "community," sociologist George Hillery found that most encompassed three elements: social interaction, relational ties, and a common locale.[1] Other dimensions of community include self-sufficiency, shared goals and ways of being, an awareness of commonalities, a sense of collective identity, and a defined territorial area with shared institutions.[2] Some theorists consider community a political unit, concerned with ideals of democracy and civic participation[3] or unified by a collective political power.[4] Others understand it as a common identity, constructed and communicated through symbols and rituals that promote solidarity.[5] This identity is often bound to a narrative or "story of us" that names shared values[6] or a "community of memory" that links a common past to a common future.[7] Tied to all of these components, though, is social interaction—this gives meaning to community.[8]

This interaction can evoke an emotional experience—a "sense of community,"[9] a concept closely aligned with theories of social capital[10] or notions of "communion."[11] This sense of community—"a feeling that members have of belonging, a feeling that members matter to one another and to the group, and a shared faith that members' needs will be met through their commitment to be together"[12]—is a positive emotion that often accompanies, and likely motivates, community membership. It is also associated with a range of other emotions and behaviors: participation in community associations, activities that address community problems, and feelings of control in the face of external threats.[13] Not all communities evoke these sorts of positive sentiments[14]—nor is community the idyllic experience romanticized by popular nostalgia[15] or tied to rural mythologies[16]—but for many community members, this sensation of belonging and security defines and inspires their membership.

With any social or emotional entity also come boundaries—a community's edges. Group members, sociologists and psychologists argue, construct communities with clear symbolic boundaries that distinguish between "us" and "them."[17] These symbolic boundaries—"lines that people draw when they categorize people"[18]—can rely upon any number of characteristics, whether relatively apparent distinctions, such as ethnicity and gender, or more subjective determinations based on morality or culture or values.[19] Boundaries are also determined by institutional and temporal factors: if and when and how individuals interact with others, for example, influence the shape and nature of the boundaries drawn.[20] Thus, these boundaries are a matter of structure and interpretation, and they reveal a social identity that categorizes and brands a group of individuals,[21] both reflecting and determining how members define themselves and others, what characteristics they base these definitions upon, what the group considers meaningful and worthy. Though boundaries sometimes challenge existing social orders, such as those tied to race or class, they typically reflect and reinforce these divisions. Boundaries can also provide a structure for the unequal distribution of resources,[22] constraining the opportunities of some groups and providing unfair advantages to others. These are the boundaries of slavery and segregation, the boundaries of private discriminations and institutional inequities, the boundaries of economic, political, and social stratification. A community's boundaries, then, broadcast its very substance and image—what the community is and why, and how others understand it. They explain a collective identity, reveal values, and expose an entire architecture of power and inequality.

Historically, of course, these communities—and all of their boundaries, their emotions, their social and political dimensions—were located in rural areas. These communities were the organizing unit of early America, and they often became a focus of study,[23] interesting because they reflected the experiences of so many, with small and bounded geographies that afforded manageable units of study. Researchers embarked on close, ethnographic studies of particular rural communities, while novelists wrote their rural tales, exploring these communities as microcosms of society. Frequently, though, their interest stretched beyond the merely academic or narrative. It was practical, too, and paternalistic—an attentiveness that

manifested in the early 1900s with a flood of reports, as eager reformers documented the "rural problem" and sought to improve and enhance
these rural communities.[24]

Gradually, though, the academic interest in community turned away
from rural communities—a relief, perhaps, to many of these "reformed"
rural locales—and toward urban centers, a shift that likely reflects the urbanization of American society.[25] But this urbanization—the diversity of
individuals and groups living in a city, the myriad interactions and countless influences—has also, it seems, resurfaced arguments about what actually makes up a community. Recently, the local, spatial dimension of
community[26] has fallen from popular understanding. Some argue that
increased globalization, long-distance communication, and the growing
complexity of social interactions render locality meaningless.[27] The bureaucratic and industrial institutions that have accompanied urbanization
and now shape social interaction may also serve to disentangle community
from place,[28] and technology, too, has redefined the role of place and interaction in creating community, as many argue that "virtual" communities
are no less real or significant than more traditional communities.[29] Yet
others believe that a consideration of locale remains crucial to any study of
community; no matter how isolating or technologically advanced society
has become, most meaningful interaction still occurs within a particular
space[30]—families still gather in their kitchens, children still play soccer at
their ball fields, and old folks still sit on their porches and front stoops.
And space and place might continue to remain particularly important to
the understanding of rural communities, for these communities are, in
many ways, defined by their geography.[31]

Beyond these arguments about the definitions and delineations and
meanings of community lies a deeper, more fundamental debate: does community even still exist? Anxiety about the loss of community is an old theoretical concern, one that dates to the distinction between *Gemeinschaft*—
community tied by organic bonds, long associated with country life—and
Gesellschaft—society organized for social and political purposes, a charac-
teristic of urban living—and the late-1800s concerns over the slow replacement of the former with the latter.[32] But even today, many Americans—
and many researchers—feel that community, whether spatial or relational,
whether bound by commonality or inequality, is dying.[33] Political scientist
Robert Putnam, for example, traces declines on a number of indices—
political, civic, and religious participation; relationships in social networks
and the workplace; philanthropic acts and volunteering; levels of trust—to

conclude that the communities that have long characterized American life are endangered.[34] Individualism, many argue, is replacing collective concern, threatening the fabric of American society.[35] Others worry that urbanization and its more recent partner—suburbanization—not only remove place from community, but also actually jeopardize the connections and embeddedness of community.[36] The concept of community itself may soon be so changed as to be rendered nearly unrecognizable: the communities of America's future may be of a qualitatively different sort than the communities of its past.

Yet, amid all of these academic conceptions of community, despite all of the concerns about the effects of urbanization, "community" continues to be defined and redefined, enacted and reenacted, across vast geographies and sprawling social networks, across wide spaces and places. It is here, within these communities, where "community" hardly seems like a dying concept, that "community" finds meaning. And, within these communities, within the Delights and Earles of America, schools often seem very tied to these meanings, linked to the creation or maintenance of communities and community boundaries. Yet here, also, public awareness is limited. This isn't to say that researchers and practitioners don't recognize the institutional promise schools might hold for their communities: a recent movement of school reformers and community-based organizations, for example, seeks to equip schools so they may deliver various services to their local communities, offering everything from neighborhood medical care to adult education classes at night.[37] These "community schools" reconceptualize schools as service providers, as central institutions that offer an array of amenities. But, in many communities, and rural communities in particular, the relationship between community and school seems more fundamental, less about discrete services and more about communion, common identity, shared story, and collective action. It's a type of community-school relationship long noted in rural communities,[38] the type of relationship that we often assume once shaped all of America's small towns.

These descriptions are not simply long-gone characterizations, fleeting and nostalgic memories of what was. Still now, today, in Earle and Delight, and in other rural communities, I hear, *The school is the community.* It's not medical services or nighttime GED classes that sustain a community; this is about gymnasiums packed on Friday nights, about traditions spanning decades and generations, about old graduation photos on hallway walls, about hopes and fears, about lives lived in and around a particular place. The school defines a community in both Delight and

Earle, communities different in substance, shaped by the particulars of their contexts and defined by boundaries distinct and consequential. These communities are different, too, in construction, in the manner by which the schools make and remake them, processes unique to the resources and constraints of the immediate surrounds but also, it seems, somehow shaped by the larger rural setting. Here, in Delight and Earle, the academic confusions about community seem to lose their relevance; here, we learn the meaning of community.

THE DELIGHT COMMUNITY

The buses idle in the early morning darkness, surrounded by a low rumble of engines and the narrow beams of headlights. Soon they'll roll out of the still lot and begin their long crawl over these Arkansas hills, a route that snakes across two counties and through six little towns. As the blackness quietly lifts, the four streets surrounding the school will fill with the traffic of slow cars, cars of parents and grandparents leaving children on the way to jobs in Murfreesboro or Arkadelphia, cars of teachers and staff parking for the day, cars spilling open with juniors and seniors and book bags and sports equipment, cars stopped for quick conversation or reminders yelled after children. The block will grow quiet during the day, though a few cars always seem to be rolling down East Cherry, dropping someone off or picking something up, and then it'll be the crowd of dismissal and sports practices and meetings. Later in the evening, too, there will be cars, parents attending games after work or congregations gathering for Wednesday services. There's an inevitability to these routines, the school extending a gravitational pull that stretches from Billstown over to the Meeks Settlement, a community formed through the school's reach.

These routines have structured life in Delight for generations. There's little transience here: a few folks move away, some for good and others just temporarily, and a few move in, often drawn by relatives. Generations occupy the community, and stories of parents and grandparents and great-grandparents linger. Children long grown and moved remain tethered by updates from family members and school homecomings. But this sense of rooted permanence belies a newness: this is a new community, a community created through school restructurings and changes, expanded with the Okolona consolidation and swollen a bit with international students, then shrunk some from choicing to Murfreesboro. With this new community come changed attitudes, too: it's much more likely now for black children and white children to spend the night at one another's houses, for black and white parents to run into each other at Mom's Diner. Some folks have struggled to get used to this kind of mixing, this new "mingling," especially the older folks, but the children are showing them how—how to be a member of an integrated community.

It's not a wealthy community; no one here has much. Incomes are low, most all of them well below the national average, and, if you don't work for the school or drive a truck for the lumberyard or own one of the small businesses in town, you'll probably have to ride a bit to find a job. But it's a quiet community, a community where you can leave your doors un- locked, a community that will organize a benefit supper for a sick child or a family coming on hard times. It's the sort of place where your neighbors know you, a place with shared values—the right values—a place where everyone's "keeping an eye on your kids." The children tell me it's boring, and parents concede that there's little for kids to do. But they fill their time cruising down the rural highway running through town or spend- ing the night at friends' houses, and parents tend not to worry, for they all went to school together, too. Even newcomers feel welcome, so long as they're gracious and don't mind pointed questions about where they came from and why they're here. The community has its separations and neighborhoods—Pisgah's white, Antoine's black—residential separations that go unquestioned, but folks are friendly, regardless of color. It has its rifts and arguments—some controversies about the school—but, resi- dents ask, doesn't any town? It's a good place to live, most agree, a good community, a community to be proud of.

And it's the school that remains the community's center, that serves as the "focal point." School sports fill the weekends of students, families, grandparents and cousins, friends, and alumni—basketball in the fall and winter, baseball in the spring. During the week, life for students, parents, and staff is structured around the rhythms of a school day, the hours of practices and club meetings, carpools and field trips. The distinction be- tween "school" and "community" is blurry, even for community members not enrolled or working or parenting in the school, with church services held in the library, equipment borrowed from the gym, benefit suppers and fund-raiser breakfasts hosted by the cafeteria. The campus always seems crowded with people: crowds generated not so much by issues of the classroom—parents rarely drop in on teachers, it seems—but fueled more by the buzz of activity in and around the school, its assemblies and events and the meetings and associations and events that just happen to occur there. Relationships begun within the school's walls spill beyond it, as students run into teachers after school at McKnight's or near home on weekends, as alumni maintain close friendships with old classmates. Students remain Bulldogs long after they graduate—socialized less through curriculum than through school rules and culture and traditions—and it's an identity they keep. There's a pride here, a sense of specialness, and community members consistently vote to raise the millage to fund their school well. This is a community threatened, though, endangered through district consolidation with Murfreesboro—an athletic rival, but now also a political rival.

The boundaries of the Delight community are clear, bright and harsh in their delineations, notable not just for whom they include but also for whom they keep out. The community encompasses all six towns in the area, and all of the little houses in between—an area southeast of Murfreesboro, northwest of Gurdon, straddling the line between Clark and Pike Counties. What ropes this mix of settlements and towns and empty land into a community is the school district: community boundaries originate with these district lines. These lines have changed over the years, reconfigurations due to desegregations and consolidations, but for now, since the latest consolidation with Okolona, here they rest, tying these six towns together into one cross-racial community. These boundaries also explicitly separate Delight from Murfreesboro, separate the familiar "us" from the threatening "them," separate "us" from a town, I was often told, that thinks a little too much of itself, a town a little bit racist and a little bit classist, a town very different than "us."

But the boundaries don't completely mirror these district lines; they're not quite so simple or linear. A bumpy terrain of allegiances and betrayals lies beneath the district's smooth surface: this community broaches racial lines, but not rifts of disloyalty. And so, the community's boundaries seem to carefully exclude those who have choiced their children to Murfreesboro, a district "licking their chops," lying in wait to consume the underenrolled Delight. These boundaries, too, appear just as defined as district lines, tinged with anger and betrayal and guilt and maintained by social distancing and abruptly ended business relationships. Yet it's within the jagged edges of these boundaries that some fuzziness emerges. There have always been small disagreements, disputes going back to allegations against a former coach, differences of opinion about leadership styles and decisions, but, as the district consolidation with Murfreesboro looks more and more imminent, greater numbers leave. Confusion and disagreement mount: is consolidation inevitable? Should we try to fight it? How? What if we became a charter school—would that prevent closure? The ideas seem to languish, though; nothing is done, and an unhappy uncertainty spreads throughout the community. Some of the unity, once simply assumed, seems to unravel—the fate of the community a loose end.

EARLE'S BLACK COMMUNITY

Long before the black community could attend any of the school campuses in Earle, they had Dunbar. Back in the fifties and sixties, there was no cafeteria or gym at Dunbar—the basketball team went over to Parkin to practice—and the textbooks were old and outdated. But teachers cared, and the classrooms were disciplined, orderly, professional, a place to raise the next generation of African American scholars. The school sustained the black community and served as its social and cultural center. And still today, decades after desegregation, the closure of Dunbar, and "a complete shutdown of the black culture," many pin their hopes, and the hopes of the community, to this vision. Black folks attend all of the Earle schools now; in fact, they occupy nearly every classroom seat, most of the teachers' desks, and all three of the principals' offices. The white community is long gone: a ghostly presence, seen and heard in the town's banks and offices, but absent from the schools. These schools now belong to the black community; once more, it has the schools, schools that have written its past and will shape its future. This is a community slowly re-created by its schools.

The community is struggling, anyone will tell you—and it has been for a while now. Economically, things are weak and "the town looks a little bad": there are some funeral homes, L&J Soul Food, a couple Laundromats, and the schools, of course, but most everything else is owned and run by white folks. It's been that way for generations, ever since the plantations. The black community is now "off the plantations": they went on strike during the 1930s to protest landowners' pocketing of federal assistance meant for sharecroppers, and they abandoned the small stores and white merchants in Earle, the businesses that relied on their credit. But now most of downtown Earle lies empty. The white families are mostly gone. The cotton gins are rusty and silent, and the jobs have left; farming has dried up, and the last factory closed after the tornado. Land still sits in the hands of a few white families, families that often no longer live in Earle, and many of the community's now-grown students are idle, wandering the streets with little to occupy them. Poverty levels are high, and folks worry about the rise in crime and drug use. Scores of residents have left, headed to nearby Memphis or to the cities and jobs up north. A few have returned, rejoining generations of family in Earle, but, with all the moving in and out, people often keep to themselves, and, jobs being so scarce and commutes so long, many lack the time or energy to socialize.

But this is also a community slowly reuniting, reawakening, a community struggling and surviving. It's a community where neighbors helped one another after the tornado, a community of families, a community that people have come back to. And it's a community where folks turn out. They turn out on weekend nights, filling the bleachers that line the high school football field during the fall, the gym for the winter basketball games—that's where "the heart and soul of the community is," the place to visit and socialize, to catch up with folks you don't see at church, to rally behind a team that will soon become the state champions. And it's not only on the weekends that the community turns out. I see parents in the schools, checking up on a student's grades or called in to fuss at an unruly child; pastors come by to keep an eye on gang activity, and others stop by the offices to use the fax machine or the copier. The community turns out at the ballot box, too, voting for higher millages to fund new facilities, voting in school board members seen as responsive to the needs of the community. The community turned out, back in 1970, to fight a costly desegregation; it turned out for decades after, despite the long bleed of white students from the schools; and it turns out now, unsteady, perhaps unsure, slowly rallying around the schools that anchor it.

It's a community a little down on itself, I often hear, a community that could have more. The stigma of the failing test scores is inescapable, a brand seared into the public identity of the community—for many, a confirmation of Earle's steady decline. Yet smart people have graduated here, I'm told again and again, important people, lawyers and doctors and statesmen. And the students are bright, parents and teachers tell me: we could be a model school system. There's pride here, pride in the schools: "It looks more like us. . . . We love that school, because it represents us." Back in 1970, these families, the parents and grandparents of today's students, organized to protest the educational inequities of the system, and now they systematically oppose closure of their schools, a threat that always seems to loom, whether tied to academics or finances or enrollments. Graduates are encouraged to go to college and then to return, to serve their community and its schools, to lead and to mentor and to teach—and a number do. The schools hold the collective aspirations of the community, just as Dunbar did back before desegregation, before the "gradual exodus" of white families. They provide the opportunity to reverse the economic stagnation, to build leadership, to rebuild the town, to create a future. The schools are more than buildings, more than a handful of classrooms: they are the identity of a community, its history and its future.

The schools write the boundaries of this community, too, boundaries that seem stark and rigid, cut deep by so many other rifts—rifts of color, rifts of inequality, rifts stretching back for generations. The schools bound Earle's black community, for they remained when white residents left. Regardless of intention, white families used the schools to reject integration, to reject the possibility of one larger, cross-racial Earle community, to reject, it sometimes feels, the black community itself. So now this black community uses the schools to inspire its children to seek an education and serve the town, to embrace a common history and write a shared future, to engage in a collective struggle for redefinition and survival in the face of economic decline and continued inequity. These schools, then, re-create the black community, re-create a community that existed before the turmoil and trauma of desegregation.

But all of these so-stark boundaries—community boundaries written by the schools, racial boundaries built on a system of exploitation, class boundaries constructed over hundreds of years—mask the uncertainties and gradations and exceptions within them. White families were not the only ones to leave the Earle schools: a number of middle-class black folks have also left, moving out of Earle or just taking their children to another district. Those who remain understand the reasoning of these families— it's an opportunity to give their children "a better learning environment"— but there's still some resentment. Most of Earle's teachers don't live in the district, either: "they scatter like roaches on Friday afternoon," says a landlord. Senator Crumbly, as superintendent, hired faculty from across the region—good teachers, strong leaders, people he felt had promise—but many didn't grow up in Earle and have few ties to the area. And among the families who have lived in Earle for generations, who send their children to the schools, there are also divisions: those who side with Senator Crumbly, appreciate his leadership of the district, and doubt the recent allegations against him, and others who oppose him; those who feel the schools are now on a path of achievement and excellence, and others who remain unconvinced. For all of the starkness of the boundary between white and black, between white flight and black ownership, I struggle to understand these smaller rifts and differences within the black community—who belongs and who doesn't, who's in and who's not. Perhaps I am sensing a lack of cohesion, or maybe the boundaries are simply a bit fluid, forgiving. But, even with these differences and disagreements, there's a sense of promise and restoration in the community, a feeling that, just maybe, something better lies ahead.

COMMUNITY CREATION AND RE-CREATION

That school, it represents us. It's a home, the heart of the community.

In so many ways, I was told what some said plainly, "The school *is* the community." In both Delight and Earle, the school structures relationships and patterns routines, defines aspirations and provides an identity, a sense of self. It builds a community—a community very much alive and well—in the most literal sense, by fostering social interaction,[39] and it ties this community to a particular place.[40] These schools also provide concrete, institutionalized borders: district lines circumscribe a particular geographic area, marking a locale as a district and forcing students and families into contact with one another, linking them in shared fate. Consolidations and desegregations and choicing policies and white flight shift these borders, complicating the simple geography of districting. Delight's cross-racial community has its roots in the Okolona consolidation, when boundaries were rewritten to include that town and those families, and it is now also shaped by the choicing policy, as the families who have transferred from Delight for Murfreesboro are excluded, no longer a part of the community. Earle's desegregation was also an opportunity for expanding community borders, but it was a missed opportunity, a risk not taken by most white families; Earle now maintains two communities, a black one and a white one, one centered on the school, the other scattered loosely throughout the area. With each shift in boundaries, the community is rewritten, the geography changed, the "us" and "them" redefined.

But it's not simply school attendance that makes a community. The schools of these towns do more than lay boundaries; these schools *construct* a community, tying a particular collection of individuals together, writing a particular community with a particular substance. In Delight, the school, it seems, builds a community through the relationships it fosters within the space it provides. Community members see and interact with one another at the school, and they form and maintain relationships that are lasting and meaningful. Through the school—its rules, its hallway culture, its recognition and care—they come to adopt similar values and beliefs, the orientation of a family, a sense of belonging. The distinctions between school and community are blurred: what happens in the school is what happens in the community. For Earle, the schools represent a shared history and common aspirations. From its beginning, Dunbar has been tied to hopes of racial uplift, and during desegregation, the community rallied to demand educational equity within the school system. Now the schools are a site of struggle for political representation, fair funding, and academic achievement. These schools maintain a common past, a collective remembering, and inspire a linked future, a future tied to college-going and new industry. This is a community re-created—once defined by its school, then threatened by the losses of desegregation and the closure of this school and the ensuing political turmoil and abandonment, and now redefined by its schools. The schools knit this community through a common narrative of both hope and struggle, of both trauma and pride. In Earle and Delight, then, the school is more than an institution of the community: in so many ways, it constructs the community, it *is* the community.

Yet this community hardly has one shape, one substance, one construction, and Delight and Earle feel like qualitatively different kinds of places. These different processes of community making—a relational one in Delight, one of shared narratives in Earle—both reflect and, in turn, influence these communities' different contexts. In Delight what is so striking is its sense of community, an emotional experience of closeness and acceptance and relatedness.[41] This emotion is, in part, a feeling of belonging. This sensation is what community members describe when they call Delight "welcoming" or when they talk about how everyone knows one another, what students mean when they describe the school as "just like one big family." The Bulldog sweatshirts and the long-standing traditions, the shared values and the rivalry with Murfreesboro—all of these indicate one's membership in Delight. A sense of community depends, too, on a kind of mutual influence: community members believe that they can, to some degree, shape the community, that their voice will be heard and will matter, and this community, in turn, also shapes their beliefs and behaviors and identity. This is that sensation of recognition and acceptance, and also its correlate: a sometimes-oppressive pressure to conform, to adopt the mores and habits of the group. A sense of community is also tied to the fulfillment of members' needs, whether psychological—the very human need to belong, for example—or the more elemental needs of survival, needs the Delight community satisfies through its communal resources, from organizing benefit suppers to providing a positive identity that one is proud to adopt. And, finally, there is the shared emotional connection, built through interaction, through real—not virtual—contact, through time donated and crises weathered, through afternoons spent on the playground swings or evenings of lining the street with signs for a millage increase.

And it's the school that fosters these elements of this sense of community. In the school, relationships are built and maintained, alumni stay in touch with one another, parents talk with teachers, children see their cousins; here, community members adopt the identity that marks them as belonging to the Delight community. Here, students feel recognized as individuals—they're given the individual attention that allows them to feel that they matter—yet through a hefty student handbook and Kathy's dress-code enforcement and a welcoming school culture, they also learn the values and norms of the community, perhaps feeling the strictures of convention. Adults, too, may feel this contradiction: they can vote for school board members and voice opinions at school board or community meetings, yet dissent might not always be welcome, especially on school-related issues. But, though conformity has its costs, it also brings benefits, as the school meets the needs of both children and adults, lending that Bulldog identity, providing that care and love, hosting all the suppers and fund-raisers, raising the next generation of Delight. And, perhaps most important, the school fosters the emotional connection: it's at the school that community members see one another, where they engage in activities—from manning a raffle ticket booth to playing on the baseball team—that unite them behind common goals, where they endure the community's largest crisis—consolidation. The school, then, demarcates a community and promotes a particular, shared, emotional sensation: it's what makes Delight, Delight.

Earle's black community is created—re-created—differently, through a shared narrative that describes a long, common struggle for racial justice. I heard this narrative, decades untangled and explained, across conversations and interviews, through stories and recollections. This community of memory ties the past to the future; it links shared suffering to common hope and relates the experiences of generations past to the educational opportunities of students today.[42] It is a narrative of place,[43] starting in the cotton fields of plantations, starting with exploitation and the struggle to end this exploitation.[44] It begins in plantation schools, the schools that educated the children of slaves and sharecroppers. These were small schools, organized by community leaders, often held in a church and resourced by the community itself, schools like so many others across the rural black South.[45] From these schools grew Earle's formal segregated system, Dunbar and the white elementary and high schools, a system both separate and unequal. Black children were cared for at Dunbar, the narrative explains, but ignored by this segregated system and its white school board. The narrative is also one of resistance—resistance to landowners' greed in the 1930s, resistance to the credit system choking the fortunes of Earle's black farmers, resistance to the district's educational inequities. This narrative tells of one night in 1970 and the fear and frustration that sent the black community to the streets—a night to protest the old textbooks and inadequate facilities and articulate concerns of unequal treatment in a newly desegregated system. This narrative was about desegregation—about struggle, about Dunbar's closure and a small black school unrecognized, about fear and suffering, about a threatened community—and then abandonment—a fleeting desegregation followed by a growing resegregation. It's a complicated story of economic decline, of an industry changed and an era ended, of businesses moved out and landowners no longer hiring—a decline fostered by the schools, many believe, schools that push families and businesses away with their failing test scores or by simply allowing black children into their halls and sparking white flight. Yet, now, this is also a narrative of a community renewed, a story of pride and power, a story of political power gained, of collective action and the black vote and black leadership. Here, again, the schools feature prominently; they've become institutions of this black community, institutions reclaimed. They are linked to voice and agency, providing a long-awaited foothold in a highly controlled political and economic structure. The narrative is incomplete, the struggle still unfolding. Power remains limited, compromised by the state government, meager educational funding, and Earle's white landowners and tainted by the public stigma of low test scores and the label of "black school." And so this narrative is a narrative of the future, too—a future that hangs in balance, tied to aspirations for college-ready graduates and newly opened factories, for economic development and financial prosperity, for service and power, for sustenance and survival.

This is a narrative of the community, a connective thread that links the community of today to the community of the past. I heard it, again and again, told by Mrs. Jessie Maples and her daughters and granddaughter, told by past and present superintendents, told by young teachers and older pastors. I heard various facts and subtle nuances, told in different voices—but, together, these details form a narrative arc that bends from past to future, from plantation to now. And I heard this narrative from those who had grown up here and those who hadn't: you inherit this narrative, it seems, when you enter this community—partly, perhaps, because it so defines Earle, and partly because it so defines the black experience in the South. It tells of Earle's institutions and residents, its ways of being and meanings—white families and black families, farms and churches and railroads and factories, routines and boundaries and patterns; nothing is untouched. It makes sense of the community and its struggles and its hopes; it is an anchor in the midst of change, transience, and conflict. It inspires continued resistance and precludes defeat. It defines the community, describes its shape and its textures, explains how it arrived at now and what it still faces. It writes a path for Earle's children and restores the community, remaking today's community as a product of the past. And this narrative's connecting thread is the schools: from small plantation schoolhouses to test scores in the newspaper, this is a story of Earle's schools.

These distinctions of community making do not, of course, mean that Earle lacks a relational community, or that Delight has no common narrative. Many members of the black community in Earle articulate feelings of belongingness and influence, of fulfillment and emotional connectedness, just as members of the Delight community describe a shared history and future. And, certainly, in both towns, smaller communities are nested within these larger ones—communities related to church, to family, to neighborhood, communities each with their own boundaries and characteristics and organizations. But, still, in each town a larger, school-related community exists, and what is most salient about each of these communities is different: in Delight, the school fosters a relational sense of community, palpable and real, and in Earle, the schools shape a narrative, a story authentic and grounded. How the school knits these communities, how it holds them together, is different.

These differences likely have many sources; these communities and schools are situated in very different economic, social, and political contexts, contexts with different resources and constraints. One variation may be geographic: Delight and Earle are both rural, but differently so. One is uplands and the other, floodplains, and Delight's hilly location may lend itself to a sense of community. Delight is far from any major city, and the jobs in town provide an income to a substantial proportion of its residents. Children spend their weekends at classmates' houses or dragging down

Delight's main stretch of road—the relative isolation of the town keeps them in Delight. Delight is a tight unit, distant spatially and economically, closed culturally and socially.[46] Earle, though, is close to Delta cities, only forty-five minutes from Memphis, twenty-five from West Memphis, and twenty from Marion. The town's lack of ready employment forces residents to commute long distances for jobs in factories or warehouses that often require long days and difficult work, and Memphis and the surrounding towns also provide options for socializing and entertainment. Many of Earle's residents find themselves spending many hours, both work hours and play hours, away from Earle. Earle's black community, too, also appears more transient than Delight's residents. Like a number of black folks living in the Delta,[47] many left the area during Reconstruction and the early 1900s, searching for jobs and racial equity, a part of the Great Migration northward,[48] and now, some drift back. And so, Delight's isolation may foster a sense of community, just as Earle's transience precludes it: Delight has a heightened feeling of mutual dependence—residents' loyalties are little diluted or compromised by competing economic allegiances or time spent away—yet the movement in Earle, the churn of long hours worked elsewhere or years spent up North or simply the pressures of financial hardship, may create feelings of anonymity and impermanence that compromise a sense of trust and belonging.

Also, Earle's shared narrative may be tied to another narrative, a larger, broader narrative of black experience in the United States. Though understandings of power and justice and equality vary over time and within the African American population, these ideologies forge a common narrative that motivates collective action and influences political thought.[49] This narrative may originate with the remembered trauma of slavery, a shared memory with shared meaning and shared resonance that shapes a collective identity,[50] and it unfolds throughout the Delta, across Reconstruction and the civil rights movement, detailing decades of struggle and resistance. It defines narratives of the present and future, too, as individuals make sense of experiences and harbor aspirations through this common understanding. In some respects, it is a narrative of necessity, making salient the still-unfolding struggle for racial equity and political opportunity that each successive generation must undertake and continue. This broader narrative serves to unite African Americans into a common, nationwide community, and it may also structure the narrative told within Earle's black community, providing a familiar and accessible template to authentically organize the experiences of community members, no matter the hours they work or the years they live away. The narrative has its own texture and shape in Earle, a telling largely recounted through the schools, but the importance and prominence of this narrative, that the community itself is maintained by narrative, may be due to the existence of this broader cultural frame. A parallel narrative, one that would explain uneasy steps toward integration, one that could perhaps explain Delight, simply may not be written.

And, finally, importantly, the schools' different kinds of community making may also relate to differences in boundary writing. The boundaries of Delight, historically, have separated two school districts, Delight and Murfreesboro, two collectives relatively equal in political status and resources. The boundaries are largely symbolic,[51] distinctions between "us" and "them" based on perceived values and priorities, rivalries that reflect allegiances and emotions. This close, somewhat sentimental rivalry heightens feelings of group belongingness, building the sense of community the school already fosters. But in Earle the boundaries are more than symbolic. They are racialized boundaries that carry political and economic meaning. White residents have more land, more wealth, more influence, and more control than black residents in Earle—these boundaries have import beyond moral distinctions or emotional rivalries; these boundaries are consequential, stratifying. These boundaries are also marked by trauma, the trauma of a painful desegregation, of a white abandonment, of a long economic decline; these boundaries are meaningful, costly. Yet the boundaries themselves, and the resegregation that reinforces them, are a part of the black community's narrative: the narrative explains these divisions and their meaning and offers a way to resist and survive, by reclaiming the schools as places of pride and achievement. The black community in Earle may not have the luxury of cultivating emotional connections and allegiances; instead, it uses a school-centered narrative to efficiently and effectively fold new members into a community struggle for power and justice.

THE RURAL COMMUNITY

Though it seems reasonable to assume that an urban school can foster contact and relationships and a sense of shared fate among its students, families, and faculty, this role of community making and remaking might favor rural schools. Rural populations, despite their variations,[52] are often tightly rooted to place,[53] and their relative isolation and shared history may foster the interaction and intimacy, the ties of common interest and mutual concern, that turn a loose collection of individuals into a community. Community is enacted through its spaces and institutions,[54] and, in a rural town, these are numbered—few other institutions or networks exist to divide the interests and loyalties of residents. Historically, rural schools have fostered the social interactions and cultural ties of rural communities,[55] and today they continue as one of a handful of common spaces and institutions—public places more encompassing than any church or civic association—that can bring a community together.

Rural schools may take on an added significance in rural communities, for they lend both political power and identity. A school—and especially a school district—gives a rural community state money and creates leadership positions: it provides resources, the ability to control them, and a voice. Just as the schools offered Earle's black community a political foothold, rural schools can give rural communities agency and leverage, the ability to speak back to the state, a precious—and scarce—resource. These schools keep individuals rooted to the area and linked in common interest and mutual dependence; they lend the identity that keeps these communities on the Arkansas map.

These aren't characteristics that are necessarily absent or impossible in urban contexts; indeed, these might be features to mimic or foster within city schools and neighborhoods. Yet rural residents might depend on their schools to build their communities in a way that few urban communities do. These rural communities *need* their schools to make a community, either through creating a sense of belonging or by writing a shared narrative, for these schools supply the promise of a recognized identity, the promise of survival.

THE FUTURE OF COMMUNITY

Like homes offering shelter or families providing care, the schools sustain Delight and Earle. These schools build and maintain these communities, communities rooted in a place, communities defined by social interaction, communities with a degree of power and voice. In Delight, the school links six towns by fostering a sense of belonging and mutual commitment; in Earle, the schools unite the black community by recounting a shared narrative linking past to future. In both towns, these institutions write the boundaries of a community, boundaries that can mark power differentials and resource inequities between communities, and they provide a political identity, an identity that promises a measure of control and influence. These schools, residents believe, keep these road signs meaningful, defining this space, marking a community that still exists.

These communities—their boundaries and their qualities, how they are defined and maintained—matter, both to their residents and to outsiders. They shape daily life, patterning and explaining interactions and events. This process of community making and remaking ties rural school and rural community into a close, mutual, dependent relationship: these schools knit together these communities, creating a sense of community or featuring in a narrative, and so any perceived threat to the schools—consolidation or state takeover, desegregation, even the threat of stigma or public censure—becomes a threat to the community. Delight's residents worry that consolidation will destroy a sense of community—"you just can't put bees and wasps together and expect them to work"—and that they will lose what binds these six towns together. They sense a shift in the rivalry with Murfreesboro, a shift forced by the state's Act 60, a shift from boundaries with symbolic meaning to ones with political meaning: Murfreesboro may soon hold a political power over Delight, wielded through a shared school board with greater Murfreesboro representation and a superintendent loyal to Murfreesboro's interests. Earle's residents fear that state takeover will fundamentally rewrite—and perhaps conclude—their narrative, forcing an end that may be little related to racial uplift or political power or economic renewal. It's this fear of a changed or lost community that likely sparked Earle's white flight a generation ago, and it's the reality of stigma that may cause rifts within the black community today. And the boundaries, too, have significance. Throughout Earle's history, the boundaries marked by the schools reflect power relationships: they adhere to centuries-old power differentials, bringing a new weight and inequity to these relationships—and now, soon, Delight may find itself on the losing end of a power struggle. The schools' role in community making, then, is a consequential role, a role with profound effects for these communities.

Here, in these communities, the question isn't whether community exists. Here, the question is whether it will continue to exist. For, not far from Delight and Earle are other schools, schools that were also once families and centers, hearts and homes. Today, though, they're closed and not much else remains, and the message is again starkly plain: no school, no community.

CHAPTER EIGHT

Our Only Hope

If there is a road sign, there is a school . . . or there was. Every road sign standing at a town's edge, every green rectangle with a town name and a population number, also means a schoolhouse, a school noisy with the growl of buses and shouts of children or a school closed, an empty building silent in a weed-covered lot.

It is only after several years of driving through rural Arkansas that I finally realize this. The road signs for the big towns, the towns where I see people and a hum of activity, towns like Delight and Earle, always seem to have a school nearby. And then there are the other road signs, the road signs without much else. In these places, people tell me, after the school closed, things just kind of shut down, and, before you knew it, the community was gone. Now it is just a lonely road sign with a forgotten town name.

This loss feeds a story told in small towns throughout the state, in all of the blink-and-you'll-miss-it towns tucked deep within the Arkansas green. The story—almost unusual in its commonness and the ordinariness of its telling—is about fear, about what happens when one of these small towns loses its small school, how things just kind of shut down. And in the lucky small towns that still have their small schools, small towns from Bismarck to Elaine, from Carthage to De Witt, from Delight to Earle, the story underscores just how much depends on these schools, just how much these places would lose if the state ever took their school.

If the state took us over . . . This is the third and final narrative I heard in Delight and in Earle, one I've heard echoed in other rural communities across Arkansas. After the stories of race and community, of unity and division, I'd hear this story, a story pressing and urgent. It is a remarkably consistent narrative, a narrative unique in the particulars it lacks, unique in its uniformity across individuals in both Delight and Earle, unique in its shared vocabulary and common structure and inevitable conclusion. It is a narrative of reform anxiously told and retold in rural communities across Arkansas—across much of rural America, I would imagine. It is recounted with a particular voice and from a particular perspective—that of rural community. It is a lopsided, emotional, partial account of the anticipated, dreaded consequences of reform, yet, still, it resonates with a century and a half of rural reform and echoes with the undeniable realities of today's education policies. Its words hang heavy over rural towns, for this is the narrative that enumerates exactly what's at stake with such a threat, when a rural town stands to lose the institution that unites and divides it, when a rural community stands to lose the institution that defines and maintains it. It is a narrative that exposes the wide chasm separating rural community from state, a boundary unsteadily straddled by the school, a narrative that explains the fears and tallies the costs of finally losing this institution to the state.

A NARRATIVE OF LOSS

The narrative always begins with the state. No matter the town or the individual, no matter the setting, no matter whether I was sitting on a couch in a living room in Earle or behind a bin of nails and pyramid of paint cans at the Delight hardware store, conversation would usually get here—to "the state." The state is an abstract entity, fuzzy and lumpy, inconsistent in definition and tellingly broad in scope. The state, I'd come to learn, is the state legislature, the one hundred representatives[1] and thirty-five senators[2] that hear the pleas of constituents and weigh interests and draft legislation, that craft Act 60 and write school-funding policy. But the state, as the label is applied in Delight and Earle, goes well beyond the legislature; it's a veritable laundry list of other officials. It includes the governor and his staff, the Department of Education, and the State Board of Education; these are the officials responsible for translating and enforcing state and national law, the ones that set educational standards and achievement test cut scores and approve or deny consolidation plans. The state even reaches beyond the borders of Arkansas and any other particular state. It stretches all the way to Washington to encompass the federal government—the president and his cabinet, the nation's senators and representatives, the Department of Education and its officials, those responsible for No Child Left Behind and all the mandates and rules and sanctions that accompany it—an entity that seems, to folks in Delight and Earle, as remote as

Arkansas's own government.[3] The state, then, is that abstract and powerful policy-writing unit, populated with bureaucrats and politicians from "away" or "off" who write the legislation that matters so much here.

Though the state reaches far beyond Arkansas, its symbolic location is Little Rock. The city is about 120 miles from Earle, 90 from Delight—from either, it's first a wandering drive to the interstate and then a long, straight shot to the center of Arkansas. It sits here in a tangle of highways ringed by suburban strip malls and megachurches; at its center, this snarl of interstate holds a neat grid of city blocks that organizes a collection of tall government buildings and banks. The capitol building presides over one edge of this grid, dignified beneath its gold cupola and behind its limestone walls, representing a sprawling and powerful state.

Stories of the state start with distance. The state these stories describe is detached and far away, and its remoteness is communicated through a well-worn and shared language: the impersonal formality of "the state," the distance implicit in "the folks in Little Rock" or simply "Little Rock," the otherness suggested by "they" or "them." This remoteness, it's believed, is tied to both geography and representation: these legislators and officials are from "large cities" and "big towns," answering to mostly urban constituents and responding to mostly urban pressures, "not affected in any way, shape, or form" by the realities of local, rural communities.

But, no matter the state's remoteness, its power is clear. The state, this story goes, sets "mandates that have changed a lot of things." These mandates have changed what is taught and how it's taught and when it's taught; they've changed who is taught and where they're taught and why they're taught. The state "puts pressure on us," a mounting pressure of accreditations, credentials, threshold scores, curricular standards, underfunded mandates, and minimum enrollments. And with this pressure comes "fear." The state, these communities explain, identifies weakness—low test scores, dropping enrollments, fiscal distress—and it uses this weakness to force compliance or, worse, closure. For Delight and Earle, the state makes existence a matter of "keeping our head above water," of "giv[ing] the state nothing to work against us," of "survival."

But, still, the state often does "come in" to sanction and punish and close. The state comes in assuming it knows what's best for these students and these schools—and assuming these rural communities don't know. It comes in, it seems to these residents, because it misunderstands Delight and Earle; it misreads these rural communities and their schools and the close relationships they share. The state imagines these communities are

"uneducated," figures they are "a group of hillbillies that don't know anything," grounding its judgments in tests "not designed for us." It ignores
the value and worth these communities find in their schools—that "we
have a great school district in spite of what test scores might say"—and
forces these small schools to provide the same opportunities and programs
and produce the same test scores and enrollment numbers as the larger,
richer, more urban schools. These requirements have an effect, residents
believe: "all that stuff affects the small schools and helps close us down."
It's as if the state has "been gunning for these schools," as if the state "is
pretty much squeezing us out," as if "the state government is going [and]
closing down all these small schools." The state, in all its remote power, has
"no idea what it means to a community to have that school."

But the communities know, they tell me. They see the results, how
"there's nothing in Okolona" and "there's no development going on in
Parkin," how rural communities throughout the state are "beginning to
diminish because they have no school district." The examples are legion,
and the lessons, to them, clear: "if you lose your school, you're going to
lose your community." This school is "the only hope for our community"—
and without a school, these folks fear, a rural community disappears. The
community "will go down like a one-egg pudding. There won't be nothing
here."

READING THE NARRATIVE

I hear this narrative again and again, in conversation after conversation,
in both Delight and Earle. It is the first story I hear—the threat of consolidation in Delight, told on my very first visit—and it is the last story I
hear—weary updates communicated through worried emails and frantic
phone calls for months and months after I've left these towns. I am struck
by the consistency of the story and its undercurrents of urgency and fear.
I know that its accuracy—whether a remote state is actually "gunning
for these schools," whether state mandates lead to school closure and
whether closure leads to a community disappeared—is an open question. I realize that its counterpart—the state's opinions and interpreta-
tions and understandings—is missing; this rural narrative tells only one
side of a complicated relationship. And I think, too, of the many coun-
terarguments and objections and complexities I could raise—that consolidation, so feared in Delight, is the reform that long ago produced the
unique demographics the community now values, or that standardized

test scores, so reviled in Earle, are the catalysts that sparked a new attention to educational quality. I recognize these complexities, and residents, when they're not knee-deep in a retelling of this story, do too.

Yet, still, this narrative is instructive and important, for in all of its simple starkness is written a layer of understanding, perception, and experience usually overlooked. In it we hear a rural community's story of school and school reform. We hear the remove of the state, the meaning of a school, the losing battle for control, and a rural community's fears for its future. And, with this narrative, the equation tallying the effects of education policy seems that much more complex.

A Distant State

The narrative starts with distance: the state, it seems, is significant in its remoteness and, also, its power. In both Delight and Earle, residents describe a detached and mighty state that endangers the schools and, therefore, threatens the community itself. The particulars of these perceptions vary, as the nature of these state threats differs—consolidation the most immediate in Delight, academic sanctions in Earle—but these perceptions all originate with distance. This great distance felt between community and state appears structured by boundaries,[4] careful delineations that separate a local, rural "us" from a very official, very powerful "them." These boundaries, like the boundaries cordoning off Earle's black community from its white families or the ones that separate Delight from Murfreesboro, are consequential constructions; they are social and cultural and demographic demarcations that categorize and construct group identities, that can legitimize and perpetuate inequities. These boundaries, and the vast distances they perpetuate, are meaningful, multiple, and overlapping.

These boundaries are rooted in misunderstanding. The state simply fails to understand them, it seems to residents of Delight and Earle; it doesn't understand who they are and what they value, and it certainly doesn't comprehend the realities they face as rural communities and, particularly for Earle, rural communities of color. These misunderstandings are often bred in the easy stereotypes that residents know shape public perceptions about rural communities, especially the rural stereotypes about uneducated backwoods people unable to recognize what's in their own best interest and the Delta-specific stereotypes about the inevitable failure of black schools. And these misunderstandings are furthered by the distance keeping "them" so far from "us," the ignorance of a state so physically removed from the dynamics and realities of Delight and Earle; this distant state never learns its errors. Not everyone within the state is misguided—residents could usually name a handful of legislators and officials friendly to rural communities and their needs, some of them from their own remote locales—and community members often explained, too, that the state might not always act on its bias. But, usually, it does: residents suspect that these misunderstandings—a failure to recognize a rural community's economic reliance on its school, or an assumption that rural residents don't value education—inform state policy; these misunderstandings fuel the consolidation legislation and the academic sanctions.

As I hear this story, even recognizing its blunt one-sidedness, I still find it difficult to dismiss these fears and perceptions as inaccurate. There's a logic to this understanding of the state and its actions, and a whole host of literature to add its weight. With "rural" so often absent from research and debate,[5] the state—Arkansas, the federal government, any extralocal policy-making entity—*can* overlook its rural communities, simply forgetting these places exist. Simplistic definitions and assumptions then substitute for real knowledge and experience. The state, in its own guidelines and policies, relies on coarse constructions of "rural" that distinguish only between urban and rural or metropolitan and nonmetropolitan, definitions tied to population and distance from urban centers.[6] These delineations reflect the government's understandings of what is unique and salient about rural places, disregarding what may matter more to those within these communities: the vast diversity of rural locales, the possibilities and challenges afforded by the land and its people, and the meaning that rural lends to a place. Stereotypes[7]—the images of backwardness or the pastoral nostalgia perpetuated by a far-away media and consumed by a far-away public—also fill the long distance between a rural community and the state. They shape popular perspectives, defining a "rural problem" a century ago and fueling understandings of "poor white trash" and "rural deprivation" today. And, as one social scientist after another has concluded, they influence policy making and rural reform, both then and now.[8] The state may feel so remote to rural communities because, simply, it is so remote, so far from the realities these communities experience and the identities these communities value.

But I don't think that misunderstanding is the only source of this distance; it's not simply that the state may fail to recognize or understand the dynamics that construct life in Delight and Earle. The state and rural communities confront different pressures, dynamics both economic and political in nature, and this contextual discrepancy reinforces this boundary and creates more distance. In Delight and Earle, the economic pressures are urgent and local—a particular factory slowing its last assembly line, a specific street filling with empty storefronts, a certain family losing its home. The larger economic context fades, and the most immediate concern here, in these two communities, is sustenance. Residents worry about attracting a Dollar General to the town, and they rebuild the burnt-out home on Third Street; they struggle to keep that last lumber yard open, and they fight the new Walmart the next county over. These small particulars slowly add up to survival, preserving the relationships and the narratives that sustain these communities. These needs are pressing, critical, and local, for there's little separating these communities from when "there won't be nothing here."

The state, though, must address other economic pressures, pressures vastly different in scale and scope. Its concern is not particular jobs or particular Main Streets or even particular communities; it must sustain entire state and national economies. And so the state may worry little over one farm in Earle or a single hardware store in Delight. Instead, it focuses on broad trends across communities, about industrialization and urbanization, about the forces that will carry it from one decade to the next. This focus isn't new: after the Civil War, Arkansas turned its attention from rural communities and set its sights on cities and factories, hoping to attract business and industry and buoy a failing postwar economy.[9] As the state's cities and industries grew, prospered, and thrived, cotton fell further, farmers and sharecroppers suffered, and rural poverty ballooned.[10] The nation, too, answered to the economic and political demands of an industrial society.[11] It built factories and promoted industrial and governmental efficiency; it Americanized immigrants and prepared workers[12]— demands large in scale and broad in scope, demands largely managed and addressed through its cities. Today, it's the demands of globalization that preoccupy the state and federal government,[13] the demands of outsourcing to India, of competing with China, of remaining a worldwide power. For the government, the focus is competition and innovation, corporate growth and the global marketplace—these are the pressures it faces, the forces it reckons with.

And so, as the state prioritizes corporatization and urbanization and globalization, Delight and Earle—and rural communities throughout the country, it seems—face the immediate and local effects of these remote economic forces. The mechanization of farming and the rise of agri-business, a turn from agriculture to technology, an economy located in cities—these are the realities. The cotton gins rust, and a feed store closes—these are often the local meanings of state and national economics. The state's economy grows more competitive, the national economy grows stronger, and the local rural community just "dries up." These forces, it seems, pull the state from particular, local rural interests and stretch wider the boundary between community and state.

This boundary is not a simple symbolic construction; it is tied to inequities in resources and power.[14] The state seems to write the terms of its relationship with localities. For over a century, the state has named the problems of rural communities—a fundamental "rural life problem" of population loss and demographic change, "the corruption of a rural Eden."[15] And the state has determined the solutions: modernization, a faith in capitalism, a focus on the national economy. Preoccupied with the economic demands of the twentieth and twenty-first centuries, it embraced—and continues to embrace—industrialization and urbanization, and these forces often carry rural losses. The state writes policies—programs developed, regulations delineated, assistance offered or denied—that eventually trickle down to rural communities. These dictates rarely originate in these communities, yet this is where they play out, here in Delight and Earle. And then these communities feel powerless, as if they exist at the mercy of the state.

A Contested Institution

As this narrative tells of tensions between the state's understandings and local understandings, conflicts between the forces that drive the state's decisions and the pressures that shape life in Delight and Earle, imbalances between the state's power and a community's diminishing control, it also explains the meaning of this boundary for the school—because somewhere in this distance, caught somewhere within this boundary, is this school, a contested institution, so necessary to the community and so subject to the state.

It's not difficult to understand why Delight and Earle value their schools and why, I imagine, many other rural communities also appreciate and need theirs. Through this connection between community and school, children are looked after and community members cared for. Old relationships are sustained, new ones shaped. Small businesses lining rural highways remain open, and teachers are employed. These schools cast the racial topography of a town; they can fracture, but they also unite; they can segregate, but they also integrate. And, as they bind and cleave, they define a group of individuals as a whole and then sustain this community through relationships and stories, through the resources and leverage of a political identity, through hope and a shared future. A town's political interests and assets are redefined, and the careful organization of a society retained or restructured. These schools are consequential, meaningful to these communities, for these functions determine the material and social resources of these rural communities, the quality of life they offer and the shape of the future they promise. And no other institution plays these roles. Churches reach particular pockets of the community, and the few cafés draw the same old crowds, narrow groups often determined by race and loyal patronage. Grocery stores and banks don't provide the collective activities or voice that can generate a larger, shared purpose and political power; they offer no narrative, build no relationships, foster no community. In these small and isolated rural towns, the schools become a shared space, a place to locate fund-raiser suppers and community meetings, one of the few places where it's possible to come together, to unite across geography and maybe even race, to gather as a community. Long tied to these rural places, these schools amply fill their social and cultural and economic and political roles in the communities; whether by default or purpose—or, perhaps, both—these rural communities are dependent upon their schools. These schools mean noisy gymnasiums and a bead of light on a dark horizon; they mean a community aside a small green road sign. These communities need these schools.

And the stories and lessons of Delight and Earle reiterate themes heard across two hundred years of rural education. There has long been a social,[16] cultural,[17] and economic[18] necessity to rural schools. These schools have afforded rural communities some measure of power in the context of much powerlessness—some security in the midst of economic storms and social upheaval, some certainty among much uncertainty. These schools have provided employment and trained local workers and fostered a small economy; they have sustained relationships and built new connections. They have tied this group of individuals to one another and to this place; they have fostered hope. Their effects are not always positive—these schools can segregate, separate, stratify. But these schools are always meaningful, because, through their district lines and school boards and superintendents and budgets, they provide these rural communities with a political identity and voice—an identity that, no matter how many mandates and sanctions, the state is still forced to recognize. A rural community with a school exists—economically, socially, and politically. No school, these residents fear, no community.

Yet the state has an interest in these schools, too. This interest has roots over a century old, roots that date back to 1896, when, faced with an unwieldy and uneven school system scattered across a vast and changing countryside, the state recognized a "rural school problem."[19] These rural schools—with curricula and staff, purpose and function dictated by communities themselves[20]—were a problem, the state said, in their inefficiency and outdatedness, in their academic shortcomings and educational inadequacies,[21] a problem of too much local control and too little professional oversight.[22] In identifying this "problem," the state located the deficiency within rural communities—communities that simply "didn't know what was good for them in a complex new society."[23] And it identified the "solution" as involvement from faraway experts, the bureaucrats and commissioners of the state itself. To bring these communities under governmental control, the state launched a century and a half of consolidation and standardization,[24] one-size-fits-all reforms meant to bring uniformity to an uneven system and progress to backwoods schools—reforms that reorganized rural schools, reshaped rural schools, and closed rural schools. As the state's economic priorities shifted toward industrialization and, later, globalization, the state worked to craft a single type of schooling.[25] The state's power—furthered through governmental reports and Supreme Court cases and the rise of federal funding, wielded through school closures and curricular standards and state achievement tests—ensures that, regardless of context, schools secure the state's priorities.[26] Now, it's no longer just the rural community, just Delight or Earle, that relies upon its school to meet so many economic and civic needs. Now, through school funding, organization, and purpose, the state also uses these schools; it uses them to shape the economic and political conditions of our nation and, it seems, to fix the rural school problems—underenrollment and academic failure—of today. Through its mandates, it determines, more and more, the teachers hired, the curriculum taught, and the standards addressed—all to build a national citizenry and national economy.

And so the institutions that structure and organize and lend meaning to rural communities are also institutions of the state. It's as if, in the vast distance between the state and rural community, hangs the school, and over the past century, through trends of urbanization and standardization, the state has pulled these schools near. These institutions now sit at the state's end of this yawning distance, under the state's control.

THE NARRATIVE'S END

And here this narrative recounted by the residents of Delight and Earle comes to an abrupt end. The state—wielding its power, responding to economic and political pressures, operating with limited and faulty knowledge of rural communities—makes its decisions and mandates its policies. The state comes in, maybe closes the school. And, then, that's it. Soon, residents explain, "there won't be nothing here." Soon, it's all lost.

Another narrative can be told, of course. No matter the losses and however imperfect the implementation, the rise of state and federal control had had its indisputable benefits. It's led to an expansion of educational services, to desegregation, to a new attention to equity. And the priorities of the state and the priorities of the community are not always misaligned, their goals not always opposing, this boundary not always conflict filled. Sometimes state and community share needs—perhaps a new factory both furthers national economic competitiveness and furnishes local jobs—and the school—by preparing students for this work—can happily and readily meet these needs. Sometimes a state's priority—a workforce prepared for a wide range of careers or the racial integration of schools—and its associated educational policy—state standards, desegregation—may benefit a rural school and community in ways residents never anticipated. Or perhaps a community's priority—a senior class focused on college—aligns with important state goals. Or maybe what is so necessary to the community—the presence of its school—and the lengths residents will go to meet that need—doggedly attending school board meetings and raising millages—are not so incompatible with state interests, like an active and engaged citizenry. State and community aren't always at odds.

But this narrative—this rural narrative that fills Friday night bleacher conversation and feeds early morning coffee shop tirades—focuses on the conflict. It explains the disparity between the needs and desires of the state and those of a local community. It tells of a state, fiscally strapped and budget worried, that is pushed to cut excess and appease a large and anxious public. The state chooses consolidation—a well-worn route politically palatable to its mostly urban constituents, a route that, at least in rhetoric, promises money saved. It sets a minimum district size and closes districts. And the community, desperate to preserve its identity and political power, desperate to ensure the continued existence of its school, does what it can to fight back or quietly, simply suffers. Or perhaps the state, foreseeing the technological needs of new industries, mandates a whole host of high school curriculum requirements, advanced classes that would prepare students for engineering and communication jobs. The community, though, frightened by the shuttered stores on Main Street, wants its high school to offer a new vocational program, to prepare a handful of graduates to reopen a welding business or a restaurant here in town, and maybe start one in the next town over, too. And besides, even if it did offer these new advanced courses, where would it find—and how would it fund—all of the teachers required? But when needs conflict, when the intentions of Delight and Earle and so many other small rural communities stand opposite the intentions of the state, for better or for worse, the state usually wins, for it holds power. And with this distance, this contested school, this fraying relationship between rural community and school, with all of this, there are losses.

For the state, this contentious boundary and contested school imply a policy risk. The state, sitting far beyond a rural community it rarely sees, hears, or experiences, makes policy that, unsurprisingly, often fails to reflect this rural reality, that assumes an urban context or presumes context-lessness.[27] It's an oversight that has existed for decades. Desegregation, for example, missed the realities of racialized history that colored the rural landscape. The state's desegregation policies offered little support to the reluctant and fearful towns that couldn't shake off their histories; these generic policies offered little nuance to match differences in motivation and context. They failed to help these small rural towns fully and fairly carry out such seismic reorganizations, failed to help desegregate the Earles of rural America.

And, today, the oversight seems to continue. In this era of academic accountability and standardization, recent policies, including the Highly Qualified Teacher provision of No Child Left Behind,[28] often fail to grapple with the challenges facing rural contexts. This provision, requiring a teacher to hold state-approved credentials in all areas of teaching, assumes a ready supply of fully credentialed teachers, an impossibility in areas without universities churning out teachers or the tax base to offer high salaries, in the many rural towns forced to find one teacher capable of covering three or four different subject areas. These kinds of policies trap communities like Delight and Earle between mandate and reality, demanding what's often impossible. And, too, these policies often miss the small line of shops and banks kept open by a school's business, miss the small cluster of houses that cling close to this school, miss the community dependent upon a school. With every impossible requirement, they push these schools toward closure and, many fear, these communities toward extinction.

And so these communities take control where they can. As these policies wend their long way to these communities, communities like Delight and Earle often appropriate them, resist them, change them. Decades of local history weigh heavily, and contextless policies quickly become context specific: curricular standards are worked around or adapted; building regulations overlooked or modified; cafeteria requirements ignored. In one rural white community, a superintendent embraces new black students and this new multiracial community, and desegregation encourages tolerance and understanding; in another community, promises are unfulfilled and the leadership conflicted—desegregation causes a resegregation. These implementations may look little like the state's intentions—the long distance between state and community, ironically, allows the community to retain some agency, to foster some specificity, to turn a generic mandate into a contextual structure. Perhaps these communities retain some power through implementation, writing subtlety and nuance into a mandate, adapting it to better fit their particular contexts. Or, sometimes, these rural communities may undermine their own future, forsaking long-term welfare for short-term comfort or hastening closure by noncompliance. And the state's best policy-making intentions—its responsibilities to promote opportunity and equity—are lost. Implementation has wandered far from intent, leaving a messy trail of unintended consequences.

And, then, there is the loss to community that this distance implies. The boundary that separates rural community from state, a boundary maintained by misunderstanding and contradictory pressures and unequal power, also endangers the important and consequential relationship shared by community and school. With each state mandate, even the mandates that foster educational equity and academic rigor, these rural communities lose a measure of local control, and their schools may be less devoted to local purposes or less able to meet local needs.[29] Students may feel forced into a false choice between community and a life lived elsewhere,[30] and communities may suffer the costs of "brain drain."[31] The close relationship between school and community may be threatened, then, as these state mandates crowd out the social and cultural functions of a rural school[32] and rural communities grow disconnected from the institutions that were once so close.[33] Rural communities may lose the social capital[34] and political power these schools promote; rural towns may lose the relationships these schools foster and the narratives these schools write. All of this may be lost, as the community's school gradually becomes the state's school.

But alienation isn't the only cost. With the sanctions of the state, with oversight increased and state control expanded, with test score thresholds set and budgets restricted and minimum enrollments determined, come closed schools. School improvement lists and required expenditures and consolidation laws can all spell closure. And then, rural communities fear, it's only a matter of time until they go, too. Much of the concern is economic, of course: a closed school means the loss of what is often the town's largest customer. Mom's no longer has a three o'clock dining room crowded with children to feed; the garage no longer has the school buses to maintain; the bank no longer has a district's budget to manage. The businesses slowly shut, residents fear, and families move away. Soon the community will endure a slow decline, an economic death. And the concern is political, too: a community needs some political tether tying it to the map, something that assures permanence. For a rural community, this political tether is often its identity as a school district. This identity has a symbolic import,[35] for the simple act of recognition from the state confers status, but this political identity is also power, promising resources and control. It allows a rural community to anticipate some governmental aid—in the form of Title I and other state and federal monies—that will then go to serve the children and the school, aid that will directly serve the community's future. It provides a political capital, a capital that Earle's black community used to speak back to white business owners and landowners, a political power the community used to exercise and strengthen its agency and voice. District boundaries circumscribe a realm of decision making, a set of responsibilities and judgments to be made by a group of elected community representatives. This area of decision making, though often crowded by state mandates, ensures that some small measure of local control remains within a rural community; within the strictures of the government, this community can still influence some decisions about hiring and textbooks, about budgets and buildings. This local control allows for a measure of local flexibility and responsiveness—it allows Earle to set a college-focused agenda, Delight to grow its international program—decisions that, then, define and shape this community and its future. The political identity provided by these school districts is a political and symbolic weight; it keeps these communities alive and active, seen and recognized. It keeps these communities on the map.

For, no matter how much the policy makers and their policies suffer from this vast distance between state and rural community, in this narrative, these communities lose more. With encroaching state control, with all of the mandates and sanctions, with the threat of consolidation and state takeover, they stand to lose this relationship that means so much, these institutions that mean so much. These communities bear the brunt of ill-fitting policies or flawed implementations, and they endure the silent gymnasiums and empty classrooms and still parking lots. They're the ones to lose the political identity—their district, their school, their community—that keeps them recognized, alive, meaningful.

I remind myself of the assumptions lacing the fears that conclude this narrative: district consolidation doesn't mandate school closure, nor does it seem like school closure has to require the disappearance of a rural community. These reminders feel comforting in the midst of so much anxiety and loss. But, as I listen to this story told once more, I don't raise these objections. They seem weak and unimportant in the face of one reality: that these communities have witnessed this sad progression over and over. They've watched the disappearance of districts and schools to the north, the south, the east and west, and they've watched the disappearance of those communities, too. The schools go and the communities just dry up, they tell me—and, as I drive past, I can see it, too, that there's nothing to give meaning to the little green sign aside the narrow rural highway.

NOTHING HERE

This is the narrative I heard again and again, told while sitting over sweet tea in Delight or shouted over the noise of a game in Earle, a narrative uniform in its vocabulary and consistent in its arc and final in its end: a faraway state threatening to control and even close a rural community's schools, a powerful and distant state taking "the only hope for our community" so that "there won't be nothing here." It may be an incomplete and stark account, but it's a revealing one, for, with this narrative, we begin to recognize the state's power and the communities' fear. We can see the boundary the state constructs and the school uneasily straddling this boundary. We see the costs of distances wide with stereotype and misunderstanding, contextless policies, and zero-sum struggles for educational control. And as the state pulls this school close through requirements and sanctions and regulations, the rural community suffers the effects—some a distant and vague danger, still more imagined than actual, and some a clear reality. Policies may lose their meaning; implementations may lose their intent. A relationship—a unique and complex and necessary relationship between community and school—is threatened. A school may close; a community may disappear. And this, so many communities fear, is how their narrative ends.

CHAPTER NINE

The Possibility of Public Education

Should our investment in public schools be about communities or students?

Senator Jim Argue asks me this as we sit in his office, a large, comfortable room in the back corner of the United Methodist Foundation. The foundation, a barely marked building in a leafy Little Rock neighborhood, seems more house than headquarters, and the three-term state senator—president of the foundation and a former banker—is a tall man with casually professional clothing and a firm handshake, a friendly man who uses your name when he speaks.

Even after only one trip to Delight, I know who Senator Argue is: chair of the Senate Education Committee, responsible for many of Arkansas's recent reforms, instrumental in writing Act 60. It is his name and his legislation that are linked to the consolidation threatening Delight, his name and his legislation that feature in the stories I am beginning to hear—stories of a distant and powerful state, stories of consolidation and academic sanctions, stories of fear and loss. I want to better understand these policies unsettling rural Arkansas, and see how the state explains the distance and pressures and closures these rural communities are experiencing. So we sit on plush living room furniture in his office, and this term-limited senator reflects on his eighteen years in the legislature, eighteen years of state education reform and "consolidation wars" and school closures.

COMMUNITIES OR STUDENTS?

Senator Argue sought office because he wanted "to move the state forward in doing a better job of educating our children." Arkansas was "chronically forty-ninth or fiftieth" on indicators like income levels and college degrees. In "fail[ing] to give educational opportunity to children," the state was "squandering human capital" and jeopardizing its future: "either we do a better job of educating our children, or we continue to be virtually a third world country right here in America." And so he ran for the Arkansas State Senate, soon becoming something of an "education specialist." Some people, he tells me, get involved in education reform for economic reasons— "they want a healthier marketplace"—and others for personal reasons—for "*my* children and *my* grandchildren." But for him, education "is a moral issue." "I don't worry about the environment or tax policy," he says. "I just spend all my time on education."

In late 2002, a few months before he began as chair of the Senate Education Committee, the Arkansas Supreme Court decided the *Lake View* case, ruling that Arkansas's funding of its public schools was unconstitutional, both inadequate and unequal. The court's decision inspired—and justified—a series of state-led reforms, the senator explains, that represented "incredible" progress and "basically put an end to local control": multiple expansions of the state's education budget, increased teachers' salaries, investments in school buildings, a new prekindergarten initiative, greater advanced placement offerings, and the consolidation of many school districts. He's pleased with the results: "We're seeing academic achievement improvements in Arkansas"—gains in state test scores— "really more quickly than I had anticipated."

Later in our conversation, I return to consolidation, a topic he has mentioned only briefly, in passing references to the state's "consolidation wars" and "the most politically difficult reform we pursued." And so I ask to hear more, to understand how the state justifies this practice that I can already see weighs so heavily in Delight. Senator Argue begins a long description of the benefits of consolidation, citing the "curriculum that those students deserve" but that small schools can't deliver and the "economies of scale" that larger facilities bring. A mandated consolidation can bring about racial justice, he explains, telling me about a small white town just outside of Hope that had, for years, resisted merging with a nearby, mostly black district. And consolidation is about fairness. He "took to heart the Court's language that a child's educational opportunity should not be an accident of residence"—a key conclusion of the *Lake View* case—and pushed for the expansion of the state's education fund, but also insisted that, "when we export those dollars from my affluent district to the Delta to better fulfill our moral obligation to educate those children, let's use those dollars efficiently." Consolidation, he argues, ensures that schools are equitable, just, and efficient.

I ask him about the drawbacks of consolidation, and he explains: "Well, what you're going to hear . . . in rural Arkansas, somebody's going to say, 'Those bigger schools aren't safe; there are safety issues.' Or 'if you take away our school, our community's going to die.' Or you'll hear the small town Chamber of Commerce types say, 'You can't take away our school. It's our biggest employer.'" But, he continues, he would have to ask these rural Arkansas residents one question: "A or B, take your pick—multiple choice. Should our investment in public schools be about certain communities or students?"

These small, rural, property-poor communities, he continues, "want their own schools and . . . they want someone else to pay for it." Rural parents, even those willing to drive many miles for groceries or the doctor or work, are too worried about what's "geographically convenient." And, consolidation wars or not, "education is valued less in rural areas," he says, and "they're not all that committed to curriculum quality." These rural communities don't care about academic achievement; they are simply "determined to protect their inferior, small school." But he wonders, "All this investment . . . in public schools, is it about serving the students, or is it about serving adults?" The money the state provides, he asks, the reforms it writes, the schools it supports—for whom? Whom should these schools serve? Students or communities? Children or adults? He provides his own quick response: "For me, the answer's clearly the students. At whatever costs a community might suffer, I can't imagine the immorality of compromising a child's educational opportunity in order to prop up a declining community."

I'm suddenly uncomfortable sitting on the senator's plush couch. Far from the hills of Delight and the floodplains of Earle, I find myself—a longtime skeptic of consolidation and state-mandated school closures— listening to this dedicated, decent man and wondering if I've been too sentimental, taken by the excitement of a few basketball games and assemblies and a long-ago beans and greens supper. Maybe I'm too generous, overlooking too many failing test scores, forgiving too many resistant school boards. Maybe I'm not seeing these communities and their schools for what they really are.

Like the senator, I can't justify limiting a student's educational opportunity. And, as a child of the South, I know the great lengths that some white families and white politicians will go to tip the balance of opportunity in their favor or to avoid racial integration. Of course I believe in the right of every child—regardless of race or class or geography—to a full, well-resourced, rigorous education. And now, faced with his question, I wonder if I've been too sympathetic to rural communities. Am I failing to properly value academic achievement and educational opportunity? Am I choosing communities over children?

CHOICES AND DOUBTS

I will remember the senator's question as I spend the next few years flying back and forth to Arkansas. His question—are these schools for communities or students?—echoes my own interest in understanding why rural schools matter, and it resonates with a rural education debate that has occupied policy makers and reformers for over 150 years: what purpose should rural schools serve? And whose purpose? His question seems significant and worthy, and it becomes something I listen for and ask about, a question lying just below my conversations and interviews and observations. After I talk with Delight students or parents in Earle, as I sit on Kathy's couch or drive the flat miles of the Delta, I sift through the stories they have shared and the things they haven't, tracing the knotty patterns, looking for the complex and tangled roles these schools play in their communities, trying to understand if these schools matter and why they matter and to whom they matter. And then, somewhere during this hearing and re-hearing, I take these richly complicated narratives, and I sort them: is this a school for students, or one for community?

It's easy at first. I listen to the complaints of high schoolers in Earle about more rules and discipline, about the new principal who is "doing it for academics"—this is a school clearly about students. I attend a cemetery dinner in Delight, the cafeteria filled with food and chatter and aging white folks, and see a school for community. This sorting becomes habitual, nearly unconscious.

But, after a while, after more time in each town and more conversation with residents, the sorting gets difficult. I talk with a Delight teacher that lives just a few miles from school, who routinely sees her students at games or McKnight's and frequently drops them off at home after church—is this an opportunity for students to be fully recognized and cared for by a teacher, or is this about an adult's convenient employment and jobs for a community? Or when the superintendent in Earle tells me of a partnership between the high school and a nearby community college, explaining how much Earle needs its graduates to attend college and then come back to serve this community, I wonder, is this school serving its students or its community? The longer I stay in Arkansas, the muddier this choice seems, tricky even to isolate children from their community or a community from its children.

Other details of the senator's reasoning also lose their clarity. The argument, I discover, seems to misunderstand these rural communities' resistance to school closure. Race is certainly a factor, but not for the reasons he described: Delight appears to value the school's role in integrating the community, while Earle's black community uses the school for political leverage and empowerment in a system still controlled by white interests. Geographic convenience is, in fact, rarely mentioned: many students, those on the districts' edges, could actually find themselves with shorter bus rides after consolidation. And I have a hard time seeing these two communities as "dying": their economies may be weak, their schools may be threatened, but, for now, each is vibrant, active, and alive.

I also begin to wonder if this argument relies too heavily on measures of achievement as indicators of academic progress. Test scores, while informative, seem unreliable, as Delight's have been mostly high, and scores in Earle, for all its relentless push, fluctuate, even as parents and teachers and students describe stronger teaching and greater learning. And on one important count—the assumption that rural communities don't value education—this argument, I find, is simply wrong. These communities pay mightily for their schools: both communities tax themselves dry, with millage rates among the highest in the state.[1] With all of the talk of college and test scores, the clear respect for teachers and school leaders, the passion and care of these educators, the lengths these communities will go just to keep their schools, it's clear these communities value the education these schools provide their children. They may sometimes oppose the state's determination of that education—questioning the relevance of its new standards or the fairness of its tests—but they recognize the value of that education.

And so, after years of conversation and meals and classroom visits in Delight and Earle, I return to the senator's question, and finally, I hear it differently. The senator, in all of his earnest effort and commitment to educational change in Arkansas, subscribes to an argument long told by policy makers, researchers, and rural reformers, an argument that recasts the complicated, tangled issue of whom schools should serve as an easy, one-or-the-other choice—*should our investment in schools be about communities or students?* The narrative he tells is simple: schools are for students, and not for communities.

It's a deft political move. This narrative imposes order on a messily fraught analysis. Through arguments of morality and efficiency, it delineates a "right" side—for students—and a "wrong" side—for communities. The senator aligns himself and his policy with that right side, while positioning small, rural towns—towns in danger of losing their schools—with that other, faraway, wrong side. The narrative is uncomplicated and effective, its framing politically powerful and convincing. It wins legislative support for Act 60 and eliminates dozens of districts across Arkansas.[2]

But its argument is flawed. It's inaccurate in many of its details—district consolidation often saves no money,[3] bigger schools guarantee nothing academically,[4] and low-income children often fare better in smaller facilities.[5] It's faulty in many of its assumptions—large, consolidated districts were, in fact, first created "for adults," reflecting reformers' understandings of what school should look like and accomplish,[6] and still today these districts serve adults' bureaucratic and political purposes.[7] Even more fundamental, its easy narrative—that schools are for students, not communities—is faulty. It's faulty because the choice itself is false, because schools like Delight and Earle exist—schools that, imperfectly and enthusiastically, serve *both* children and communities.

THE FEDERAL NARRATIVE

The senator's argument is, of course, only one argument, one conversation with one voice, one justification of a policy that many rural residents believe is "squeezing out" rural communities. But another policy, the federal No Child Left Behind Act, also figures into the closures that rural communities face. Adopted with bipartisan support in early 2002, NCLB requires states to test their students in reading and math and track and report the progress of students' scores, with the goal of all students reaching "proficiency."[8] If schools or districts fail to make adequate yearly progress toward this goal, they face increasingly harsh sanctions: they must allow students to transfer, must provide them with tutoring services, must undertake "corrective action" such as changes in staff or curriculum. The final sanction is school "restructuring," which includes shutting and reopening as a charter school, firing the principal and teachers and hiring new staff, surrendering control to a private entity or the state, or submitting to some other type of reorganization; this final sanction is, essentially, closure. This threat looms over Earle—as its schools have all logged time on the state's lists of failure, the middle and high school for many years—and the policy and its tests cast a long shadow over both towns. It surfaces, again and again, in my conversations with parents and teachers, students and administrators; it figures into their narrative of a distant and threatening state, of fear and closure, of everything that could be lost.

But the federal policy makers, in justifying their policy, also have a narrative, a story to tell about the meaning of schools. It is a story told by President George W. Bush, as he signed the bill into law at Hamilton High School in Hamilton, Ohio.[9] To a crowd yelling "U-S-A," he declared, "We owe the children of America a good education. . . . As of this hour, America's schools will be on a new path of reform and a new path of results." The No Child Left Behind Act, he explained, centers on accountability: "Every school has a job to do. And that's to teach the basics and teach them well. If we want to make sure no child is left behind, every child must learn to read. And every child must learn to add and subtract." At the core of NLCB is the expectation that "every child can learn, we expect every child to learn, and you must show us whether or not every child is learning." He ended with a plea: "And now it's up to you, the local citizens of our great land, the compassionate, decent citizens of America, to stand up and demand high standards, and to demand that no child—not one single child in America—is left behind."

This back-to-basics rationale of high expectations and accountability, of leaving no child behind, is offered again and again over the next decade, even stretching into Barack Obama's presidency and his Race to the Top initiative.[10] It's offered even as tens of thousands of schools are designated as failing and local schools across the country face closure.[11] It's offered even as Earle begins its long march through sanctions, years of hard work bringing, it seems, only more penalty. It's offered even as many critics argue that, despite all good intentions, some children are, in fact, still being left behind. It's offered even as the act, more than a decade after its adoption, fails to be reauthorized.[12]

The argument persists because it's persuasive—it's difficult to argue against the equity of accountability, against recognizing the potential of all children and the urgency of serving them—and its underlying assumption, that the job of schools is teaching students basic math and reading, seems unassailable and self-evident. Like the senator's rationale, it's a tidy imperative of an argument. But this argument, too, is flawed. Its sides are too clean, its promises too sweeping, and, perhaps most significantly, its narrative too simple. This narrative ascribes, without question or debate, a function—a single and very narrow function—to schools, and, in doing so, it eliminates all of the other important functions a school carries out, the multiple roles it plays, the myriad purposes it serves. This narrative is narrow, limiting, and reductive, for, like the senator's, it overlooks the schools of Delight and Earle, schools with roles more numerous than one, purposes more consequential than basics.

FAMILIAR NARRATIVES, FAMILIAR CONSEQUENCES

These policies—Act 60 and NCLB—are separate, distinct in scope and intent. Act 60 is a state consolidation policy; NCLB is a federal policy of educational accountability. But both policies increase state control and reduce the power of local communities, and both promise school closures, and, for this, both feature in the narrative Delight and Earle tell about distant, powerful, threatening governments.

And the arguments for these policies—the rationale a state senator uses to defend a landscape of school districts tallying student enrollments and fearing closed schools, the justification a president gives for stacks of math and reading tests and long lists of failing schools—are also similar. Both arguments cast the government—state or federal—as leading actor, a responsible and righteous hero doing the right thing for children. Both arguments rely upon themes of equity and sensibility, of child-centeredness and responsibility. And both arguments share a timeworn grammar: they echo with the moralistic justifications that have inspired rural reform for nearly 150 years. I hear the accusations of parochialism and ignorance often levied upon rural communities and the assumptions of failure often tied to rural schools and those in them. Still today, it seems, local schools and communities need rescue by a watchful and efficient state or federal government—rescue or, as it often turns out, closure—and questions of schooling—whom and what it is for—are not for local determination, not for local consideration or for local answers.

These policy arguments also depend upon the same sort of dichotomous framing that has defined the debates of rural school reform for generations, stark oppositions that rural communities themselves often slip into: state and federal priorities versus local ones, state and federal needs versus local ones, state and federal actors versus local ones. Today's policy debates fragment into the same sorts of adversaries, with state and federal government assuming the moral advantage: a noble state serving its children versus a dying rural town saving a few jobs, a wise and just federal government focusing on academics versus some unpatriotic and provincial adults distracting the work. The policies are new, but the arguments old—these are the rationales that have been given for decades, the labels applied for years, the language that has always been used to justify the reform of rural schools.

And, at the heart of these arguments, lie simple policy narratives—that schools are for students, that schools are for teaching students basic reading and math. They are parallel narratives, one dictating whom schools serve, the other determining what they do. Together, they establish customer and product, client and service. And students are, of course, worthy constituents, and basics a sound goal.

But these are narrow narratives, with so much missing. Because, on a Friday night in Delight, the boys' basketball team runs and jumps and sweats its way through a game, with their families and neighbors and teachers, both black and white, all wearing Bulldog T-shirts and caps, crowded into the bleachers lining the gym. As the players shoot and miss, excite and disappoint, they grow closer, and those watching, cheering, and gossiping do, too. And, on Monday, teachers will congratulate these players on their game, and these students will feel more connected to school—and they will likely stay through school and graduate.[13] The parents and neighbors will recognize one another in the carpool line, and they will stop to talk, maybe plan a team fund-raiser—and they will likely grow more tolerant and accepting.[14] And the children of the family that owns the printing shop in town, the shop that churns out all of those Bulldog T-shirts and caps, will climb off the bus, and they will be well rested and well fed, secure in the knowledge that their parents have jobs—and they will likely see academic benefits.[15]

And just before lunch in Earle, the students of Dunbar Middle School, joined by a few parents and volunteers, file through a hallway lined with graduates' photographs and college fliers and fill the bleachers of the gym, gathering to hear the campaign speeches for that afternoon's student elections. Their principal quiets their chatter and cheering, welcomes the parents and visitors, and introduces the candidates, who, nearly hidden behind a podium, deliver their speeches. The children will see their mothers and fathers sitting in those bleachers, and they will watch their families participate in this and other school activities—and they will likely see scholastic advantages for this involvement.[16] And, later that afternoon, these students will cast their votes, and they will feel more engaged in their school—and they will likely sustain their academic motivation, too.[17] These middle schoolers will spend another four or five years surrounded by these same college fliers, and they will begin to feel that college might be a worthy and attainable goal—and they will likely explore this option.[18] And this black community will witness the power of a strong, effective, black principal and the growth of a new generation of young leaders, and it will feel represented and hopeful—and it will likely watch the old racial order of Earle slowly shift.[19]

The meaning of these schools is not singular[20]—those served are not only students, what's accomplished is not only basics. These schools don't force simple choices, nor follow simple narratives. The schools of Delight and Earle play multiple and inseparable roles for multiple and inseparable groups. These purposes are academic and social, economic and civic, for children and for adults. These schools sustain the town's economy while focusing on college preparation; they welcome new community members while empowering leaders; they foster common values while challenging tradition. They promote academic achievement *because* they build relationships; they inspire generational support *because* they nurture youth. These purposes are local and state: these schools shape local racial boundaries while fulfilling federal desegregation policies, they buoy local hopes while raising academic standards. These schools are essential and multifunctional, useful to many people and for many purposes, and they are meaningful and necessary precisely for that boundlessness and complication.

But these narratives, the narratives of Delight and Earle, are getting lost, going unheard, crowded out by the louder, easier narratives of state and federal policy makers, the narratives that insist upon narrow definitions of whom a school serves or what a school does. Policy makers are, of course, tasked with devising solutions to complex problems. In doing so, they must identify and define these issues and marshal support for policies, and sharply written narratives are useful, providing clarity within otherwise murky political terrain. And these narratives have accomplished some important victories for educational equity: Arkansas's reforms have led to better teacher salaries and a more rigorous high school curriculum,[21] and NCLB has brought to the public school system a sorely needed transparency and attention to equity.[22] These narratives have raised important and necessary questions about the rigor and quality of public education.

But as these narratives define the terms and dictate the choices, they diminish the meaning of a rural school. These policy narratives—so persuasive in their uncomplicated simplicity, so inarguable in their apparent morality—begin to circumscribe how we think about school, to reduce what we think it can accomplish. We—policy makers and the public—lose sight of the Delights and Earles, everything they do and everyone they serve. We forget that equity and opportunity are the responsibility and aspiration of both community and state. We mistake ease for virtue, pursue a stark minimalism over a much more complicated balance. We begin to separate what's inseparable—children from communities, communities from schools. And then we close these schools, losing the institutions that raise and educate a generation, that bind and sustain a community.

AN URBAN SCHOOL PROBLEM, TOO

For decades, these trends—the erosion of local control, the narrowing of meaning, the closures of schools and districts—have typically been understood as a "rural issue." Rural communities have borne the brunt of assumptions of ignorance and school failure, and for a century and a half, the dominant model of reform was "the one best system," a system controlled by urban elites and designed to meet the educational, social, and economic needs of burgeoning cities and an industrializing nation.[23] A long, slow conflict simmers between local, rural communities and an urban-focused state: the state acts on behalf of its cities, its urban-centric policies further urban-centric objectives,[24] and, in the process, rural schools are "improved out of existence."[25] This conflict has existed for generations, and it still persists, still pushes the state to standardize and close rural schools, still stokes uneasy fears in rural communities. But, increasingly, state and federal education policy seems to fail American cities, too.

As politicians, operating under the mandates of NCLB, have moved to close "underperforming" schools in New York City, Chicago, and Washington, D.C.,[26] these urban communities have erupted in protest. Parents, teachers, and community members—children and adults—have organized to fight sanctions and closures, forming groups such as the Coalition for Educational Justice, Parents Across America, and Save Our Schools. In what has become an annual event, Save Our Schools hosted a four-day rally in Washington to protest NCLB, its testing and sanctions, and the closures of neighborhood schools.[27] Thousands of teachers, academics, and activists from cities across the country attended, and they organized rallies, delivered speeches, and held a march that ended at the Department of Education.[28] And others have registered their dissent in quieter ways: many parents have just refused to transfer their children from schools labeled failing.[29]

Policy makers appear surprised and angered by this resistance.[30] New York City mayor Michael Bloomberg, responding to a lawsuit filed by parents and teachers to block the closure of twenty-two city schools, argued that community members "don't understand the value of education."[31] In responding to criticism of NCLB, former secretary of education Rod Paige asked, "Would parents, educators, taxpayers, and state and local policymakers have any expectations for student performance on their own accord, absent federal law?"[32] These local folks don't hold the proper regard for academics, for education, for schools, these comments suggest—echoing the same complaints levied against rural residents for generations.

Yet these urban communities must understand something policy makers don't. If urban schools mattered only for their ability to teach basic reading and math, closures would be welcomed, and opportunities to transfer readily taken. But, often, they aren't, and instead, urban reformers meet with a fierce and defiant commitment to a kind of urban school that means more than just its test scores. These communities, it seems, understand quite well everything at stake with a school's closure.

And with these protests come other calls from urban communities and urban activists—demands for more expansive, more responsive city schools.[33] Many urban communities want schools that are more welcoming to students and families, with student handbooks translated into multiple languages, school leaders that know students' names, and music lessons offered after school. They, too, understand the benefits of schools that serve as community centers, benefits for both children and adults, and they are organizing into powerful, community-led school reform movements, fighting for nighttime classes and parent meeting spaces and extended school days.

And these appeals for an expanded understanding of educational purpose are not limited to parents and residents. Sociologists and demographers, alarmed by the growing segregation of urban schools, call for a renewal of *Brown*'s promise,[34] asking schools to dismantle the racial inequalities that structure American society. Urban leaders and doctors look to schools to curb obesity, instill healthy eating habits, and educate about sex and HIV. City planners hope strong schools will boost housing prices and spark urban renewal. Political scientists appeal to schools to teach civics, to provide community service opportunities, to offer extracurriculars—all to end urban isolation and repair a democracy civically and socially unraveling.[35] These calls aren't new;[36] for generations, the American public has placed its faith in schools, looking to these institutions for prosperity, for democracy, for hope. These are the sorts of multiple, overlapping goals and priorities that American communities, rural or urban, have always had for their schools. But today, these founding principles are threatened by simplistic narratives that promise a partially educated, profoundly fragmented society.

THE CANARY IN THE COAL MINE

Long miles separate these city schools and urban communities from Delight and Earle. These two rural communities are distant and different, and the relationships they share with their rural schools may be uniquely close and interdependent. But still—it's not just the Friday night bleachers of rural schools that are so tightly packed, not just the elections of rural school boards that are so closely followed, not just the boundaries of rural school districts that are so often contested. And it's not just the closures of rural schools that bring protest and fear.

Urban communities also rely upon their schools for shape and structure, for substance and sustenance—perhaps not as heavily or exclusively as rural communities, maybe a bit more quietly and subtly, but still, it seems, they do. And, it seems, these urban schools are also under threat, the threat of sanctions and closures, the threat of a persuasive narrative that writes these schools into a narrow insignificance. The realities that rural communities have lived with since the 1800s—the reduction of a school's meaning, the school closures it brings—are quickly becoming urban realities, American realities.

These rural schools are a miner's canary—the first to go, their sacrifice a warning to others. They tell a cautionary tale, a tale of everything that can be lost with the narrow circumscription of a school's purpose. They ask not for sentimentalism, nor extreme localism, nor utopianism—these are not perfect schools, and schools are not perfect institutions. Instead, they offer a call to question the prevailing narratives of policy, to hear counternarratives and write new narratives. They remind us to see the complexity and possibility beyond the simple packaging, to believe again in the vast potential of public schools to serve students and transform society.

But these schools offer more than just their warnings. Two small, rural communities in the vast green of Arkansas depend on these schools. Their rhythms pattern these communities, their spaces structure these communities, their ties bind these communities—and for this reason, for these two communities, these rural schools matter.

Epilogue

The decision was final in March 2010, just as I was finishing my last trips to Arkansas. Delight would be consolidated. When the school year began in the new South Pike County School District, nothing was too different, from what I heard—the Delight school opened its doors, just like any August, and buses snaked through familiar routes, children filled familiar classrooms, and families crowded a familiar gym. By September, though, word got out: this would be the high school's last year. Next August, all of the seventh through twelfth grade students, all of their teachers and their parents, all of their basketball games and their traditions—all would go to Murfreesboro High.

And Earle—only two schools opened there in August, the elementary and the high school. Dunbar's doors remained shut, its students split between the other schools and its staff scattered—some rehired by the district, others moving on. The closure is surely an indicator of the district's shrinking population. And some wonder what else it might mean—whether it is a financial decision driven by landowners eager to curb rising property taxes, or perhaps a final parting slight to Senator Crumbly. Either way, the closure has an eerie historical resonance—Dunbar, once the black school, was last closed after desegregation, an act of retribution, it seems, for the protests of 1970. Regardless of the motivation, when the year's test results are finally released, the decision seems short-sighted: the high school still fell short of adequate yearly progress—it's now in its sixth year of corrective action—and the elementary school's scores also faltered, putting it back in school improvement. But Dunbar had raised its scores, made adequate yearly progress, become an "achieving" school. Had it remained open, it would have been removed from the state's list.

I hear this news, communicated across thousands of miles, in phone calls and emails, through Department of Education websites and Arkansas media—news buried in the halting silences of uncertainty, news found at the bottom of long lists. There's a weight to these updates, the crushing weight of a state's blunt policies. There's an irony, too, the irony of a state-recognized "achieving" school—a school with such symbolic and cultural importance—closed, the sharp irony of good work unrecognized. And, of course, there's sadness and fear. Are these the first sentences of the final chapter of Delight and Earle, the chapter that ends the stories of all ghost towns sitting aside little green road signs?

It doesn't have to end this way; this doesn't have to be the final chapter. These communities have never told simple stories and never accepted others' stories of them. They reject the myths and stereotypes; they refuse the foregone conclusions.

This narrative, too, can be rewritten. We can edit out the distance separating community and state, reduce the boundary, put community and state in dialogue, force some accountability and compromise and understanding. We can revise for complexity and multiplicity. We can explain our interests as shared and our fates as tied. We can develop a more nuanced and connected approach to education policy, writing reforms that balance individual and collective needs, support local and national goals, foster racial and geographic justice.

We can tell a story of the possible—the possibility of crowded Friday night gymnasiums, of bleachers filled with black and white students and black and white parents, of a community that's like family. The possibility of gowned alumni in faded hallway pictures, of eighth grade campaign slogans, of a community that marches. The possibility of a beans and greens supper, of steaming Styrofoam trays and rising piles of donated cookies, of a community that turns out.

The possibility of public education.

Notes

CHAPTER ONE

1. Flora and Flora, *Rural Communities*, 7.
2. Cromartie and Bucholtz, "Defining the 'Rural.'"
3. Reynnells and John, "What Is Rural?"
4. As Cromartie and Bucholtz describe, the Census Bureau draws upon a land-use concept and defines urban areas as those with more than 2,500 residents. The OMB, relying upon an economic definition, designates metropolitan counties as those core counties containing an urban area with at least 50,000 residents or counties with economic ties to a core county (determined by proportion of residents commuting to a core county for employment); in 2000, it added a designation for micropolitan areas, a label that follows these same criteria, though with a lower threshold of 10,000 residents.
5. Haas, "Leaving Home," 8.
6. Brown and Schafft, *Rural People and Communities*, 8; Johnson and Strange, "Why Rural Matters 2009," 25; Reynnells and John, "What Is Rural?"
7. Coladarci, "Improving the Yield of Rural Education Research," 2; Howley, Theobald, and Howley, "What Rural Education Research," 1–2.
8. Howley, Theobald, and Howley, "What Rural Education Research," 1.
9. hooks, *Belonging*.
10. For the remainder of this chapter and in others, when describing research work, I use the same "urban," "rural," "metropolitan," and "nonmetropolitan" designations authors employed in their studies. In the community portraits and my later analysis, I rely upon participants' own perceptions of living in and identifying as a rural community.
11. Johnson, "Rural Demographic Change in the New Century," 1.
12. Flora and Flora, *Rural Communities*; Isserman, "Getting State Rural Policy Right"; Johnson, "Demographic Trends."
13. Housing Assistance Council, "Race and Ethnicity in Rural America," 1. These categories reflect census-defined racial and ethnic designations.
14. Economic Research Service, "Rural Hispanics at a Glance."
15. Economic Research Service, "Rural America at a Glance."
16. Hamilton, Hamilton, Duncan, and Colocousis, "Place Matters."
17. Haas, "Leaving Home," 8–9; Howley, Theobald, and Howley, "What Rural Education Research," 5; Johnson, "Demographic Trends," 7; Theobald and Wood, "Learning to Be Rural," 17–33.

18. Arnold, Newman, Gaddy, and Dean, "Condition of Rural Educational Research," 1; Isserman, "Getting State Rural Policy Right"; Kannapel and DeYoung, "The Rural School Problem in 1999," 70; Silver and DeYoung, "Ideology of Rural/Appalachian Education"; Tyack, *One Best System*, 21–27.

19. Wray, *Not Quite White*, 1–20.

20. Johnson and Strange, "Why Rural Matters 2009," 1.

21. Ibid.

22. Johnson, "Unpredictable Directions," 21.

23. Henderson and Mapp, "A New Wave of Evidence"; Oakes and Rogers, *Learning Power*; Warren, Hong, Rubin, and Uy, "Beyond the Bake Sale."

CHAPTER TWO

1. Corbett, *Learning to Leave*, 8.

2. Tyack, *One Best System*.

3. Zimmerman, *Small Wonder*, 18–19.

4. Ibid., 20–26.

5. Tyack, *One Best System*, 14.

6. DeYoung and Howley, "Political Economy of Rural School Consolidation," 67.

7. Silver and DeYoung, "Ideology of Rural/Appalachian Education," 59; Tyack, "The Tribe and the Common School," 3–12; Tyack, *One Best System*, 15–21; Zimmerman, *Small Wonder*, 28–32.

8. Tyack, "The Tribe and the Common School," 9.

9. Edmondson, *Prairie Town*.

10. Tyack, *One Best System*, 15.

11. Howley, Johnson, and Petrie, "Consolidation of Schools and Districts," 5.

12. Tyack, *One Best System*, 19.

13. As quoted in ibid., 15–16.

14. Ibid., 16.

15. Zimmerman, *Small Wonder*, 37.

16. As quoted in ibid.

17. Tyack, *One Best System*, 17; Zimmerman, *Small Wonder*, 41–42.

18. Graham, *Schooling America*, 13.

19. Anderson, *Education of Blacks in the South*, 4; Graham, *Schooling America*, 19.

20. Anderson, *Education of Blacks in the South*, 148.

21. Butchart, *Schooling the Freed People*, 2.

22. Perry, "Freedom for Literacy," 13.

23. Anderson, *Education of Blacks in the South*, 4–32; Butchart, *Schooling the Freed People*, 1–16.

24. Perry, "Freedom for Literacy," 11.

25. Graham, *Schooling America*, 14; Tyack, *One Best System*, 29; Zinn, *A People's History*, 253.

26. Theobald, *Teaching the Commons*, 74–87; Theobald and Wood, "Learning to Be Rural," 18–24.

27. Graham, *Schooling America*, 9.

28. Silver and DeYoung, "Ideology of Rural/Appalachian Education," 54.

29. Tyack, *One Best System*, 31.

30. Ibid., 29.

31. Silver and DeYoung, "Ideology of Rural/Appalachian Education," 52; Tyack, *One Best System*, 14.

32. Graham, *Schooling America*, 27–35; Tyack, *One Best System*, 39–59.

33. Bauch, "School-Community Partnerships in Rural Schools," 206–7; Graham, *Schooling America*, 27–35; Kannapel and DeYoung, "The Rural School Problem in 1999," 70.

34. DeYoung and Howley, "Political Economy of Rural School Consolidation," 68–69.

35. Tyack, *One Best System*.

36. Theobald, *Teaching the Commons*, 92–115; Theobald and Wood, "Learning to Be Rural," 22–24.

37. Silver and DeYoung, "Ideology of Rural/Appalachian Education," 52.

38. Theobald and Wood, "Learning to Be Rural," 24–25.

39. Tyack, *One Best System*, 22.

40. As quoted in Theobald, *Teaching the Commons*, 104.

41. Tyack, *One Best System*, 22.

42. Theobald, personal email.

43. Edmondson, *Prairie Town*, 63–64; Theobald, *Teaching the Commons*, 103.

44. Theobald and Wood, "Learning to Be Rural," 25.

45. As quoted in Theobald, *Teaching the Commons*, 103.

46. Kannapel and DeYoung, "The Rural School Problem in 1999," 67; Silver and DeYoung, "Ideology of Rural/Appalachian Education," 55; Tyack, *One Best System*, 23.

47. "Report on Rural Schools," 19–20.

48. Cubberley, *Rural Life and Education*, 102.

49. As quoted in Tyack, *One Best System*, 23.

50. Theobald, *Teaching the Commons*, 104.

51. Tyack, *One Best System*, 24.

52. Cubberley, *Rural Life and Education*, 106.

53. Howley, Johnson, and Petrie, "Consolidation of Schools and Districts," 5.

54. Ibid., 6.

55. Bard, Gardener, and Wieland, "Rural School Consolidation," 40.

56. DeYoung and Howley, "Political Economy of Rural School Consolidation," 69.

57. Tyack, *One Best System*, 43–44.

58. Theobald, personal email.

59. Tyack, *One Best System*, 24.

60. Anderson, *Education of Blacks in the South*, 22.

61. Ibid., 153.

62. Walker, *Their Highest Potential*.

63. Anderson, *Education of Blacks in the South*.

64. Ibid., 114.

65. Ogden, as quoted in ibid., 89.

66. Washington, as quoted in Anderson, *Education of Blacks in the South*, 77.

67. Anderson, *Education of Blacks in the South*, 115.

68. Adams, *Education for Extinction*, 44.

69. Kannapel and DeYoung, "The Rural School Problem in 1999," 67.

70. Theobald, *Teaching the Commons*, 112.

71. Salamon, *Newcomers to Old Towns*, 8.

72. Edmondson, *Prairie Town*, 26; Falk, Talley, and Rankin, "Life in the Forgotten South," 64.

73. Edmondson, *Prairie Town*, 26.

74. Ibid., 27.

75. Ibid.

76. Kannapel and DeYoung, "The Rural School Problem in 1999," 67.

77. Economic Research Service, "Rural America at a Glance," 1.

78. Johnson, "Demographic Trends," 13.

79. Falk, Talley, and Rankin, "Life in the Forgotten South," 71; Hyland and Timberlake, "Mississippi Delta," 79–80; Lemann, *Promised Land*.

80. Budge, "Rural Leaders, Rural Places," 4–5; Corbett, *Learning to Leave*; Edmondson, *Prairie Town*, 81; Howley and Howley, "Poverty and School Achievement," 46; Theobald, "Forces Supporting Consolidation."

81. Haas, "Leaving Home," 8.

82. Theobald, "Forces Supporting Consolidation."

83. Budge, "Rural Leaders, Rural Places," 4; Corbett, *Learning to Leave*; Howley and Howley, "Poverty and School Achievement," 46.

84. Graham, *Schooling America*, 150–52.

85. Brewster, "Toward a Critical Agricultural Literacy," 40–41; Edmondson, *Prairie Town*, 81; Edmondson and Butler, "Teaching School in Rural America," 162; Kannapel, "Standards-Based Reform," 2; Schafft, "Economics, Community, and Rural Education," 278–80; Theobald, *Education Now*, 103; Woodrum, "State-Mandated Testing and Cultural Resistance," 7.

86. Brewster, "Toward a Critical Agricultural Literacy," 33–36; Corbett, "Wharf Talk, Home Talk, and School Talk," 119; DeYoung, Howley, and Theobald, "Cultural Contradictions of Middle Schooling," 33–34; Edmondson, *Prairie Town*, 80; Faircloth, "Re-visioning the Future of Education," 1; Woodrum, "State-Mandated Testing and Cultural Resistance," 6.

87. Woodrum, "State-Mandated Testing and Cultural Resistance," 9.

88. Corbett, *Learning to Leave*, 34; Seal and Harmon, "Realities of Rural School Reform," 123; Theobald, "Forces Supporting Consolidation."

89. Carr and Kefalas, *Hollowing Out the Middle*, 20.

90. Faircloth, "Re-visioning the Future of Education," 2.

91. Edmondson, *Prairie Town*, 91; Eppley and Corbett, "I'll See That When I Believe It," 3.

92. Edmondson, *Prairie Town*, 91.

93. Strange, "Funding Fairness for Rural Students," 14–15.

94. Eppley, "Rural Schools," 7; Monk, "Recruiting and Retaining High-Quality Teachers," 159–60.

95. Beck and Shoffstall, "How Do Rural Schools Fare," 9–10.

96. Edmondson, *Prairie Town*, 97.

97. Bard, Gardener, and Wieland, "Rural School Consolidation," 40; Howley, Johnson, and Petrie, "Consolidation of Schools and Districts," 4.

98. Bard, Gardener, and Wieland, "Rural School Consolidation," 40; DeYoung and Howley, "Political Economy of Rural School Consolidation," 70; Howley, Johnson, and Petrie, "Consolidation of Schools and Districts," 3.

99. Bard, Gardener, and Wieland, "Rural School Consolidation," 43–44; Howley, Johnson, and Petrie, "Consolidation of Schools and Districts," 8.

100. Bard, Gardener, and Wieland, "Rural School Consolidation," 42; DeYoung, Howley, and Theobald, "Cultural Contradictions of Middle Schooling," 32.

101. Howley, Johnson, and Petrie, "Consolidation of Schools and Districts," 5.

102. Nitta, Holley, and Wrobel, "Phenomenological Study of Rural School Consolidation."

103. Eyre and Finn, "Closing Costs."

104. Howley, Johnson, and Petrie, "Consolidation of Schools and Districts," 9.

105. Cecelski, *Along Freedom Road*, 57; Graham, *Schooling America*, 131–32.

106. Graham, *Schooling America*, 21; Walker, *Their Highest Potential*, 1–2.

107. Falk, *Rooted in Place*, 77–83; Graham, *Schooling America*, 131–32.

108. Cecelski, *Along Freedom Road*, 82.

109. Graham, *Schooling America*, 138–39; Stockley, *Ruled by Race*, 392.

110. Orfield and Lee, "*Brown* at 50," 16.

111. Duncan, *Worlds Apart*, 193; Hyland and Timberlake, "Mississippi Delta," 82; Reardon and Yun, "Integrating Neighborhoods, Segregating Schools," 1582.

112. Edmondson, *Prairie Town*, 81; Hamann, Wortham, and Murillo, "Education and Policy," 1.

113. Kannapel and DeYoung, "The Rural School Problem in 1999," 74–75; Miller, "Role of Rural Schools"; Schafft, "Economics, Community, and Rural Education," 281; Theobald, "Forces Supporting Consolidation"; Theobald, *Teaching the Commons*, 112.

114. Kannapel, *Standards-Based Reform*, 4–5; Theobald, *Teaching the Commons*, 132–59.

115. Pitzl, "Revitalizing Communities in New Mexico," 19, 21.

116. Miller, "Role of Rural Schools," 166; Wigginton, "Foxfire Grows Up."

117. Schafft, "Economics, Community, and Rural Education," 282.

118. Kannapel and DeYoung, "The Rural School Problem in 1999," 73; Miller, "Role of Rural Schools," 166.

119. Bauch, "School-Community Partnerships in Rural Schools," 215–16; Butler and Edmondson, "Sustaining a Rural Pennsylvania Community," 223; Pitzl, "Revitalizing Communities in New Mexico," 21.

120. Bustamante, Brown, and Irby, "Advocating for English Language Learners," 242–43.

121. Hammer et al., "Rural Teacher Recruitment and Retention Practices," 6–8; Monk, "Recruiting and Retaining High-Quality Teachers," 169.

122. Monk, "Recruiting and Retaining High-Quality Teachers," 160.

123. Hammer et al., "Rural Teacher Recruitment and Retention Practices," 13.

124. Kannapel and DeYoung, "The Rural School Problem in 1999," 74; Rao, Eady, and Edelen-Smith, "Creating Virtual Classrooms," 23–25; Seal and Harmon, "Realities of Rural School Reform," 124.

125. DeYoung and Howley, "Political Economy of Rural School Consolidation," 63.

126. Lyson, "What Does a School Mean," 133.

127. Peshkin, *Growing Up American*.

128. Howley and Howley, "Poverty and School Achievement," 40–41.

129. Orfield and Frankenberg, "The Last Have Become First," 3.

130. DeYoung and Howley, "Political Economy of Rural School Consolidation," 65, emphasis in original.

131. Schafft, "Economics, Community, and Rural Education," 275–89.

132. Paige, "No Child Left Behind," 465; Ravitch, *Great American School System*, 3.

CHAPTER THREE

1. Welty, *One Writer's Beginning*, 14.

2. Lawrence-Lightfoot, *The Good High School*, 3–26, 369–78; Lawrence-Lightfoot and Davis, *Art and Science of Portraiture*.

3. Lawrence-Lightfoot and Davis, *Art and Science of Portraiture*, 3.

4. Ibid., 9.

5. Ibid., 243.

6. Geertz, *Interpretation of Cultures*, 3–30.

7. Lawrence-Lightfoot, *The Good High School*, 6; Lawrence-Lightfoot and Davis, *Art and Science of Portraiture*, 12.

8. Tieken, "The Distance to Delight."

9. Community members of both Delight and Earle uniformly describe their locales as "rural." Depending on the official government definition used, the Earle area is only sometimes classified as rural, and its county (Crittenden) is considered metropolitan due to the presence of West Memphis and Marion (Cromartie and Bucholtz, "ERS/USDA Data—Rural Definitions"). The Delight area receives both a rural and a nonmetropolitan designation, regardless of definition.

10. Cromartie and Bucholtz, "ERS/USDA Data—Rural Definitions."

11. Gatewood, "Arkansas Delta," 4.

12. Ibid., 9.

13. Moneyhon, *Arkansas and the New South*, 5–6.

14. Arnold, "The Delta's Colonial Heritage," 58.

15. Richter and Clark County Historical Association, *Clark County Arkansas*, 7.

16. Gatewood, "Arkansas Delta," 4.

17. Roberts, "'Desolation Itself,'" 72.

18. Graves, *Town and Country*, 14–27.

19. Stockley, *Ruled by Race*, 255.

20. Gatewood, "Arkansas Delta," 3.

21. Holley, "Plantation Heritage," 252–53.

22. Gatewood, "Arkansas Delta," 22.

23. Ibid.; Hyland and Timberlake, "Mississippi Delta," 79.

24. Holley, "Plantation Heritage," 262.

25. Gatewood, "Arkansas Delta," 23–24.

26. Foti, "The River's Gifts and Curses," 41.

27. Graves, *Town and Country*, 5.

28. Moneyhon, *Arkansas and the New South*, 5.

29. Graves, *Town and Country*, 6.

30. Rural Policy Research Institute, "Demographic and Economic Profile: Arkansas," 4.

31. Graves, *Town and Country*, 34.

32. Bass and DeVries, *Transformation of Southern Politics*, 87; Gatewood, "Arkansas Delta," 19; Graves, *Town and Country*, 5; Lancaster, "'Negroes are Leaving Paragould,'" 3.

33. Gatewood, "Arkansas Delta," 15.

34. Roberts, "'Desolation Itself,'" 72.

35. Graves, *Town and Country*, 19.

36. Gatewood, "Arkansas Delta," 19.

37. Graves, *Town and Country*, 98.

38. Ibid., 99.

39. Ibid., 10–52.

40. Ibid., 54.

41. Gatewood, "Arkansas Delta," 17; Graves, *Town and Country*, 199.

42. Graves, *Town and Country*, 84.

43. Gatewood, "Arkansas Delta," 13; Graves, *Town and Country*, 33–34.

44. Graves, *Town and Country*, 110.

45. Ibid., 95.

46. Anderson, *Education of Blacks in the South*, 153.

47. Gatewood, "Arkansas Delta," 13; Hyland and Timberlake, "Mississippi Delta," 82.

48. Stockley, *Ruled by Race*, 255–71.

49. Gatewood, "Arkansas Delta," 13; Stockley, *Ruled by Race*, 399.

50. Carr, "In Southern Towns"; Nevin and Bills, *Schools That Fear Built*; Reardon and Yun, "Private School Racial Enrollments," 12; Stockley, *Ruled by Race*, 398; Walters, "Educational Access and the State," 43.

51. Stockley, *Ruled by Race*, 386.

52. Ibid., 407.

53. Ibid., 426.

54. Strange, "Funding Fairness for Rural Students," 10; Terry, "Inadequate and Inequitable," 245.

55. Ledbetter, "Fight for School Consolidation in Arkansas," 45–46; Strange, "Funding Fairness for Rural Students," 10.

56. Ledbetter, "Fight for School Consolidation in Arkansas," 45.

57. Jimerson, "Impact of Arkansas' Act 60 Consolidation," 2; Strange, "Funding Fairness for Rural Students," 10.

58. In 2011, the federal government began offering state waivers that provide increased flexibility in meeting some of the act's requirements, including the 2014 deadline; however, as of publication, the act has not been revised and reauthorized, and its core provisions remain in place.

59. Ravitch, *Great American School System*, 97–98; Rhodes, *An Education in Politics*, 1–8.

60. Johnson and Strange, "Why Rural Matters 2007," 44.

61. Rural Policy Research Institute, "Demographic and Economic Profile: Arkansas," 2, 7, 12.

62. Johnson and Strange, "Why Rural Matters 2007," 44.

63. Stockley, *Ruled by Race*, 431–60.

64. Ibid., 448.

65. Ibid., 452.

66. Jimerson, "Impact of Arkansas' Act 60 Consolidation"; Strange, "Funding Fairness for Rural Students," 11.

67. Maxwell, *Qualitative Research Design*, 88.

68. Maykut and Morehouse, *Beginning Qualitative Research*, 57.

69. Fine and Weis, "Writing the 'Wrongs' of Fieldwork," 266.

70. Alinsky, *Reveille for Radicals*, 64.

71. Maxwell, *Qualitative Research Design*, 89–90.

72. Charmaz, "Grounded Theory"; Charmaz, *Constructing Grounded Theory*.

73. Page, Samson, and Crockett, "Reporting Ethnography to Informants," 299.

74. Lawrence-Lightfoot and Davis, *Art and Science of Portraiture*, 12.

75. Milner, "Race, Culture, and Researcher Positionality," 391.

76. Hillery, "Definitions of Community," 111.

77. Thomas, Lowe, Fulkerson, and Smith, *Critical Rural Theory*, 5.

CHAPTER FOUR

1. Advocates for Community and Rural Education, "ACRE's First Rural Community Revitalization Project," 1.

2. Ibid.

3. This is a pseudonym, used to respect the children's privacy.

CHAPTER FIVE

1. Pugh, "Sketch of Earle."

2. Cleave, "Earle Public Schools."

CHAPTER SIX

1. Weber, "Class, Status, Party."

2. Anyon, "Social Class and School Knowledge"; Bowles, "Unequal Education"; Collins, "Functional and Conflict Theories"; Duncan, "Social Capital," 193; Kozol, *Savage Inequalities*; Kozol, *Shame of the Nation*.

3. Kozol, *Savage Inequalities*.

4. Oakes, *Keeping Track*, 13.

5. Anyon, "Social Class and School Knowledge."

6. Bourdieu, "Forms of Capital," 242–43; MacLeod, *Ain't No Makin' It*, 140.

7. Wells and Crain, "Perpetuation Theory," 531.

8. Anderson, *Education of Blacks in the South*, 147.

9. Ibid., 156.

10. Wells and Crain, "Perpetuation Theory," 531.

11. Nevin and Bills, *Schools That Fear Built*, 1–2; Walters, "Educational Access and the State," 43.

12. Stockley, *Ruled by Race*, 251–71.

13. Orfield, "Growth of Segregation," 10.

14. Street, *Segregated Schools*.

15. Orfield, "Growth of Segregation," 22.

16. Wells, Holme, Revilla, and Atanda, *Both Sides Now*, 221–35.

17. Stockley, *Ruled by Race*, 448–60.

18. Hanifan, "The Rural School Community Center," 130.

19. Ibid.

20. Ibid., 130–31.

21. Putnam, *Bowling Alone*, 19.

22. Coleman, "Social Capital," S102.

23. Putnam, *Bowling Alone*, 20.

24. Woolcock, "Social Capital and Economic Development," 163.

25. Putnam, *Making Democracy Work*, 173.

26. Putnam, *Bowling Alone*, 22.

27. Noguera, "Transforming Urban Schools," 199; Warren, Thompson, and Saegert, "Role of Social Capital," 8.

28. Putnam, *Bowling Alone*, 22.

29. Ibid.

30. Tate, Ladson-Billings, and Grant, "The *Brown* Decision Revisited," 34.

31. Reardon and Yun, "Integrating Neighborhoods, Segregating Schools," 1582.

32. Hyland and Timberlake, "Mississippi Delta," 82; Stockley, *Ruled by Race*, 397.

33. Wells, Holme, Revilla, and Atanda, *Both Sides Now*, 273.

34. Stockley, *Ruled by Race*, 448.

35. Duncan, *Worlds Apart*, 74; Hyland and Timberlake, "Mississippi Delta," 85.

36. Bankston and Caldas, "Majority African American Schools," 552; Borman et al., "Accountability in a Postdesegregation Era," 626; Committee on Social Science Research Evidence, "Race-Conscious Policies," 18.

37. Anyon, "Social Class and School Knowledge"; Bowles, "Unequal Education"; Collins, "Functional and Conflict Theories"; MacLeod, *Ain't No Makin' It*, 140.

38. Warren, Thompson, and Saegert, "Role of Social Capital," 11.

39. Committee on Social Science Research Evidence, "Race-Conscious Policies," 25; Wells and Crain, "Perpetuation Theory," 552.

40. Anderson, *Education of Blacks in the South*, 283; Cecelski, *Along Freedom Road*, 9; Walker, *Their Highest Potential*.

41. Putnam, *Bowling Alone*, 22.

42. Loomer, "Two Conceptions of Power"; Warren, Thompson, and Saegert, "Role of Social Capital," 9.

43. Hanifan, "The Rural School Community Center," 130.

44. Ibid.

45. Rodriguez, "Struggling to Recognize Their Existence," 439.

46. Noddings, *The Challenge to Care in Schools*.

47. Allport, *Nature of Prejudice*, 250–84; Dovidio, Gaertner, and Kawakami, "Intergroup Contact," 8; Emerson, Kimbro, and Yancey, "Contact Theory Extended," 757.

48. Dovidio, Gaertner, and Kawakami, "Intergroup Contact," 7, 8.

49. Putnam, *Bowling Alone*, 22.

50. Woolcock, "Social Capital and Economic Development," 163.

51. Coleman, "Social Capital," S102.

52. Pfeffer and Parra, "Strong Ties, Weak Ties," 254; Saegert, "Building Civic Capacity in Urban Neighborhoods," 291.

53. Wilson, "Impact of School Desegregation Programs," 151–52.

54. Allport, *Nature of Prejudice*, 281.

55. Putnam, *Making Democracy Work*, 177.

56. Duncan, "Social Capital," 90–123; Hyland and Timberlake, "Mississippi Delta," 79.

57. Gatewood, "Arkansas Delta," 14; Hyland and Timberlake, "Mississippi Delta," 79; Stockley, *Ruled by Race*, 40.

58. Duncan, "Social Capital," 91; Graves, *Town and Country*, 87; Holley, "Plantation Heritage," 238.

59. Stockley, *Ruled by Race*, xv–xxiii.

60. Gatewood, "Arkansas Delta," 19.

61. Pike County Archives and History Society, *Pike County Archives*.

62. Schafft and Brown, "Social Capital, Social Networks," 333.

63. Hero, *Racial Diversity and Social Capital*, 113.

64. Fine, *Theories of Social Capital*, 4; Schafft and Brown, "Social Capital, Social Networks," 333.

65. Warren, Thompson, and Saegert, "Role of Social Capital," 8.

66. Loomer, "Two Conceptions of Power."

67. Warren, Thompson, and Saegert, "Role of Social Capital," 6.

68. Lyson, "What Does a School Mean," 133.

69. Kannapel and DeYoung, "The Rural School Problem in 1999," 70.

70. Cecelski, *Along Freedom Road.*

71. Seal and Harmon, "Realities of Rural School Reform," 122.

72. Flora and Flora, *Rural Communities*, 6; Isserman, "Getting State Rural Policy Right," 73; Johnson, "Demographic Trends," 13.

73. Wilkinson, *Community in Rural America*, 9.

74. Duncan, *Worlds Apart.*

75. Harris and Worthen, "African Americans in Rural America," 35.

76. Russell and Tieken, "'Weaving a Tapestry That Won't Unravel,'" 135.

77. hooks, *Belonging*, 9–11.

78. Russell and Tieken, "'Weaving a Tapestry That Won't Unravel,'" 136.

79. Duncan, *Worlds Apart*, 192; Wellstone, *How the Rural Poor Got Power*, xiv.

80. Duncan, *Worlds Apart*, 193.

81. Orfield, "Growth of Segregation," 61; Orfield and Frankenberg, "The Last Have Become First," 2.

82. Vidich and Bensman, *Small Town in Mass Society*, 227.

83. Pfeffer and Parra, "Strong Ties, Weak Ties," 256.

84. Orfield, "Growth of Segregation," 61; Orfield and Frankenberg, "The Last Have Become First," 2.

85. Allport, *Nature of Prejudice*, 250–84; Dovidio, Gaertner, and Kawakami, "Intergroup Contact," 8; Emerson, Kimbro, and Yancey, "Contact Theory Extended," 757.

86. Emerson, Kimbro, and Yancey, "Contact Theory Extended," 753.

87. Wells, Holme, Revilla, and Atanda, *Both Sides Now*, 7.

88. Ibid., 16.

CHAPTER SEVEN

1. Hillery, "Definitions of Community," 118.

2. Ibid., 114–15.

3. Fowler, *Dance with Community*, 1.

4. Heller, "Return to Community," 3.

5. Cohen, *Symbolic Construction of Community.*

6. Ganz, "Leading Change," 543.

7. Bellah et al., *Habits of the Heart*, 138.

8. Wilkinson, *Community in Rural America*, 13.

9. McMillan and Chavis, "Sense of Community"; Sarason, *Psychological Sense of Community.*

10. Putnam, *Bowling Alone.*

11. Herman Schmalenbach, "Communion," in Luschen and Stone, *Herman Schmalenbach on Society and Experience*; Wilkinson, *Community in Rural America*, 16.

12. McMillan and Chavis, "Sense of Community," 9.

13. Ibid., 7.

14. Wilkinson, *Community in Rural America*, 17.

15. Bender, *Community and Social Change in America*, 8.

16. Brown and Schafft, *Rural People and Communities*, 8–11.

17. Cohen, *Symbolic Construction of Community*, 12.

18. Lamont, *Money, Morals, and Manners*, 1.

19. Cohen, *Symbolic Construction of Community*, 12–13; Lamont, *Money, Morals, and Manners*, 4; Lamont and Molnar, "Study of Boundaries," 168–69.

20. Lamont, *Money, Morals, and Manners*, 11.

21. Tajfel, "Social Identity and Intergroup Behaviour," 69.

22. Lamont and Molnar, "Study of Boundaries," 168.

23. Salamon, "From Hometown to Nontown," 5; Wilkinson, *Community in Rural America*, 41–42.

24. Cubberley, *Rural Life and Education*; Edmondson, *Prairie Town*, 63–64; Galpin, *Rural Life*; Theobald, *Teaching the Commons*, 102–4.

25. Friedland, "Who Killed Rural Sociology?," 84.

26. Gusfield, *The Community*, xv–xvi.

27. Bender, *Community and Social Change in America*, 6; Wilkinson, *Community in Rural America*, 5.

28. Wellman and Leighton, "Networks, Neighborhoods, and Communities," 367.

29. Wellman and Gulia, "Net-Surfers Don't Ride Alone."

30. Keller, *Community*, 6; Liepins, "New Energies for an Old Idea," 32; Wellman and Leighton, "Networks, Neighborhoods, and Communities," 365; Wilkinson, *Community in Rural America*, 57.

31. Falk, *Rooted in Place*, 18; Wilkinson, *Community in Rural America*, 57.

32. Tonnies, *Community and Civil Society*.

33. Heller, "Return to Community," 4; Putnam, *Bowling Alone*; Theobald, *Teaching the Commons*, 53; see chapter 2 of Fowler's *Dance with Community* for a review of these arguments.

34. Putnam, *Bowling Alone*.

35. Bellah et al., *Habits of the Heart*, 23; Theobald, *Teaching the Commons*, 31.

36. Bender, *Community and Social Change in America*, 3; Salamon, *Newcomers to Old Towns*, 11–22; Theobald, *Teaching the Commons*, 15–16.

37. Dryfoos, "Full-Service Schools"; Warren, Hong, Rubin, and Uy, "Beyond the Bake Sale," 2210.

38. Hanifan, "The Rural School Community Center"; Peshkin, *Growing Up American*; Tyack, *One Best System*, 15.

39. Hillery, "Definitions of Community," 115; Wilkinson, *Community in Rural America*, 14.

40. Keller, *Community*, 6; Wilkinson, *Community in Rural America*, 23.

41. McMillan and Chavis, "Sense of Community," 9.

42. Bellah et al., *Habits of the Heart*, 138.

43. Falk, *Rooted in Place*, 18; Wilkinson, *Community in Rural America*, 23.

44. Eyerman, *Cultural Trauma*; Eyerman, "Cultural Trauma."

45. Anderson, *Education of Blacks in the South*, 4–32; Cecelski, *Along Freedom Road*, 59–68; Walker, *Their Highest Potential*.

46. Coleman, "Social Capital," S105.

47. Lemann, *Promised Land*, 6.

48. Holley, "Plantation Heritage," 259.

49. Dawson, *Black Visions*.

50. Eyerman, *Cultural Trauma*; Eyerman, "Cultural Trauma."

51. Lamont and Molnar, "Study of Boundaries," 168.

52. Flora and Flora, *Rural Communities*, 6; Isserman, "Getting State Rural Policy Right," 73; Johnson, "Demographic Trends," 13.

53. Wilkinson, *Community in Rural America*, 57.

54. Liepins, "New Energies for an Old Idea," 32.

55. Hanifan, "The Rural School Community Center"; Tyack, *One Best System*, 17.

CHAPTER EIGHT

1. State of Arkansas, "Arkansas House of Representatives."

2. Arkansas Senate, "About the Arkansas Senate."

3. Throughout this chapter, I use the term "state" as these communities do. When I am referring only to the federal government or one of its constituent parts, I use a more precise term to reflect this reference.

4. Lamont, *Money, Morals, and Manners*, 1, 2; Lamont and Molnar, "Study of Boundaries," 168–69.

5. Arnold, Newman, Gaddy, and Dean, "A Look at the Condition," 1; Coladarci, "Improving the Yield," 1; Stern, "Condition of Education in Rural Schools," iii; Thomas, Lowe, Fulkerson, and Smith, *Critical Rural Theory*, 7–11.

6. Haas, "Leaving Home," 8; Johnson and Strange, "Why Rural Matters 2009," 25; Reynnells and John, "What Is Rural?"

7. Haas, "Leaving Home," 8–9; Howley, Theobald, and Howley, "What Rural Education Research," 5; Johnson, "Demographic Trends," 7; Thomas, Lowe, Fulkerson, and Smith, *Critical Rural Theory*, 23.

8. Edmondson, *Prairie Town*; Isserman, "Getting State Rural Policy Right"; Seal and Harmon, "Realities of Rural School Reform," 119–20; Theobald, *Teaching the Commons*, 102–4; Tyack, *One Best System*, 21–27; Wray, *Not Quite White*, 1–15.

9. Graves, *Town and Country*, 98–99.

10. Ibid., 134.

11. Silver and DeYoung, "Ideology of Rural/Appalachian Education," 52; Tyack, *One Best System*, 30.

12. Graham, "Schools," 7–50.

13. Edmondson, *Prairie Town*, 21–22; Schafft, "Economics, Community, and Rural Education," 276; Theobald, *Teaching the Commons*, 107.

14. Lamont, *Money, Morals, and Manners*, 12; Lamont and Molnar, "Study of Boundaries," 168–69.

15. Edmondson, *Prairie Town*, 63–64; Silver and DeYoung, "Ideology of Rural/Appalachian Education," 55; Theobald, *Teaching the Commons*, 103; Theobald and Wood, "Learning to Be Rural," 25; Tyack, *One Best System*, 22.

16. Hanifan, "The Rural School Community Center"; Tyack, *One Best System*, 15.

17. Cecelski, *Along Freedom Road*, 60–68; Peshkin, *Growing Up American*; Walker, *Their Highest Potential*, 213–14.

18. Lyson, "What Does a School Mean."

19. DeYoung and Howley, "Political Economy of Rural School Consolidation," 69; Tyack, *One Best System*, 21.

20. Tyack, *One Best System*, 21.

21. Kannapel and DeYoung, "The Rural School Problem in 1999," 67.

22. Tyack, *One Best System*, 14.

23. Ibid., 21.

24. DeYoung, *Life and Death of a Rural American High School*, 295–98; Kannapel and DeYoung, "The Rural School Problem in 1999," 67; Tyack, *One Best System*, 23–29.

25. Tyack, *One Best System*, 39–59.

26. Edmondson, *Prairie Town*, 81–91; Theobald, *Teaching the Commons*, 102–8; Anderson, *Education of Blacks in the South*, 82; Graham, *Schooling America*.

27. Bryant, "Dismantling Rural Stereotypes," 56.

28. Eppley, "Rural Schools."

29. Corbett, *Learning to Leave*, 10; DeYoung and Howley, "Political Economy of Rural School Consolidation," 68–70; Edmondson, *Prairie Town*, 80–82.

30. Budge, "Rural Leaders, Rural Places," 4–5; Corbett, *Learning to Leave*, 8; Hektner, "When Moving Up Implies Moving Out," 3.

31. Carr and Kefalas, *Hollowing Out the Middle*.

32. Cecelski, *Along Freedom Road*, 60–68; Tyack, *One Best System*, 17.

33. Woodrum, "State-Mandated Testing and Cultural Resistance," 2.

34. Hanifan, "The Rural School Community Center."

35. Cohen, *Symbolic Construction of Community*.

CHAPTER NINE

1. Assessment Coordination Department, "2010 Millage Report."

2. Jimerson, "Impact of Arkansas' Act 60 Consolidation," 2; Strange, "Funding Fairness for Rural Students," 10.

3. Howley, Johnson, and Petrie, "Consolidation of Schools and Districts," 8–9; Strange, "Funding Fairness for Rural Students," 11; Young and Green, "School System Consolidation," 6.

4. Elder and Conger, *Children of the Land*, 186; Lee and Smith, "Effects of High School Restructuring," 157; Lee and Smith, *Restructuring High Schools*, 257.

5. Bickel and Howley, "Influence of Scale on School Performance," 22; Howley, "Compounding Disadvantage," 28.

6. Graham, *Schooling America*, 27–35; Tyack, *One Best System*, 21–30.

7. Strange, "Funding Fairness for Rural Students," 11.

8. Ravitch, *Great American School System*, 97–98.

9. Bush, "President Signs Landmark Bill."

10. Rhodes, *An Education in Politics*, 159–82.

11. Darling-Hammond, "From 'Separate but Equal,'" 654.

12. Rhodes, *An Education in Politics*, 178–82.

13. Croninger and Lee, "Social Capital"; Elder and Conger, *Children of the Land*, 244–46.

14. Allport, *Nature of Prejudice*, 250–54; Dovidio, Gaertner, and Kawakami, "Intergroup Contact," 8; Emerson, Kimbro, and Yancey, "Contact Theory Extended," 757.

15. Schmitt et al., "Parental Employment," 750.

16. Henderson and Mapp, "A New Wave of Evidence," 24.

17. Eccles et al., "Development During Adolescence," 92.

18. What Works Clearinghouse, "Helping Students Navigate the Path," 5.

19. Dillard, "Leading with Her Life"; Stockley, *Ruled by Race*, 442–43.

20. Schafft, "Economics, Community, and Rural Education," 286.

21. Ritter, "Education Reform in Arkansas," 36, 40–41.

22. Darling-Hammond, "No Child Left Behind," 646; Paige, "No Child Left Behind," 465–66; Rhodes, *An Education in Politics*, 154.

23. Silver and DeYoung, "Ideology of Rural/Appalachian Education"; Tyack, *One Best System*.

24. Thomas, Lowe, Fulkerson, and Smith, *Critical Rural Theory*, 178.

25. DeYoung and Howley, "Political Economy of Rural School Consolidation," 63.

26. Ravitch, *Great American School System*, 204; Save Our Schools, "Save Our Schools."

27. Save Our Schools, "Save Our Schools."

28. "Save Our Schools Rally."

29. Ravitch, *Great American School System*, 99.

30. Paige, "No Child Left Behind"; Santos, "Mayor Is Criticized for Comments"; Turque and Anderson, "Former D.C. Schools Chancellor Michelle Rhee."

31. Santos, "Mayor Is Criticized for Comments."

32. Paige, "No Child Left Behind," 466.

33. Dryfoos, "Full-Service Schools," 18–19; Shirley, *Community Organizing for Urban School Reform*, 76; Warren, Hong, Rubin, and Uy, "Beyond the Bake Sale," 2210; Warren, Mapp, and the Community Organizing and School Reform Project, *A Match on Dry Grass*, 3–4.

34. Eaton, *The Children in Room E4*, 343–54; Orfield and Lee, "*Brown* at 50," 40–41; Wells, Holme, Revilla, and Atanda, *Both Sides Now*, 5–11.

35. Putnam, *Bowling Alone*, 404–5.

36. Graham, *Schooling America*, 1, 2; Larabee, "Public Goods, Private Goods," 31.

Bibliography

Adams, David Wallace. *Education for Extinction: American Indians and the Boarding School Experience 1875–1928*. Lawrence: University Press of Kansas, 1995.

Advocates for Community and Rural Education. "Delight Begins ACRE's First Rural Community Revitalization Project." *Advocates for Community and Rural Education Newsletter*, October 12, 2008, 2–3.

Alinsky, Saul. *Reveille for Radicals*. Vintage ed. New York: Vintage Books, 1989.

Allport, G. W. *The Nature of Prejudice*. Cambridge, MA: Addison-Wesley, 1954.

Anderson, James D. *The Education of Blacks in the South, 1860–1935*. Chapel Hill: University of North Carolina Press, 1988.

Anyon, Jean. "Social Class and School Knowledge." *Curriculum Inquiry* 11, no. 1 (1981): 3–41.

Arkansas Senate. "About the Arkansas Senate." http://www.arkansas.gov/senate/about_senate.html (January 22, 2011).

Arnold, Michael L., John H. Newman, Barbara B. Gaddy, and Ceri B. Dean. "A Look at the Condition of Rural Educational Research: Setting a Direction for Future Research." *Journal of Research in Rural Education* 20, no. 6 (2005).

Arnold, Morris S. "The Delta's Colonial Heritage." In *The Arkansas Delta: Land of Paradox*, edited by Jeannie Whayne and Willard B. Gatewood, 58–69. Fayetteville: University of Arkansas Press, 1993.

Assessment Coordination Department. "2010 Millage Report." Little Rock, AR: State of Arkansas, 2011.

Bankston, Carl, and Stephen J. Caldas. "Majority African American Schools and Social Injustice: The Influence of De Facto Segregation on Academic Achievement." *Social Forces* 75, no. 2 (1996): 535–55.

Bard, Joe, Clark Gardener, and Regi Wieland. "National Rural Education Association Report: Rural School Consolidation: History, Research Summary, Conclusions, and Recommendations." *The Rural Educator* 27, no. 2 (Winter 2006): 40–48.

Bass, Jack, and Walter DeVries. *The Transformation of Southern Politics: Social Change and Political Consequence since 1945*. New York: Basic Books, 1976.

Bauch, Patricia. "School-Community Partnerships in Rural Schools: Leadership, Renewal, and Sense of Place." *Peabody Journal of Education* 76, no. 2 (2001): 204–21.

Beck, Frank, and Grant W. Shoffstall. "How Do Rural Schools Fare under a High Stakes Testing Regime?" *Journal of Research in Rural Education* 20, no. 14 (2005).

Bellah, Robert N., Richard Madsen, William M. Sullivan, Ann Swidler, and Steven M. Tipton. *Habits of the Heart: Individualism and Commitment in American Life.* 2nd ed. Berkeley: University of California Press, 1996.

Bender, Thomas. *Community and Social Change in America.* New Brunswick, NJ: Rutgers University Press, 1978.

Bickel, Robert, and Craig Howley. "The Influence of Scale on School Performance: A Multilevel Extension of the Matthew Principle." *Education Policy Analysis* 8, no. 22 (2000).

Borman, Kathryn M., Tamela McNulty Eitle, Deanna Michael, David J. Eitle, Reginald Lee, Larry Johnson, Deidre Cobb-Roberts, Sherman Dorn, and Barbara Shircliffe. "Accountability in a Postdesegregation Era: The Continuing Significance of Racial Segregation in Florida's Schools." *American Educational Research Journal* 41, no. 3 (Fall 2004): 605–34.

Bourdieu, Pierre. "The Forms of Capital." In *Handbook of Theory and Research for the Sociology of Education*, edited by John G. Richardson, 241–58. New York: Greenwood Press, 1986.

Bowles, Samuel. "Unequal Education and the Reproduction of the Social Division of Labor." In *Power and Ideology in Education*, edited by Jerome Karabel and A. H. Halsey, 137–53. New York: Oxford University Press, 1977.

Brewster, Cori. "Toward a Critical Agricultural Literacy." In *Reclaiming the Rural: Essays on Literacy, Rhetoric, and Pedagogy*, edited by Kim Donehower, Charlotte Hogg, and Eileen E. Schell, 34–51. Carbondale: Southern Illinois University Press, 2012.

Brizuela, Barbara M., Julie Pearson Stewart, Romina G. Carrillo, and Jennifer Garvey Berger, eds. *Acts of Inquiry in Qualitative Research.* Cambridge: Harvard Educational Review, 2000.

Brown, David L., and Kai A. Schafft. *Rural People and Communities in the 21st Century: Resilience and Transformation.* Malden, MA: Polity Press, 2011.

Bryant, James A. "Dismantling Rural Stereotypes." *Closing Opportunity Gaps* 68, no. 3 (November 2010): 54–58.

Budge, Kathleen. "Rural Leaders, Rural Places: Problem, Privilege, and Possibility." *Journal of Research in Rural Education* 21, no. 13 (2006): 1–10.

Bush, George W. "President Signs Landmark No Child Left Behind Education Bill." http://georgewbush-whitehouse.archives.gov/news/releases/2002/01/20020108-1.html (December 1, 2013).

Bustamante, Rebecca M., Genevieve Brown, and Beverly J. Irby. "Advocating for English Language Learners: U.S. Teacher Leadership in Rural Texas Schools." In *Rural Education for the Twenty-First Century: Identity, Place, and Community in a Globalizing World*, edited by Kai A. Schafft and Alecia Youngblood Jackson, 232–52. University Park: Pennsylvania State University Press, 2010.

Butchart, Ronald E. *Schooling the Freed People: Teaching, Learning, and the Struggle for Black Freedom, 1861–1876.* Chapel Hill: University of North Carolina Press, 2010.

Butler, Thomas, and Jacqueline Edmondson. "Sustaining a Rural Pennsylvania Community: Negotiating Rural Literacies and Sustainability." In *Reclaiming the Rural: Essays on Literacy, Rhetoric, and Pedagogy*, edited by Kim Donehower, Charlotte Hogg, and Eileen E. Schell, 223–37. Carbondale: Southern Illinois University Press, 2012.

Carr, Patricia J., and Maria J. Kefalas. *Hollowing Out the Middle: The Rural Brain Drain and What It Means for America*. Boston: Beacon Press, 2009.

Carr, Sarah. "In Southern Towns, 'Segregation Academies' Are Still Going Strong." *The Atlantic*, December 12, 2012. http://www.theatlantic.com/national/archive/2012/12/in-southern-towns-segregation-academies-are-still-going-strong/266207/ (November 20, 2013).

Cecelski, David S. *Along Freedom Road: Hyde County, North Carolina, and the Fate of Black Schools in the South*. Chapel Hill: University of North Carolina Press, 1994.

Charmaz, Kathy. *Constructing Grounded Theory: A Practical Guide through Qualitative Analysis*. Thousand Oaks, CA: Sage Publications, 2006.

———. "Grounded Theory." In *Handbook of Qualitative Research*, edited by N. Denzin and Y. Lincoln, 509–35. Thousand Oaks, CA: Sage, 2000.

Cleave, O. E. Van. "The Earle Public Schools." In *Historical Record and Survey of Crittenden County, Arkansas*, edited by A. A. Weeks. Earle, AR: 1919.

Cohen, Anthony P. *The Symbolic Construction of Community*. New York: Routledge, 1985.

Coladarci, Theodore. "Improving the Yield of Rural Education Research: An Editor's Swan Song." *Journal of Research in Rural Education* 22, no. 3 (May 24, 2007): 1–9.

Coleman, James S. "Social Capital in the Creation of Human Capital." *American Journal of Sociology* 94, Supplement (1988): S95–S120.

Collins, Randall. "Functional and Conflict Theories of Educational Stratification." *American Sociological Review* 36, no. 6 (1971): 1002–19.

Committee on Social Science Research Evidence on Racial Diversity in Schools. "Race-Conscious Policies for Assigning Students to Schools: Social Science Research and the Supreme Court Cases." Edited by Robert L. Linn and Kevin G. Welner. Washington, DC: National Academy of Education, 2007.

Corbett, Michael. *Learning to Leave: The Irony of Schooling in a Coastal Community*. Halifax: Fernwood Publishing, 2007.

———. "Wharf Talk, Home Talk, and School Talk: The Politics of Language in a Coastal Community." In *Rural Education for the Twenty-First Century: Identity, Place, and Community in a Globalizing World*, edited by Kai A. Schafft and Alecia Youngblood Jackson, 115–31. University Park: Pennsylvania State University Press, 2010.

Cromartie, John, and Shawn Bucholtz. "Defining the 'Rural' in Rural America." Economic Research Service, http://www.ers.usda.gov/AmberWaves/June08/Features/RuralAmerica.htm (August 1, 2010).

———. "ERS/USDA Data—Rural Definitions: State-Level Maps: Arkansas." United States Department of Agriculture, http://www.ers.usda.gov/data/ruraldefinitions/AR.pdf (February 19, 2011).

Croninger, Robert G., and Valerie E. Lee. "Social Capital and Dropping out of High School: Benefits to at-Risk Students of Teachers' Support and Guidance." *Teachers College Record* 103, no. 4 (2001): 548–81.

Cubberley, Ellwood P. *Rural Life and Education: A Study of the Rural-School Problem as a Phase of the Rural-Life Problem.* Cambridge, MA: Riverside Press, 1914.

Darling-Hammond, Linda. "From 'Separate but Equal' to 'No Child Left Behind': The Collision of New Standards and Old Inequalities." In *Many Children Left Behind: How the No Child Left Behind Act Is Damaging Our Children and Our Schools,* edited by Deborah Meier and George Wood, 3–32. Boston: Beacon Press, 2004.

———. "No Child Left Behind and High School Reform." *Harvard Educational Review* 76, no. 4 (Winter 2006): 642–67.

Dawson, Michael C. *Black Visions: The Roots of Contemporary African American Political Ideologies.* Chicago: University of Chicago Press, 2001.

DeYoung, Alan. *The Life and Death of a Rural American High School: Farewell Little Kanawha.* New York: Garland Publishing, 1995.

DeYoung, Alan, and Craig Howley. "The Political Economy of Rural School Consolidation." *Peabody Journal of Education* 67, no. 4 (Summer 1990): 63–89.

DeYoung, Alan, Craig Howley, and Paul Theobald. "The Cultural Contradictions of Middle Schooling for Rural Community Survival." *Journal of Research in Rural Education* 11, no. 1 (Spring 1995): 24–35.

Dillard, Cynthia B. "Leading with Her Life: An African American Feminist (Re)interpretation of Leadership for an Urban High School Principal." *Educational Administration Quarterly* 31, no. 4 (1995): 539–63.

Dovidio, John F., Samuel L. Gaertner, and Kerry Kawakami. "Intergroup Contact: The Past, Present, and the Future." *Group Processes & Intergroup Relations* 6, no. 1 (2003): 5–21.

Dryfoos, Joy G. "Full-Service Schools." *Educational Leadership* 53, no. 7 (April 1996): 18–23.

Duncan, Cynthia M. "Social Capital in America's Poor Rural Communities." In *Social Capital and Poor Communities,* edited by Susan Saegert, J. Phillip Thompson, and Mark R. Warren. Ford Foundation Series on Asset Building. New York: Russell Sage Foundation, 2001.

———. *Worlds Apart: Why Poverty Persists in Rural America.* New Haven, CT: Yale University Press, 1999.

Eaton, Susan. *The Children in Room E4: American Education on Trial.* Chapel Hill, NC: Algonquin Books of Chapel Hill, 2007.

Eccles, Jacquelynne S., Carol Midgley, Allan Wigfield, Christy Miller Buchanan, David Reuman, Constance Flanagan, and Douglas Mac Iver. "Development During Adolescence: The Impact of Stage-Environment Fit on Young Adolescents' Experiences in Schools and in Families." *American Psychologist* 48, no. 2 (February 1993): 90–101.

Economic Research Service. "Rural America at a Glance: 2009 Edition." United States Department of Agriculture, http://www.ers.usda.gov/publications/eib-economic-information-bulletin/eib59.aspx#.U2WB3y_95IY (May 2, 2014).

———. "Rural Hispanics at a Glance." United States Department of Agriculture, http://www.ers.usda.gov/publications/eib-economic-information-bulletin/eib8.aspx#.U2WCOS_95IY (May 2, 2014).

Edmondson, Jacqueline. *Prairie Town: Redefining Rural Life in the Age of Globalization*. Lanham, MD: Rowman & Littlefield Publishers, 2003.

Edmondson, Jacqueline, and Thomas Butler. "Teaching School in Rural America: Toward an Educated Hope." In *Rural Education for the Twenty-First Century: Identity, Place, and Community in a Globalizing World*, edited by Kai A. Schafft and Alecia Youngblood Jackson, 150–72. University Park: Pennsylvania State University Press, 2010.

Elder, Glen H., and Rand D. Conger. *Children of the Land: Adversity and Success in Rural America*. Chicago: University of Chicago Press, 2000.

Emerson, Michael O., Rachel Tolbert Kimbro, and George Yancey. "Contact Theory Extended: The Effects of Prior Racial Contact on Current Social Ties." *Social Science Quarterly* 83, no. 3 (2002): 745–61.

Eppley, Karen. "Rural Schools and the Highly Qualified Teacher Provision of No Child Left Behind: A Critical Policy Analysis." *Journal of Research in Rural Education* 24, no. 4 (2009): 1–11.

Eppley, Karen, and Michael Corbett. "I'll See That When I Believe It: A Dialogue on Epistemological Difference and Rural Literacies." *Journal of Research in Rural Education* 27, no. 1 (2012): 1–9.

Eyerman, Ron. *Cultural Trauma: Slavery and the Formation of African American Identity*. Cambridge Cultural Social Studies. Edited by Jeffrey C. Alexander and Steven Seidman. Cambridge, UK: Cambridge University Press, 2002.

———. "Cultural Trauma: Slavery and the Formation of the African American Identity." In *Cultural Trauma and Collective Identity*, edited by Jeffrey C. Alexander, 60–111. Berkeley: University of California Press, 2004.

Eyre, Eric, and Scott Finn. "Closing Costs: School Consolidation in West Virginia." *Charleston Gazette*, August 25 and 30; September 8, 12, 24, and 29; October 3 and 6, 2002.

Faircloth, Susan C. "Re-visioning the Future of Education for Native Youth in Rural Schools and Communities." *Journal of Research in Rural Education* 24, no. 9 (2009): 1–4.

Falk, William W. *Rooted in Place: Family and Belonging in a Southern Black Community*. New Brunswick, NJ: Rutgers University Press, 2004.

Falk, William W., Clarence R. Talley, and Bruce H. Rankin. "Life in the Forgotten South: The Black Belt." In *Forgotten Places: Uneven Development in Rural America*, edited by Thomas A. Lyson and William W. Falk, 53–75. Lawrence: University of Kansas Press, 1993.

Fine, Ben. *Theories of Social Capital: Researchers Behaving Badly*. London: Pluto Press, 2010.

Fine, Michelle, and Lois Weis. "Writing the 'Wrongs' of Fieldwork: Confronting Our Own Research/Writing Dilemmas in Urban Ethnography." *Qualitative Inquiry* 2, no. 3 (1996): 251–74.

Flora, Cornelia Butler, and Jan L. Flora. *Rural Communities: Legacy and Change.* 3rd ed. Boulder, CO: Westview Press, 2008.

Foti, Thomas. "The River's Gifts and Curses." In *The Arkansas Delta: Land of Paradox*, edited by Jeannie Whayne and Willard B. Gatewood, 30–57. Fayetteville: University of Arkansas Press, 1993.

Fowler, Robert Booth. *The Dance with Community: The Contemporary Debate in American Political Thought.* Lawrence: University Press of Kansas, 1991.

Friedland, William H. "Who Killed Rural Sociology? A Case Study in the Political Economy of Knowledge Production." *International Journal of Sociology of Agriculture and Food* 17, no. 1 (2010): 72–88.

Galpin, Charles Josiah. *Rural Life.* New York: The Century Company, 1918.

Ganz, Marshall. "Leading Change: Leadership, Organization, and Social Movements." In *Handbook of Leadership Theory and Practice*, edited by Nitin Nohria and Rakesh Khurana, 527–68. Cambridge, MA: Harvard Business School Press, 2010.

Gatewood, Willard B. "The Arkansas Delta: The Deepest of the Deep South." In *The Arkansas Delta: Land of Paradox*, edited by Jeannie Whayne and Willard B. Gatewood, 3–29. Fayetteville: University of Arkansas Press, 1993.

Geertz, Clifford. *The Interpretation of Cultures: Selected Essays.* New York City: Basic Books, 1973.

Graham, Patricia Albjerg. *Schooling America: How the Public Schools Meet the Nation's Changing Needs.* New York: Oxford University Press, 2005.

———. "Schools: Cacophony About Practice, Silence About Purpose." *Daedalus* 113, no. 4 (1984): 27–57.

Graves, John William. *Town and Country: Race Relations in an Urban-Rural Context, Arkansas, 1865–1905.* Fayetteville: University of Arkansas Press, 1990.

Gusfield, Joseph R. *The Community: A Critical Response.* New York: Harper Colophon, 1975.

Haas, Toni. "Leaving Home: Circumstances Afflicting Rural America During the Last Decade and Their Impact on Public Education." *Peabody Journal of Education* 67, no. 4 (Summer 1990): 7–28.

Hamann, Edmund T., Stanton Wortham, and Enrique G. Murillo Jr. "Education and Policy in the New Latino Diaspora." In *Education in the New Latino Diaspora: Policy and the Politics of Identity*, edited by Stanton Wortham, Enrique G. Murillo Jr., and Edmund T. Hamann, 1–12. Westport, CT: Ablex Publishing, 2002.

Hamilton, Lawrence C., Leslie R. Hamilton, Cynthia M. Duncan, and Chris R. Colocousis. "Place Matters: Challenges and Opportunities in Four Rural Americas." In *Reports on Rural America*, vol. 1, no. 4. Durham, NH: Carsey Institute, University of New Hampshire, 2008.

Hammer, Patricia Cahape, Georgia Hughes, Carla McClure, Cynthia Reeves, and Dawn Salgado. "Rural Teacher Recruitment and Retention Practices: A

Review of the Research Literature, National Survey of Rural Superintendents, and Case Studies of Programs in Virginia." Charleston, WV: Appalachia Educational Laboratory at Edvantia, 2005.

Hanifan, L. J. "The Rural School Community Center." *Annals of the American Academy of Political and Social Science* 67, New Possibilities in Education (September 1916): 130–38.

Harris, Rosalind P., and Dreamal Worthen. "African Americans in Rural America." In *Challenges for Rural America in the Twenty-First Century*, edited by David L. Brown and Louis E. Swanson. University Park: Pennsylvania State University Press, 2003.

Hektner, Joel M. "When Moving Up Implies Moving Out: Rural Adolescent Conflict in the Transition to Adulthood." *Journal of Research in Rural Education* 11, no. 1 (Spring 1995): 3–14.

Heller, Kenneth. "The Return to Community." *American Journal of Community Psychology* 17, no. 1 (1989): 1–15.

Henderson, Anne T., and Karen L. Mapp. "A New Wave of Evidence: The Impact of School, Family, and Community Connections on Student Achievement." Austin, TX: National Center for Family and Community Partnerships, 2002.

Hero, Rodney. *Racial Diversity and Social Capital: Equality and Community in America*. New York: Cambridge University Press, 2007.

Hillery, George A. "Definitions of Community: Areas of Agreement." *Rural Sociology* 20, no. 2 (1955): 111–23.

Holley, Donald. "The Plantation Heritage: Agriculture in the Arkansas Delta." In *The Arkansas Delta: Land of Paradox*, edited by Jeannie Whayne and Willard B. Gatewood, 238–77. Fayetteville: University of Arkansas Press, 1993.

hooks, bell. *Belonging: A Culture of Place*. New York: Routledge, 2009.

Housing Assistance Council. "Race and Ethnicity in Rural America." In *Rural Research Note*. Washington, DC: Housing Assistance Council, 2012.

Howley, Craig. "Compounding Disadvantage: The Effects of School and District Size on Student Achievement in West Virginia." *Journal of Research in Rural Education* 12, no. 1 (1996): 25–32.

Howley, Craig, and Aimee Howley. "Poverty and School Achievement in Rural Communities: A Social-Class Interpretation." In *Rural Education for the Twenty-First Century: Identity, Place, and Community in a Globalizing World*, edited by Kai A. Schafft and Alecia Youngblood Jackson, 34–50. University Park: Pennsylvania State University, 2010.

Howley, Craig, Jerry Johnson, and Jennifer Petrie. "Consolidation of Schools and Districts: What the Research Says and What It Means." Boulder, CO: National Education Policy Center, 2011.

Howley, Craig B., Paul Theobald, and Aimee Howley. "What Rural Education Research Is of Most Worth? A Reply to Arnold, Newman, Gaddy, and Dean." *Journal of Research in Rural Education* 20, no. 18 (December 31, 2005).

Hyland, Stanley, and Michael Timberlake. "The Mississippi Delta: Change or Continued Trouble." In *Forgotten Places: Uneven Development in Rural*

America, edited by Thomas A. Lyson and William W. Falk, 76–101. Lawrence: University Press of Kansas, 1993.

Isserman, Andrew M. "Getting State Rural Policy Right: Definitions, Growth, and Program Eligibility." *Journal of Regional Analysis and Policy* 37, no. 1 (2007): 72–79.

Jimerson, Lorna. "The Impact of Arkansas' Act 60 Consolidation on African American School Leadership and Racial Composition of School Districts." Washington, DC: Rural School and Community Trust, 2005.

Johnson, Jerry, and Marty Strange. "Why Rural Matters 2007: The Realities of Rural Education Growth." Washington, DC: Rural School and Community Trust, 2007.

——. "Why Rural Matters 2009: State and Regional Challenges and Opportunities." Washington, DC: Rural School and Community Trust, 2009.

Johnson, Kenneth. "Demographic Trends in Rural and Small Town America." In Reports on Rural America, vol. 1, no. 1. Durham, NH: Carsey Institute, University of New Hampshire, 2006.

——. "Rural Demographic Change in the New Century: Slower Growth, Increased Diversity." Issue Brief no. 44 (Winter 2012). Durham, NH: Carsey Institute, University of New Hampshire, 2012.

——. "Unpredictable Directions of Rural Population Growth and Migration." In *Challenges for Rural America in the Twenty-First Century*, edited by David L. Brown and Louis E. Swanson, 19–31. University Park: Pennsylvania State University Press, 2003.

Johnson, Walter. *River of Dark Dreams: Slavery and Empire in the Cotton Kingdom*. Cambridge, MA: Belknap Press, 2013.

Kannapel, Patricia. "Standards-Based Reform and Rural School Improvement: Similarities, Differences, Prospects for the Future." Charleston, WV: Office of Educational Research and Improvement, 2000.

Kannapel, Patricia, and Alan DeYoung. "The Rural School Problem in 1999: A Review and Critique of the Literature." *Journal of Research in Rural Education* 15, no. 2 (Fall 1999): 67–79.

Keller, Suzanne. *Community: Pursuing the Dream, Living the Reality*. Princeton, NJ: Princeton University Press, 2003.

Kozol, Jonathan. *Savage Inequalities: Children in America's Schools*. New York: HarperPerennial, 1991.

——. *Shame of the Nation: The Restoration of Apartheid Schooling in America*. New York: Crown Publishers, 2005.

Lamont, Michele. *Money, Morals, and Manners: The Culture of the French and the American Upper-Middle Class*. Chicago: University of Chicago Press, 1992.

Lamont, Michele, and Virag Molnar. "The Study of Boundaries in the Social Sciences." In *Annual Review of Sociology*, 167–95. Annual Reviews, 2002.

Lancaster, Guy. " 'Negroes Are Leaving Paragould by the Hundreds': Racial Cleansing in a Northeast Arkansas Railroad Town, 1880–1920s." *Arkansas Review: A Journal of Delta Studies* 41, no. 1 (April 2010): 3–15.

Larabee, David. "Public Goods, Private Goods: The American Struggle over Educational Goals." *American Educational Research Journal* 34, no. 1 (1997): 39–81.

Lawrence-Lightfoot, Sara. *The Good High School: Portraits of Character and Culture.* New York: Basic Books, 1983.

Lawrence-Lightfoot, Sara, and Jessica Hoffman Davis. *The Art and Science of Portraiture.* San Francisco: Jossey-Bass Publishers, 1997.

Ledbetter, Calvin R. "The Fight for School Consolidation in Arkansas, 1946–1948." *Arkansas Historical Quarterly* 65, no. 1 (Spring 2006): 45–57.

Lee, Valerie E., and Julia B. Smith. "Effects of High School Restructuring and Size on Early Gains in Achievement and Engagement." *Sociology of Education* 68 (October 1995): 241–70.

———. *Restructuring High Schools for Equity and Excellence.* New York: Teachers College Press, 2001.

Lemann, Nicholas. *The Promised Land: The Great Black Migration and How It Changed America.* New York: Vintage Books, 1991.

Liepins, Ruth. "New Energies for an Old Idea: Reworking Approaches to 'Community' in Contemporary Rural Studies." *Journal of Rural Studies* 16 (2000): 28–35.

Loomer, Bernard M. "Two Conceptions of Power." *Criterion* 15, no. 1 (Winter 1976): 11–29.

Luschen, Gunther, and Gregory P. Stone, eds. *Herman Schmalenbach on Society and Experience.* Chicago: University of Chicago Press, 1977.

Lyson, Thomas A. "What Does a School Mean to a Community? Assessing the Social and Economic Benefits of Schools to Rural Villages in New York." *Journal of Research in Rural Education* 17 (2002): 131–37.

MacLeod, James. *Ain't No Makin' It: Aspirations and Attainment in a Low-Income Neighborhood.* Boulder, CO: Westview Press, 2004.

Maxwell, Joseph A. *Qualitative Research Design: An Interactive Approach.* 2nd ed. Thousand Oaks, CA: Sage Publications, 2005.

Maykut, Pamela, and Richard Morehouse. *Beginning Qualitative Research: A Philosophic and Practical Guide.* Philadelphia, PA: RoutledgeFalmer, 1994.

McMillan, David W., and David M. Chavis. "Sense of Community: A Definition and Theory." *Journal of Community Psychology* 14 (January 1986): 6–23.

Miller, Bruce A. "The Role of Rural Schools in Community Development: Policy Issues and Implications." *Journal of Research in Rural Education* 11, no. 3 (Winter 1995): 163–72.

Mills, C. Wright. *The Sociological Imagination.* New York: Oxford University Press, 1959.

Milner, H. Richard. "Race, Culture, and Researcher Positionality: Working through Dangers Seen, Unseen, and Unforeseen." *Educational Researcher* 36, no. 7 (October 2007): 388–400.

Moneyhon, Carl H. *Arkansas and the New South 1874–1929.* Fayetteville: University of Arkansas Press, 1997.

Monk, David H. "Recruiting and Retaining High-Quality Teachers in Rural Areas." *Future of Children* 17, no. 1 (Spring 2007): 155–74.

Nevin, David, and Robert E. Bills. *The Schools That Fear Built: Segregationist Academies in the South*. Washington, DC: Acropolis Books, 1976.

Nitta, Keith A., Marc J. Holley, and Sharon L. Wrobel. "A Phenomenological Study of Rural School Consolidation." *Journal of Research in Rural Education* 25, no. 2 (2010): 1–19.

Noddings, Nel. *The Challenge to Care in Schools: An Alternative Approach to Education*. New York: Teachers College Press, 1992.

Noguera, Pedro. "Transforming Urban Schools through Investments in the Social Capital of Parents." In *Social Capital and Poor Communities*, edited by Susan Saegert, J. Philip Thompson, and Mark R. Warren. New York: Russell Sage Foundation, 2001.

Oakes, Jeannie. *Keeping Track: How Schools Structure Inequality*. New Haven, CT: Yale University Press, 1985.

Oakes, Jeannie, and John Rogers. *Learning Power: Organizing for Education and Justice*. New York: Teachers College Press, 2006.

Orfield, Gary. "The Growth of Segregation: African Americans, Latinos, and Unequal Education." In *Dismantling Desegregation*, edited by Gary Orfield, 53–71. New York: New Press, 1996.

Orfield, Gary, and Erica Frankenberg. "The Last Have Become First: Rural and Small Town America Lead the Way on Desegregation." Los Angeles: The Civil Rights Project, 2008.

Orfield, Gary, and Chungmei Lee. "*Brown* at 50: King's Dream or Plessy's Nightmare?" Cambridge, MA: The Civil Rights Project at Harvard University, 2004.

Page, Reba N., Yvette J. Samson, and Michele D. Crockett. "Reporting Ethnography to Informants." *Harvard Educational Review* 68, no. 3 (1998): 299–333.

Paige, Rod. "No Child Left Behind: The Ongoing Movement for Public Education Reform." *Harvard Educational Review* 76, no. 4 (Winter 2006): 461–73.

Perry, Theresa. "Freedom for Literacy and Literacy for Freedom: The African American Philosophy of Education." In *Young, Gifted, and Black: Promoting High Achievement among African American Students*, 11–51. Boston: Beacon Press, 2003.

Peshkin, Alan. *Growing Up American: Schooling and the Survival of Community*. Chicago: University of Chicago Press, 1978.

Pfeffer, Max J., and Pilar A. Parra. "Strong Ties, Weak Ties, and Human Capital: Latino Immigrant Employment Outside the Enclave." *Rural Sociology* 74, no. 2 (2009): 241–69.

Pike County Archives and History Society. *Pike County Archives: A Look at the Past*. Murfreesboro, AR: Pike County Archives and History Society, 1995.

Pitzl, Jerry. "Revitalizing Communities in New Mexico." *Phi Delta Kappan* 92, no. 6 (March 2011): 16–21.

Pugh, J. R. "Sketch of Earle." In *Historical Record and Survey of Crittenden County, Arkansas*, edited by A. A. Weeks. Earle, AR: 1919.

Putnam, Robert D. *Bowling Alone: The Collapse and Renewal of American Community*. New York: Simon & Schuster, 2000.

———. *Making Democracy Work: Civic Traditions in Modern Italy*. Princeton, NJ: Princeton University Press, 1993.

Rao, Kavita, Michelle Eady, and Patricia Edelen-Smith. "Creating Virtual Classrooms for Rural and Remote Communities." *Phi Delta Kappan* 92, no. 6 (March 2011): 22–27.

Ravitch, Diane. *The Death and Life of the Great American School System: How Testing and Choice Are Undermining Education*. New York: Basic Books, 2010.

Reardon, Sean, and John T. Yun. "Integrating Neighborhoods, Segregating Schools: The Retreat from School Desegregation in the South, 1990–2000." *North Carolina Law Review* 81, no. 4 (2003): 1563–96.

Reardon, Sean F., and John T. Yun. "Private School Racial Enrollments and Segregation." Cambridge, MA: The Civil Rights Project, 2002.

"Report on Rural Schools: Conclusions of a Committee of the National Education Association." *New York Times*, June 28, 1896.

Reynnells, Louise, and Patricia LaCaille John. "What Is Rural?" Rural Information Center, http://www.nal.usda.gov/ric/ricpubs/what_is_rural.shtml (October 16, 2013).

Rhodes, Jesse H. *An Education in Politics: The Origin and Evolution of No Child Left Behind*. Ithaca, NY: Cornell University Press, 2012.

Richter, Wendy, and Clark County Historical Association, eds. *Clark County Arkansas: Past and Present*. Walsworth Publishing Company, 1992.

Ritter, Gary W. "Education Reform in Arkansas: Past and Present." In *Reforming Education in Arkansas*, edited by Koret Task Force, 27–42. Stanford, CA: Hoover Institution, 2005.

Roberts, Bobby. "'Desolation Itself': The Impact of Civil War." In *The Arkansas Delta: Land of Paradox*, edited by Jeannie Whayne and Willard B. Gatewood, 70–97. Fayetteville: University of Arkansas Press, 1993.

Rodriguez, Louie. "Struggling to Recognize Their Existence: Examining Student-Adult Relationships in Urban High School Context." *Urban Review* 40, no. 4 (November 2008): 436–53.

Rural Policy Research Institute. "Demographic and Economic Profile: Arkansas." Edited by Truman School of Public Affairs. Columbia, MO: Rural Policy Research Institute, 2006.

Russell, Kenneth, and Mara Casey Tieken. "'Weaving a Tapestry That Won't Unravel': The Transformation of Education in the Mississippi Delta." In *A Match on Dry Grass: Community Organizing as a Catalyst for School Reform*, edited by Mark R. Warren, Karen L. Mapp, and the Community Organizing and School Reform Project. New York: Oxford University Press, 2011.

Saegert, Susan. "Building Civic Capacity in Urban Neighborhoods: An Empirically Grounded Anatomy." *Journal of Urban Affairs* 28, no. 3 (2006): 275–94.

Salamon, Sonya. "From Hometown to Nontown: Rural Community Effects of Suburbanization." *Rural Sociology* 68, no. 1 (2003): 1–24.

———. *Newcomers to Old Towns: Suburbanization of the Heartland*. Chicago: University of Chicago Press, 2003.

Santos, Fernanda. "Mayor Is Criticized for Comments on Parents at Poor Schools." *New York Times*, May 20, 2011. http://cityroom.blogs.nytimes .com/2011/05/20/mayor-is-criticized-for-comments-on-parents-at-poor-schools/ (March 13, 2013).

Sarason, Seymour. *The Psychological Sense of Community: Prospects for a Community Psychology*. San Francisco: Jossey-Bass, 1974.

Save Our Schools. "Save Our Schools: On the March to Save and Transform Public Education." http://www.saveourschoolsmarch.com (July 30, 2013).

"Save Our Schools Rally Kicks Off in D.C., Teachers Invited to Meet with Arne Duncan." *Huffpost Education*, July 28, 2011. http://www.huffingtonpost .com/2011/07/28/save-our-schools-march-ki_n_912061.html (July 30, 2013).

Schafft, Kai A. "Conclusion: Economics, Community, and Rural Education: Rethinking the Nature of Accountability in the Twenty-First Century." In *Rural Education for the Twenty-First Century: Identity, Place, and Community in a Globalizing World*, edited by Kai A. Schafft and Alecia Youngblood Jackson, 275–89. University Park: Pennsylvania State University Press, 2010.

Schafft, Kai A., and David L. Brown. "Social Capital, Social Networks, and Social Power." *Social Epistemology* 17, no. 4 (2003): 329–42.

Schmitt, Neal, Joshua M. Sacco, Sharon Ramey, Craig Ramey, and David Chan. "Parental Employment, School Climate, and Children's Academic and Social Development." *Journal of Applied Psychology* 84, no. 5 (October 1999): 737–53.

Seal, Kenna R., and Hobart L. Harmon. "Realities of Rural School Reform." *Phi Delta Kappan* 77, no. 2 (October 1995): 119.

Shirley, Dennis. *Community Organizing for Urban School Reform*. Austin: University of Texas Press, 1997.

Silver, Roy, and Alan J. DeYoung. "The Ideology of Rural/Appalachian Education, 1895–1935: The Appalachian Education Problem as Part of the Appalachian Life Problem." *Educational Theory* 36, no. 1 (Winter 1986): 51–65.

State of Arkansas. "Arkansas House of Representatives." http://www.arkansas-house.org/ (May 3, 2014).

Stern, Joyce D. "The Condition of Education in Rural Schools." Washington, DC: Office of Educational Research and Improvement, 1994.

Stockley, Grif. *Ruled by Race: Black/White Relations in Arkansas from Slavery to the Present*. Fayetteville: University of Arkansas Press, 2009.

Strange, Marty. "Funding Fairness for Rural Students." *Phi Delta Kappan* 92, no. 6 (March 2011): 8–15.

Street, Paul. *Segregated Schools: Educational Apartheid in Post-Civil Rights America*. New York: Routledge, 2005.

Tajfel, Henri. "Social Identity and Intergroup Behaviour." *Social Science Information* 74, no. 13 (1974): 65–93.

Tate, William F., Gloria Ladson-Billings, and Carl A. Grant. "The *Brown* Decision Revisited: Mathematizing a Social Problem." In *Beyond Desegregation: The Politics of Quality in African American Schooling*, edited by Mwalimu J. Shujaa, 29–50. Thousand Oaks, CA: Corwin Press, 1996.

Terry, David A. "Inadequate and Inequitable: The Role of the Judiciary in Arkansas Education." *Washington University Journal of Law and Policy* 25 (2007): 245–75.

Theobald, Paul. *Call School: Rural Education in the Midwest to 1918*. Carbondale: Southern Illinois University Press, 1995.

———. *Education Now: How Rethinking America's Past Can Change Its Future*. Boulder, CO: Paradigm Publishers, 2009.

———. "Forces Supporting Consolidation and Some Alternatives." Paper presented at the Annual Rural Education Conference, Dillon, MT, 1994.

———. Personal email, March 11, 2013.

———. *Teaching the Commons: Place, Pride, and the Renewal of Community*. Boulder, CO: Westview Press, 1997.

Theobald, Paul, and Kathy Wood. "Learning to Be Rural: Identity Lessons from History, Schooling, and the U.S. Corporate Media." In *Rural Education for the Twenty-First Century: Identity, Place, and Community in a Globalizing World*, edited by Kai A. Schafft and Alecia Youngblood Jackson, 17–33. University Park: Pennsylvania State University, 2010.

Thomas, Alexander R., Brian M. Lowe, Gregory M. Fulkerson, and Polly J. Smith. *Critical Rural Theory: Structure, Space, Culture*. Lanham, MD: Lexington Books, 2011.

Tieken, Mara Casey. "The Distance to Delight: A Graduate Student Enters the Field." *Qualitative Inquiry* 19, no. 4 (April 2013): 320–26.

Tonnies, Ferdinand. *Community and Civil Society*. Translated by Jose Harris and Margaret Hollis. Edited by Jose Harris. 1887; Cambridge: Cambridge University Press, 2001.

Turque, Bill, and Nick Anderson. "Former D.C. Schools Chancellor Michelle Rhee Starts Student Advocacy Group." *Washington Post*, December 6, 2010.

Tyack, David. *One Best System: A History of American Urban Education*. Cambridge, MA: Harvard University Press, 1974.

———. "The Tribe and the Common School: Community Control in Rural Education." *American Quarterly* 24, no. 1 (March 1972): 3–19.

Vidich, Arthur J., and Joseph Bensman. *Small Town in Mass Society: Class, Power, and Religion in a Rural Community*. Princeton, NJ: Princeton University Press, 1958.

Walker, Vanessa Siddle. *Their Highest Potential: An African American School Community in the Segregated South*. Chapel Hill: University of North Carolina Press, 1996.

Walters, Pamela Barnhouse. "Educational Access and the State: Historical Continuities and Discontinuities in Racial Inequality in American Education." *Sociology of Education*, extra issue (2001): 35–49.

Warren, Mark, Soo Hong, Carolyn Leung Rubin, and Phitsamay Sychitkokhong Uy. "Beyond the Bake Sale: A Community-Based Relational Approach to Parent Engagement in Schools." *Teachers College Record* 111, no. 9 (2009): 2209–54.

Warren, Mark, Karen Mapp, and the Community Organizing and School Reform Project. *A Match on Dry Grass: Community Organizing as a Catalyst for School Reform.* New York: Oxford University Press, 2011.

Warren, Mark R., J. Phillip Thompson, and Susan Saegert. "The Role of Social Capital in Combating Poverty." In *Social Capital and Poor Communities*, edited by Susan Saegert, J. Phillip Thompson and Mark R. Warren. New York: Russell Sage Foundation, 2001.

Weber, Max. "Class, Status, Party." In *From Max Weber: Essays in Sociology*, edited by Hans Heinrich Gerth and C. W. Mills. New York: Oxford University Press, 1946.

Wellman, Barry, and Milena Gulia. "Net-Surfers Don't Ride Alone: Virtual Communities as Communities." In *Networks in the Global Village: Life in Contemporary Communities*, edited by Barry Wellman, 331–66. Boulder, CO: Westview Press, 1999.

Wellman, Barry, and Barry Leighton. "Networks, Neighborhoods, and Communities: Approaches to the Study of the Community Question." *Urban Affairs Review* 14 (1979): 363–90.

Wells, Amy Stuart, and Robert L. Crain. "Perpetuation Theory and the Long-Term Effects of School Desegregation." *Review of Educational Research* 64, no. 4 (Winter 1994): 531–55.

Wells, Amy Stuart, Jennifer Jellison Holme, Anita Tijerina Revilla, and Awo Korantemaa Atanda. *Both Sides Now: The Story of School Desegregation's Graduates.* Los Angeles: University of California Press, 2009.

Wellstone, Paul. *How the Rural Poor Got Power: Narrative of a Grass-Roots Organizer.* Minneapolis: University of Minnesota Press, 1978.

Welty, Eudora. *One Writer's Beginning.* Cambridge, MA: Harvard University Press, 1983.

What Works Clearinghouse. "Helping Students Navigate the Path to College: What High Schools Can Do." In *IES Practice Guide*, edited by Institute of Education Sciences. Washington, DC: U.S. Department of Education, 2009.

Wigginton, Eliot. "Foxfire Grows Up." *Harvard Educational Review* 59, no. 1 (Spring 1989): 24–50.

Wilkinson, Kenneth P. *The Community in Rural America.* New York: Greenwood Press, 1991.

Wilson, Franklin D. "The Impact of School Desegregation Programs on White Public-School Enrollment, 1968–1976." *Sociology of Education* 58, no. 3 (July 1985): 137–53.

Woodrum, Arlie. "State-Mandated Testing and Cultural Resistance in Appalachian Schools: Competing Values and Expectations." *Journal of Research in Rural Education* 19, no. 1 (September 7, 2004): 1–10.

Woolcock, Michael. "Social Capital and Economic Development: Toward a Theoretical Synthesis and Policy Framework." *Theory and Society* 27 (1998): 151–208.

Wray, Matt. *Not Quite White: White Trash and the Boundaries of Whiteness.* Durham, NC: Duke University Press, 2006.

Young, Ed, and Harry A. Green. "School System Consolidation." Nashville, TN: Tennessee Advisory Commission on Intergovernmental Relations, 2005.

Zimmerman, Jonathan. *Small Wonder: The Little Red Schoolhouse in History and Memory*. New Haven, CT: Yale University Press, 2009.

Zinn, Howard. *A People's History of the United States: 1492–Present*. New York: HarperCollins Publishers, 1980.

Index

effects on, 22–23; Earle and, 40, 86, 87, 88, 92, 93, 102, 148; Hampton model for, 18–19; inequities of, 18, 37, 91, 119, 148, 154; northern philanthropists and, 18, 37, 133; plantation forerunners of, 18–19, 37, 91, 153–54; social importance of, 124–25; stereotypes of, 164

Bloomberg, Michael, 187

Bonding social capital, 121, 124–25, 127, 134–35, 139

Boundaries, 8, 41, 47, 140, 141–59; community-state, 164–65, 267; determination of, 142; Earle black community, 45–46, 87, 95, 96, 148–51, 153–55, 157; symbolic, 142, 157, 159; "us" and "them" construction of, 45, 89, 90, 101–2, 130, 132, 141, 142, 147, 157, 164–65. *See also* Community-school relationship; Segregation

Boycotts, 23, 92, 103, 125

Bridging social capital, 121, 124, 127, 128–29, 131, 134–39

Brown v. Board of Education (1954), 22, 37, 119, 133, 187; unrealized promise of, 120

Brownwood, Tex., 51

Bulldog Café (Earle), 95, 136

Bulldog identity (Delight), 4, 61, 65–66, 73, 75, 131; alumni continuance of, 147, 153; T-shirts and sweatshirts, 127, 152, 184

Bulldog symbol (Earle), 96, 103, 109

Bush, George W., 182, 183

Caddo Nation, 32

Cambridge, Mass., 31, 41

Campbell, Irby, 12, 96–97, 100–101, 107

Capitalism, 14, 167

Care, culture of, 57–59, 126

Census Bureau, U.S.: definition of rural, 5; definition of urban, 191 (n. 4); rural population statistics, 6

Central High School (Little Rock), 37, 38, 119

Charter schools, 181

Childhood obesity, 187

Christian academies. *See* Segregation academies

Christian principles, 19

Churches, 137, 138, 168; racial divide and, 13, 32, 38, 95, 96, 136

Citgo gas station (Earle), 40, 89

Cities. *See* Urbanization; Urban schools

Civil Rights Act (1964), 23

Civil War, 13, 14, 32–35, 83, 87, 133, 166; postwar conditions, 14, 15, 32, 35, 36, 156

Clark, Mark, 106, 114

Clark County, Ark., 147

Class status, 95, 118, 150

Clear Spring, Ark., 49

Clinton, Bill, 103

Cliques, 129

Closures. *See* School closures

Coalition for Educational Justice, 186

Cole, Kathy, 43, 49, 51, 52, 53, 54–55, 58, 62, 63, 67, 179; on Delight's shared identity, 70; diverse student body and, 75–77; race and, 79–80, 82–83, 129; school regulations and, 68, 110, 153; school symbol and, 66; shared values and, 66, 67; transfer request and, 70, 71

Collective action, 134–35

Collective identity, 65–73, 141, 142, 144, 156

Commission on Country Life, 16

Committee of Twelve (1896), 16

Commonalities, awareness of, 141

Community, 140–59; boundaries and, 141–45; decline of, 143–44; definition of, 45, 46, 141–43; future of, 158–59; Hillery's definition of, 141; making and remaking of, 151–57, 159; political power and, 105–6, 109, 110, 119, 122–23, 124, 141,

consolidation and expansion of, 38, 70, 71, 177, 178; Country Life movement and, 17; industrial model for black schools, 18–19; locally relevant, 12, 24, 25, 26; racial divisions and, 119; standardization of, 20–21, 27, 169; state reforms and, 171, 177, 178, 185; state standards and, 162; student tracking and, 92; technological support for, 24

Cyndi (Delight teacher), 51

Deacon, Mrs. (Delight teacher), 57
Delight, Ark., 48–84, 188; and aversion to Murfreesboro, 69–70, 147, 152, 159; bridging relationships in, 134, 137; business district of, 60, 61–62; care in, 57–59, 126; cemetery dinner tradition in, 66, 67, 80, 179; choice of as research site, 31–32; close-knit relationships in, 55–56, 125–29; community boundaries of, 45; conflicts within, 59, 70–73; cross-racial support in, 49–51, 53–54, 73–83, 125–29, 137–39, 140, 141, 145–46, 147, 151, 155–56; degree of integration of, 76–83, 126, 146, 179; desegregation mandate and, 129–34; economic conditions and, 50, 60, 61–62, 64, 126, 127, 128, 133, 146, 155, 166, 173, 184, 185; family-like atmosphere of, 54–60, 67–68, 70, 152; history of, 50–51; identity linked with, 65, 66, 68–71, 72, 73; Little Rock's distance from, 162; location of, *33*, 34, 133, 155–56; population (311) of, 49, 50, 84, 145; racial dynamics of, 80–81, 82, 88, 117, 118, 121, 146; research approach to, 31–32, 40–47; researcher's relationship with, 43–44, 50–51; residential separation within, 81, 146; school's physical and psychological meaning to, 51, 61–62, 84, 144–45; as rural

locale, 196 (n. 9); setting of, 48–49, 51, 84; shared values of, 67–68, 79, 81, 152, 153; social capital in, 126–29, 134, 139; uncertainty of future of, 84; urbanization and, 36; white majority of, 81
Delight school district, 8, 9, 10, 48–84, 135; and alumni friendships, 147; black principal of, 43, 49, 51, 80 (*see also* Cole, Kathy); boundaries and, 157; bulldog symbol of, 4, 61, 65–66, 73, 75, 127, 131, 147, 152, 153, 184; cafeteria of, 54–55, 68; campus scene of, 146–47; cohesive student body of, 131, 153; common goals of, 127; common identity fostered by, 126–27, 135, 138, 153; as community focal point, 51, 61–62, 84, 126–27, 144–47, 155–56, 158–59, 179–81, 183, 188; conformity and, 153; consolidation fears of, 32, 40, 44, 50, 59–60, 61, 62, 63, 65, 69, 70, 72, 73, 84, 139, 147–48, 153, 159, 160, 162, 163–64, 176, 177; consolidation into new South Pike County School District, 189–90; demographics of student body, 32, 40, 50, 75–76, 78–83, 126, 131, 163; desegregation process of, 74–76, 129–34; district line of, 45, 68–69; economic contribution of, 61–65, 127, 128; enrollment of, 50; as essential and multifunctional, 185; faculty racial make-up of, 80; as freestanding school district, 50; handbook regulations, 68, 153; interactions within, 54–56; international student program of, 74, 75–76, 77, 126, 128, 145, 173; interracial patterns and, 73–83; local control benefits for, 173–74; location of, 34, 35, 40, 48–49, 50, 51–52; loyalty to, 63–64; meaningful interactions and, 127; multiple roles of, 185; Okolona's former

consolidation with, 84, 130–31, 145, 147, 151; past reorganizations and, 74; physical and psychological meaning of, 51–52; physical layout of, 48, 49–50, 52, 53–54; racial make-up of, 40, 50, 78–83; racially representative administration of, 78–79; sports events and, 48, 49, 51–52, 53, 80, 125–27, 184; state government mandates and, 160–75; student body openness and, 74; student "choicing" (transfer) from, 70–73, 79, 145, 147, 151; test scores and, 180; towns of, 50, 147; traditions and, 66–67; welcoming culture of, 153

Deliverance (film), 7

Delta, 6, 7, 32–39, 87, 88–89, 132, 164; continued segregation in, 136; description of, 34–35; Earle located in, 34, 40, 85, 87, 132, 156; economic decline of, 34, 166; as floodplain, 97, 132; geography and history of, 34–35; landscape of, 85; one-crop economy of (*see* Cotton farming); outmigration from, 34; poor black school districts of, 38; racialized history of, 88–89, 132; slavery and, 34, 35, 87, 132, 133–34; starkness of, 88; stereotypes of, 88, 164; uplands contrasted with, 34–36, 39, 133, 155; white control over, 36–37, 39, 136; white flight and, 38, 122. *See also* Plantation system

Democracy, 17, 22, 141, 187–88

Democratic Party, 36

Demographics, 10, 23, 167; Arkansas, 34, 35; choice of research site and, 31, 32; Delight student body, 75–76, 126, 131, 163; Earle shift in, 87, 93, 94, 95; immigration effects on, 23; risk of school closures and, 6; rural outmigration and, 15, 16; rural population by race, 6–7

Department of Education, Arkansas, 83–84, 161, 189

Department of Education, U.S., 161, 186, 187

Desegregation, 26, 28; Arkansas Delta vs. uplands region, 133; Arkansas resistance to, 32, 37–38, 119, 128, 132–33; black education and drawbacks of, 22–23, 92, 110, 123–24, 135; context and details of, 129–30, 133–34; Delight effects of, 74, 76–83, 126, 129–34, 146, 151, 179, 185; Earle 1970 protest and, 90–91, 92–93, 96, 100, 102, 116, 129, 149, 154, 189; Earle effects of, 92, 93–94, 97–102, 122, 129, 134, 150, 151, 152, 154, 157, 185, 189; Earle vs. Delight experience of, 132–34, 151; end of white lifestyle and, 98; government intervention and, 27, 91, 170; integration vs., 92; resistance to, 37, 38, 119; rural opponents of, 22–23, 171; school consolidations resulting from, 60, 130; social costs of, 38; Supreme Court 1954 ruling, 22, 37, 119, 120, 133, 187; Supreme Court 1968 ruling, 23, 37–38; voluntary, 130; white resistance to, 23, 37, 38, 119, 122 (*see also* White flight)

Diversity, 6–7, 12, 32

Dress code, 68, 110, 153

Drop-out rates, 21

Drug use, 97, 125, 149

Dunbar Middle School (Earle), 87, 88, 91, 111, 148, 154, 181; closure of, 189; description of, 86; desegregation and, 92, 129; significance of, 152, 284–85; test scores of, 122

Earle, Ark., 8, 9, 10, 85–116; black community bonds of, 134–35, 140, 141, 149–50, 153–55; black community protest (1970) as defining racial moment in, 90–91, 92–93,

Little Rock, Ark., 34, 39; school deseg-
regation resistance in, 37, 38, 119;
as state government center, 162, 176
Locale. *See* Place
Louisiana Purchase (1803), 32, 35
Lumbering. *See* Timber industry
Lynching tree, 2–3, 4

Mad Butcher (Earle business), 122,
124
Manufacturing. *See* Industrialization
Maples, Jessie Mae, 90, 94, 101, 154
Maples, Linda, 91, 92, 95, 112, 113, 154
Marion, Ark., 93, 103, 108, 125, 196
(n. 9)
McGuffey reader, 11
McKnight's Grocery (Delight), 49, 50,
60, 61, 147, 179
Meatpacking industry, 20
Meeks Settlement, Ark., 45, 49, 50, 68,
145; as black community, 57, 81, 84,
126, 127
Memorization, 11
Memphis, Tenn.: Earle's proximity to,
87, 94, 114, 124, 149
Metropolitan/nonmetropolitan cat-
egory, 5, 191 (nn. 4, 10), 196 (n. 9)
Midwestern rural communities, 6, 12
Millage rate, 63, 122, 149, 180
Mississippi floodplain. *See* Delta
Mississippi River, 34, 87, 88; first
white settlement west of, 32
Mom's Diner (Delight), 40, 50, 62,
79–80, 84, 137, 146, 173
Moore, Pastor Connie, 97, 104, 105,
106, 107, 108, 114
Mosquero, N.Mex., 24
Mt. Beulah MB church (Earle), 136
Murfreesboro, Ark., 50, 68–71, 157;
curricular offerings at, 70–71;
Delight district's potential consoli-
dation with, 62, 69, 70, 84, 147–48;
Delight rivalry with, 69–70, 147,
152, 159; Delight's consolidation
with, 189–90; Delight student

"choicing" (transfer) to, 70–73, 79,
145, 147, 151
Myths, 7, 47, 117, 142, 190

National Education Association, 16
National Guard, 37, 128
Nation at Risk, A (education report),
20
Native American census rural popula-
tion figures, 7
Native American rural communities,
6, 19
NCLB. *See* No Child Left Behind Act
New England rural communities, 6, 12
New Mexico Rural Revitalization
Initiative, 24
New York City, resistance to school
closure, 186, 187
Nicks, Ricky, 92, 93, 98, 99, 105, 106,
129
No Child Left Behind Act (NCLB)
(2002), 3, 39, 88, 109, 161, 171,
181–83; 198 (n. 58); accountability
basis of, 182, 185; protests against,
186–87
Normal schools, 14, 19
Nostalgia, 7, 16, 64, 98, 117, 142, 165

Obama, Barack, 86, 182
Office of Management and Budget
(OMB): rural definition, 5; urban
area definition, 191 (n. 4)
Okolona, Ark., 45, 49, 50, 68, 163, 190;
consolidation with Delight school
district, 84, 130–31, 145, 147, 151; as
mixed-race community, 126; school
desegregation and, 74–75, 130
One-room schools, 11, 12
Ouachita mountains, 35
Outmigration, 15, 16, 20, 25, 26, 27,
34, 156
Ozarks, 35

Paige, Rod, 187
Parents Across America, 186

148; equal opportunity and, 92; generational divides and, 95–96; historical inequities of, 30, 31, 37, 187; narratives of, 43–44, 117–39; political power and, 88, 103–10, 119, 122–23; researcher's personal relationships and, 43–44; research sites and, 31, 32 (*see also* Delight; Earle); rural divisions of, 18–19, 43–44; rural population breakdown by, 6–7, 18–19; social capital and, 121, 123, 124, 125, 132; stereotypes of, 7, 29, 88, 102–3, 114; "us" and "them" patterns and, 45, 89, 90, 101–2, 130, 132. *See also* Cross-racial contact; Desegregation; Integration; Segregation

Race to the Top (education initiative), 182

Racial epithets, 79, 129

Racism, 20, 102, 119; desegregation resistance and, 37; legacies of, 8, 83; "local control" cry of, 28

Reconstruction, 32, 35, 36, 156

Reform. *See* Education policy

Religious life, 12, 19, 129. *See also* Churches

Republican Party, 36

Research: authenticity and, 30, 31, 43, 44; development of relationships and, 30, 42–47; portraiture method of, 30–47; urban schools as focus of, 3–4, 29

Residential segregation, 81, 129, 146

Retirement communities, 7

Rice farming, 34, 87Roosevelt, Franklin D., 104

Roosevelt, Theodore, 16

Rosenwald, Julius, 18, 37, 133

Route 19 (Ark), 51, 60, 84

Route 26 (Ark.), 48, 51, 60, 84

Route 149 (Ark.), 85, 107

Route 235 (Tenn.), 1

Rural areas, 6–28; challenges faced by, 39–40; changes in, 10, 15–19; coarse constructions of, 165; definitions of, 5, 191 (n. 10); demographics of, 6–7; desegregation effects on, 22–23, 171; economic conditions and, 10, 20, 136; education and (*see* Rural schools); effects of government intervention on, 27–28; histories of, 10–28; inequities and, 20–21, 136; invisibility of, 6; losses within, 19–21; outmigration from, 15, 16, 20, 25, 26, 27, 34, 156; place and, 157–58; popular image of, 20, 25; poverty rate and, 7, 20, 21, 136; racial divisions and, 18–19, 43–44; research project design, 29–47; social stratification and, 136–37; stereotypes/misunderstandings of, 7, 15, 29, 51, 164–65, 167, 180, 183, 186, 187, 190; study of, 142–43; urban interests superseding, 13, 15–19, 35–36

Rural Life and Education (Cubberley), 16

"Rural problem," 15–16, 18, 27, 143, 165, 167

Rural School and Community Trust, 31

Rural schools: Arkansas percentage of, 39; black administrators of, 105–6, 125; of black communities, 13, 18–19; bridging potential of, 137–39; as "canary in coal mine," 188; challenges faced by, 171–72; common narratives of, 117–18; community ties and, 157–58, 159; consolidation movement, 17, 21–23; consolidation resistance, 22; constant risk of closure of, 6, 21, 172; as cultural centers, 12, 135, 137; current problems and possibilities, 19–25; desegregation of, 25, 137–38; desegregation opposition and, 22–23, 171; drop-out rate of, 21; economic meaning of, 2, 60, 62–63; emotional meaning of, 2; as focus of social life, 1–2, 12;

history of, 11–23, 37; importance of, 7–8, 24–25, 26, 28, 168, 188; local control advocates, 23, 27–28, 173–74; local control losses by, 39, 169–70, 183, 185–86; new roles for, 25; policy makers' disregard of, 3–4, 171–72; political power and, 168–69; researcher's teaching experience in, 4–9; significance of, 47, 179, 188; split sessions, 11, 91; standardization of, 20–21; state and federal policy effects on, 39, 47, 169–88; state misunderstanding of, 163–64; statistics, 7–8; tax basis of, 18, 38; unifying potential of, 121, 138–39; urbanization effects on, 15–17, 25–26. *See also* Community-school relationship; Delight; Earle

Sabbath schools, 13
Save Our Schools, 186
School: as community, 140; definition of, 46. *See also* Community-school relationship; Education policy; Public education; Rural schools
School boards, 12; black representation on, 23, 78, 93, 105–6, 107, 125; school "choicing" (transfer) petitions and, 70, 71
School buildings, 17, 18, 177; conflicts over sites for, 12, 103, 107; Delight's complex of, 48, 49; disrepair of, 119; size-success equation, 21–22
School buses: black schools and, 119; Delight community and, 45, 61, 74, 126, 145; desegregation mandate and, 37; district consolidation and, 17, 84, 130; long rides on, 22
School closures, 22, 23, 25, 26, 27, 28, 31; community dissolution resulting from, 174, 186; as consolidation effect, 39; constant threat of, 6, 21, 32, 44, 46, 108–9, 159–60, 162, 172, 173, 174–75, 189; government mandates and, 169, 181–83, 186–87; resistance

to, 180, 187; state's rationale for, 108, 178, 183; test scores determining, 39, 181; urban threats of, 186, 188. *See also* Consolidation; Delight school district; Earle school districtSchools. *See* Black schools; Education policy; Rural schools; Urban schools
School year, 11, 91
Scott (Delight coach), 51, 52, 56
Secession, 32, 34, 35
Segregation, 25, 26, 28, 32, 41, 82, 142; academic consequences of, 123–24; of churches, 136; collective resistance to, 125; Earle's history and, 86, 90–96, 122, 123, 132, 153–54; gray area between integration and, 82–83; inequalities and, 22, 119; Jim Crow and, 132; legal end to, 22, 37, 119; residential, 81, 129, 146; resistance to, 128; rural public institutions and, 136; social consequences of, 123–26; urban schools and, 187. *See also* Black schools; Desegregation; Integration
Segregation academies, 23, 38, 39, 93, 119, 122, 130, 132
Senate Education Committee, Arkansas, 176–79
Sex education, 187
Sharecroppers, 34, 37, 87, 98, 132; children's split school sessions, 91; poverty and, 166; racial oppression of, 104, 105; as replacing slavery, 132; strike (1930s) of, 104, 148, 154
Shared values, 66–68, 79, 81, 141, 142, 146, 152, 153
Shear Delight (Delight hair salon), 60, 84
Simmons, Ark., 130
Singleton, Dorothy, 31–32, 43, 46
Slavery, 83, 142, 256; Delta plantations and, 34, 35, 87, 132, 133–34; education bans and, 13; emancipation and, 132; shared memory of, 156. *See also* Plantation system